Floyd, It has been a
pleasure to fellowship
with you in the Lord
and His marvellous Word!

C. E. Mason, Jr.

Dt. 29:29

Prophetic Problems

with Alternate Solutions

Clarence E. Mason Jr.

MOODY PRESS
CHICAGO

Library of Congress Catalog Card Number: 73-7335

ISBN: 0-8024-6907-8

Printed in the United States of America

Contents

CHAPTER   **PAGE**

Foreword   5

Preface   7

Acknowledgments   10

1. God's Throne—Active but Unshaken   11

2. The Key Covenant   27

3. The Virgin Prophecy   43

4. Hosea's Heartbreak   65

5. Two Kingdoms in Matthew?   87

6. The Times of Restitution   110

7. What Kind of Body?   129

8. The Day of the Lord Jesus Christ   143

9. Are Names Significant?   152

10. The United States of the Western World   164

11. The Power Struggle of the End Time   177

12. Gog and Magog, Who and When?   192

13. The Sinister Men   204

14. The City from Outer Space   229

Scripture Index   252

Foreword

INTEREST IN PROPHECY is on the increase. Events in the Middle East and the expanding importance of the Common Market fill our newspapers almost daily and touch the lives of people everywhere. The world seems to sense that its last hours are at hand.

The Christian, of course, is not left in the dark about what is happening in the world, for the prophetic Scriptures give us a knowledge of the future. Although the outlines of prophecy are clear, not all scholars agree on every detail of interpretation. Concerning some of the problems in interpretation, Dr. Mason offers important suggestions, which are the fruit of his lifelong study of the Word.

The author, with whom I had the privilege of serving at Philadelphia College of Bible, is well known to the thousands of students whose lives he has touched during his nearly half century of teaching. Now some of this stimulating teaching is made available in this book to a wider audience. Not all will agree with the author's conclusions, but all will do well to read carefully his discussions. Whether he persuades you or not, he will provoke your thinking.

Dr. Mason was the dean during my presidency at PCB. He always called me "boss," which was somewhat embarrassing to me since I was his junior by some years. But when it comes to biblical knowledge, I rightly call him "boss." Thus I gladly commend this book of his to "all them also that love his appearing" (2 Ti 4:8).

CHARLES C. RYRIE

5

Preface

WHY ANOTHER BOOK on prophecy? Aren't there enough?

Perhaps it is precisely *because of* the large number of voices and views that I have felt increasingly impressed with the confusion in the mind of the average Bible-interested person. I make it a practice to invite questions in my prophetic conferences and "confusion" is a mild word. Often "frustration" would be a more apt description.

So many variant things are being said by good men. What about Russia? What about Israel? What about the United States? What about China? What about Africa? Who is the beast? Who is the false prophet? Will there be *one* ruler over all the world? Who is the Antichrist (the latter so often assumed to be the only *one* Antichrist that the Bible speaks of)? Who attacks whom and when? What will be the movement of nations?

I have been concerned to see if I can help clarify some of the alternate views. It would be naive and egotistical to suppose that my solutions to these variant views will satisfy every reader. But having answered thousands of students through the years, I think I know the questions, and it is my earnest hope that these chapters will provide *solutions* in the proper choice among alternate views. Hence, this book.

As a teacher since 1927, I have some very settled views on the philosophy of teaching. I cannot accept as valid the idea that a teacher has fulfilled his duty when he has presented two, three, four or more views, with the invitation to the student: "Now take your pick. Which one tickles your fancy most?"

I feel a teacher should be aware of various views, be fair with them, and should assist a student in knowing what they are. But I feel a teacher who stops there is recreant to his duty. I believe that he should have thought through the problems and come to some settled conclusion in each area. I feel that he should then *valiantly plead* for the view he understands the Bible to teach.

I am not arguing for blind dogmatism. We should never get beyond facts! We should not stubbornly resist possible change of view. If anyone comes up with more facts and/or a better use of them, we should never be afraid to change. This is exactly what my experience has been. If you will read my background in this field in the opening of chapter 11, and then read the book, you will see that the chapters indicate many changed positions from what I was taught. You will agree that my thrust has not been the maintaining of a position but arriving, hopefully and finally, at the facts on which to rest a settled, refined conviction.

Perhaps another word will be in order. Some of these messages are directed at an average interested Bible student in an average prophetic conference. They are intended to be thorough but they do not pretend to scrape the bottom of the barrel of scholarship. There are, however, a few closely reasoned and somewhat technical articles written for theological journals. An example of the first mentioned would be chapter 3, "The Virgin Prophecy," where philological data is necessarily introduced. In a different way, I would include chapters like "Two Kingdoms in Matthew?" (5), "The Day of the Lord Jesus Christ" (8), and "The Sinister Men" (13). It is not suggested that these chapters are too difficult for the average reader, but it is true that they will take more careful reading than most of the other chapters. It is the teacher's duty to challenge the student. In other words, the style of treatment is dictated by the type of subject under discussion.

It is my hope that every chapter will be read and will be

found helpful, but, naturally, some things will help some more than others. It is my prayer that many of you will find solutions to quite a number of things over which you have pondered. If so, my goal will have been attained!

Acknowledgments

The author gratefully acknowledges permissions granted to reprint, with changes, his previously published material:

Chapter 2—from *The King's Business* 51 (March 1960): 25-28, originally entitled "Was the Abrahamic Covenant Conditioned?"

Chapter 7—from *Prophecy and the Seventies,* ed. Charles Lee Feinberg (Chicago: Moody, 1971), pp. 124-37, originally entitled "The Believer's Resurrection Body."

Chapter 8—from *Bibliotheca Sacra* 125 (Oct-Dec 1968):352-59.

Chapter 9—from *Prophecy and the Seventies,* pp. 87-98, originally entitled "The Names of Christ in Revelation."

Chapter 10—from *Prophetic Truth Unfolding Today,* ed. Charles Lee Feinberg (Westwood, N.J.: Revell, 1968), pp. 101-13.

Chapter 11—from *Prophetic Truth Unfolding Today,* pp. 114-23.

Chapter 12—from *Prophecy and the Seventies,* pp. 221-32.

1

God's Throne—Active but Unshaken

THESE ARE DAYS that try men's souls. Men's hearts are failing them for fear. Everyone hears the fuse sizzling. Many have their fingers stuffed in their ears to muffle the sound of the inevitable explosion. Multitudes are walking on eggshells, not daring to look behind. Great numbers jump if anyone says, "Boo!"

And with good cause! They who know the most in international affairs are the most worried. The Far East is a bog of quicksand. The Middle East is a powder keg. Leftist groups in Japan and Latin America, to name two key areas, are steadily increasing. The Pope is demythologizing, with the attendant vacuum created. Nothing seems steady or certain.

What I have said above is the world as it is. But, sad to say, Christians—who have every reason to know better—are greatly affected by this quiet or loud hysteria (depending upon how much they know of international affairs and depending on how little they know the Lord and His Word).

These events should come as no surprise to a Bible believer. But how few Christians really read (to know) their Bibles! Jesus said things would get worse and worse, not better and better! He said that wars and rumors of wars would increase with dramatic crescendo. He said that the darkest days for the world are the end-time days. Too bad that Christians, generally, either do not really believe what Jesus said or have been too busy buying the new model cars and gadgets to bother to know what He said.

Of course, the Bible-taught person is an incurable optimist. Sure, he knows troublous times will come and increase. But he doesn't grab a "Linus blanket" of maudlin unreality and resign from the human race as being too much for him. He looks at things, if he knows God and his Bible, with eyeball-to-eyeball confrontation and doesn't even blink. He knows the world cannot be destroyed by ICBM weapons, for a great multitude of people must be around during the tribulation period for anything in prophecy to make sense (e.g., the 200 million army coming from the Far East). He knows that a great multitude of Gentiles, besides a substantial number of repentant Jews (God's Israel), will survive the awesome tribulation days and enter the millennium when Jesus comes. All this, despite the holocaust of those days, so terrible that Jesus said no flesh could survive, unless those days were shortened—cut short—by the supernatural return and intervention of the Lord Jesus Christ.

So the Christian has no right to join in the hysteria. He should be calm and a rock of comfort to those who want to know what is going to happen on earth. He knows for a certainty that the world is not going to be destroyed in an agony of nuclear dissolution. He knows that the world is going on for a thousand years after Jesus comes, in its most glorious utopian experience—that He will rule with a rod of iron from Jerusalem and smash every focus of rebellion. Indeed, earth shall yet have her golden age, poignantly wished for by men of all eras, but clearly prophesied in the sure word of prophecy. Christians are the only people who have a right to be optimists, and they have scriptural ground for it. By contrast, most realistic thinkers of the world are gloomily pessimistic concerning the future. The only non-Christians in the world of affairs who are optimistic are people who have "misty optics" and live in a dream world of fantasy.

In beginning a book like this, it seems to me very practical and basic to get a view of the majestic throne of God and see that God is neither aloof nor unconcerned nor incompetent to handle the real problems which face the world. The first chapter of Ezekiel provides just such a revelation, appropriate to our troubled times.

Get the setting. Ezekiel is with a group of Jews already in captivity. He is living by the canal Chebar that connected the two great rivers of Mesopotamia, the Euphrates and the Tigris. Here was located one of the oldest centers of human activity dating back to Babel and—indeed—to Eden. He is there because his Jewish people have incurred the judgment of God for disobedience to the Palestinian covenant. The nation has been steadily disintegrating. The cup of iniquity has been steadily filling. Shortly, God will say to Jeremiah, "Don't pray for this people. The time of delay has passed. Judgment must fall." The shadows are gathering around Jerusalem. In a little while, Nebuchadrezzar II will answer the rebellion of the puppet king Zedekiah with a siege and utter destruction of Jerusalem and its temple.

So the perspective is the fall and seeming destruction of the Jewish nation. Everything they dreamed about has gone down the drain. The throne of David and the Jewish state will come to an end. Worship will no longer be possible at the only place God has put His name and permitted official worship—the temple at Jerusalem. That temple will be torn stone from stone. Vast numbers will die in the siege from hunger and disease; a host of others will die in the successful breach of the walls and assault of the city from all sides. Those left will either be sold into slavery, taken captive to Babylon, or—a small group—will be left to till the land.

What a comedown for a people who had been assured that heaven was on their side and that the nations of the world would be subject to them when Messiah came and took the throne of David! One could scarcely blame them if they felt all hope was lost and that the heavens were brass.

It was to this time and to this generation that God vouchsafed this great message of the first chapter of Ezekiel. Though all seems lost, the throne of God is symbolically revealed in vision. A majestic throne, serene in majesty and yet related to earth and earth's affairs. It is no nostalgic, philosophical dream, in a nonexistent phantom world. It is a very pragmatic throne, however holy and awesome. As Dr. Charles C. Ryrie of Dallas Seminary has well said: "God is not *still* on the throne. He is very active on that throne!"

To calm their fears with a divine perspective, God gives this foundational vision at the opening of this prophecy and Ezekiel's ministry. God appeared to Ezekiel that He might put a bright light of hope in an otherwise dark and dismal situation, where there seemed no basis for hope. In visions of God, He spoke "expressly" to Ezekiel (1:3). And, as intended, Ezekiel passed it on to his people. In the providence of God, who knew that there would be many such distressing eras, He saw to it that it became part of His holy Word, and would be available to all His own who would follow in the course of history. This wonderful vision is just as relevant to God's people today, if not more so, since the shadows of the end-time storm are gathering, and the lightning and thunder have already started.

So, then, just what did God say to Ezekiel and his people, and to us as He looked down the corridor of the centuries? I believe there are ten things very clearly suggested by the words of this vision.

1. THERE IS A THRONE (v. 26)

Although this has already been anticipated in the introduction, it is well that we give the scriptural basis for the statement. In the quicksands of nations' kaleidoscope of experiences, rising and falling with startling suddenness, it is well to know there is something stable, something solid, something dependable, and something in authority when everything seems in chaos. However distressing the world scene, it is both instructive and comforting to know there is a throne.

Someone is in charge and in control, however it may seem otherwise. This should calm Christians, who tend to look at the paper and melt like gelatin over bad news about China, Russia, Vietnam, the Middle East, or the American scene of fiscal insanity, drug addiction, and the decay of honor in public and private life. No Christian has a right to lean over the back fence or the luncheon table and dolefully agree with an unsaved friend that everything is out of hand, especially after witnessing to this friend that we have a trustworthy God whom he needs. Why would that friend want your God, if He can't allay your fears and give you peace?

Do you really believe God is on a throne? Then quiet your fears! Someone who has power and wisdom is in on the case. He is not biting His fingernails, uneasily sitting on the edge of His throne, wondering what is going to happen and fearing that it will. He is in control! There is a throne and God is on it, as we read, "The Lord hath prepared his throne in the heavens; and his kingdom ruleth over all" (Ps 103:19).

2. There Is a Man on the Throne (v. 26)

This is evidently a Christophany, as in Isaiah 6. We could not see God in essence, "Spirit" (Jn 4:24), so God adjusts to our human limitation. On a number of Old Testament occasions, our Lord "appears" to the eye as in a body. For instance, the key visitor to Abraham, to whom Abraham prayed for the sparing of Lot (Gen 19). Again, the captain of the Lord's host who appeared to Joshua, as he reconnnoitered outside the walls of Jericho, was very evidently a preincarnate manifestation of the Lord Jesus Christ, *Ha-Malak-Jehovah,* "*the* angel of Jehovah" (Jos 5:13ff.). John emphatically tells us in his gospel that it was Christ whom Isaiah saw high and lifted up in the heavenly temple (Jn 12:41; Is 6:1-5), when he quoted Jehovah's words of Isaiah 6:9-10 (Jn 12:39-40).

This passage is not only retrospective, but anticipative and prophetic. Eventually, all judgment will be committed to the Son (Jn 5:22), but in the meantime He shares this function as co-ruler of the universe, sitting on His Father's throne, while He awaits His own throne from which He will judge the nations and rule a thousand years (Rev 3:21; 4:3-4; all of chapter 20). Men can never complain that they are being judged by One who cannot understand them, an ethereal unrelated God. There is a man on the throne who was down here and understands truly and fully, and the "Judge of all the earth will do *right*" (Gen 18:25). Thus, the throne of God is human-oriented and sympathetic, but fair, majestic, and practical.

3. God's Throne Is Related to Earth (e.g., v. 15)

The "wheels" of God's moving, non-static throne are pictured as touching the earth (vv. 15, 19). God's throne is not only human-oriented, it is also earth-oriented. Of all the galaxies of the relatively infinite universe, this small ball in space is the only place where God has been pleased to put men and give His attention. There is no possible explanation apart from the fact that God pleased to do it that way!

So the activities of God are definitely and designedly related to this earth and the affairs of earth. This is where He placed man. This is where His Son came. This is where the drama of redemption is being worked out. This is where a throne of righteousness will one day be set up in Jerusalem, over all the world (Mic 4:1-5).

But we do not need to wait for that day to see an active God in relation to earth. Providence is spelled with a capital P! Impersonal laws of nature's god (a la Declaration of Independence written by deist Thomas Jefferson) are foreign to the biblical concept. A very personal God rules and overrules in the affairs of men. That is what Nebuchadrezzar II, the first king of the "times of the Gentiles," had to learn the hard way; namely, "the most High rules in the kingdom of men, and gives it to whomsoever He will . . . the heavens do rule" (Dan 4:17, 25, 26, 32). Nothing happens but by His dictate or permission. Indeed, "the powers that be are ordained of God" and the ruler is described as "the minister of God" (Ro 13:1-7). Thus, Christians must be law-abiding citizens, not Bolsheviks. Further, we must be comforted to know that a Hitler or a Mao Tse-tung does not "happen." In the wisdom of God they are there by God's permission. God is not helpless. He lets human sin show its ugly face and the waves of wickedness beat against the shore of human affairs. But, He says, "Thus far and no further."

Of Him, it is written, "Surely the wrath of man shall praise thee: the remainder of wrath shalt thou restrain" (Ps 76:10). By the same token, the throne of God in relation to earth brings all of our blessings and benefits. Therefore, God reassures His prophet, in effect:

> Ezekiel, it may seem I have forgotten earth and Israel. It may indeed be true that there is no throne in Jerusalem. But I am above all. I am not restricted. I am on a throne and I will sovereignly guide the destinies of Israel and the nations. My promises are not forgotten. I will work all things together for your good. I will manage the world in such a way as to preserve My people and ultimately restore the throne of David, when He shall come, whose right it is, though human thrones are overturned again and again.

4. The Throne of God Is an Active Throne (v. 4)

Although the throne of God is seen in the vision as stable, in every sense of inviolability, the throne is seen to be "on wheels" (vv. 15, 16, 19-21). Of course, wheels suggest the thought of movement. Thus, the vision emphasizes the movements of God in human affairs.

We are so prone to think that God is up there and that things just "happen" down here. Ezekiel was given to see that God's throne is not static but related persuasively, meaningfully, and, in the ultimate, sovereignly to the purposes of God. And God so superintends the affairs of men, the movements of nations and men's activities, that He is never absent, as it were. He is present where the action is! Indeed,

He is the directing force of the activities, not simply the One strong enough to contain and restrain the action, though that is also true.

I certainly do not mean to suggest that God is the author of evil machinations of men, although they do not act apart from His knowledge and permission. To that extent, He is involved in the movements of men's activities. Daniel 10 gives us an insight into this matter. There, Satan's sinister "prince-ipalities" and powers seek to thwart the purpose of God, or go their way regardless of God. But God's mighty angels fight with Satan's "prince-ipalities" and powers and overcome them for the good ends of God's purpose (Dan 10:12ff.). Satan is allowed great latitude but God is there on the spot and, through the activity of His mighty angels, turns things His way. Thus, the king of Persia is led to exercise caution and graciousness toward Israel because Michael, "the great prince" who stands for "thy people" Israel (Dan 12:1), overcomes anything in the machinations of "the prince of Persia" (Satan's mighty angel) which might unfavorably affect the kings of Persia in their attitude and relation to Israel (Dan 10:13).

Thus, God does not sit by and let men act, and then try to salvage what He can out of the mess. On the contrary, He is in on the making of policy as well as the implementation of policy. This is the force of the word Providence as the personal activity of God directly and through His assigned subordinates, like the mighty angel Michael. Thus, as already quoted from Ryrie, "God is not *still* on the throne. He is very active!"

One could spin quite a list of things to illustrate this fact. Why did the Japanese not follow up their crippling blow to America at Pearl Harbor? Had they believed in themselves sufficiently to have had further ships to refuel and join the unique armada that stunned us in Hawaii, they could have hurt us painfully and caused hysterical panic by continuing on and bombing our large western cities, or one of them, as an awesome example. Why did we of the United States have just enough and no more planes and ships at Midway, when they did try to move toward our West Coast? Why did we win the battle of the Coral Sea? Why was the Remagen bridge across the Rhine left standing, permitting our tanks to get over the bridge, despite strict orders to blow it up before we arrived? Why was Paris not burned? Why did not Hitler attack England when she was helpless after Dunkirk, instead of moving first into France? Why did not the Germans first perfect the atomic bomb instead of us? Indeed, all of history is filled with mysterious providences. Certainly, the United States was not holy. But evidently God had a work of missions and mercy for much of a war-torn world which was made to praise Him, despite our own multiple sins. Since then, in Korea, Vietnam, Indonesia and elsewhere, complete Communist take-over (with the inevitable death of the church) has been forestalled. And who could ever believe that Berlin could be saved from complete Russian domination by, of all things, an utterly improbable and impractical winter airlift? "God moves in a mysterious way His wonders to perform!"

5. The Throne Is Highly Personal (v. 20)

I have already labored this point but, observe, there was "spirit" in the wheels (vv. 20-21). There are no impersonal laws of nature here. There are no forces and counterforces involved in a tug-of-war so that the force that is most powerful wins. It is true that a lion can easily kill and devour a rabbit. But it is interesting to note the number of rabbits in contrast to the number of lions. The weak are not necessarily overthrown in this wicked world. God's higher purpose and plan often contravene in human affairs and puny nations ofttimes persist when great powerful nations fall. This can only be attributed to the personal intervention of God. There is no human explanation for the phenomenon. There is life and activity, not merely the cold, cruel logic of preponderant supply of men and materiel. Things often happen that make historians' and military men's heads swim.

6. INTELLIGENCE SITS ON THE THRONE (v. 18)

We read in verse 18 that the "rings (actually, rims) were full of eyes." Eyes speak of intelligence and perspicacity. By this we understand that an omniscient God directs the activity of that throne in its relationship on the earth and human affairs. God is not driving blind with a mud-covered windshield. He sees everything and knows all things. Therefore, His actions are always appropriate to the purposes He has in mind for the individual, the family, the group, the nation, and the nations.

It is not only in relation to the irrevocable covenants, but to all of God's activities in human affairs, that the majestic paean of praise-filled words apply, when Paul by the Spirit wrote:

> O the depth of the riches both of the wisdom and knowledge of God! how unsearchable are his judgments, and his ways past finding out! (Ro 11:33).

Paul continues: "Who hath been his counsellor?" (v. 34).

The greatest minds of earth meet in counsel at the United Nations and other places. They puzzle and fret and travail to bring forth a workable plan to stem aggression, to promote security and peace. So often a London fog of baffling intensity obscures the slightest ray of light as they deliberate, yet God always has clear weather above the clouds of earth. He not only clearly sees all the present, but the past and the future are present to Him as the ever-existent, self-sufficient "I AM" of the universe!

7. THE IRRESISTIBLE GOD (v. 9)

We have a long-standing humorous incident in our family memory. An auntie who had never before been to the seashore was persuaded to go in swimming. She was encouraged

by the relatively calm flow of the surf. When she got about
waist-deep, suddenly out of nowhere a rather large wave
rolled in view. Turning, she sought to race for the beach but
found running in water is not very successful. So, looking
back over her shoulder and seeing the wave almost upon her,
she put up her hand like a traffic policeman and cried out in
fear, "Stop! Stop!" Needless to say, she was rolled over and
over, and she came up spluttering. It was quite a while before she could be persuaded to try again. You can be sure,
though, she now knew that the ocean would not obey her
commands!

This is very much like our world. Even rulers cannot im-
periously cry "Stop!" and have any assurance that another
nation will heed the command. In most cases their cry is
drowned by the cacophony of battle.

But, the throne of our God is pictured in verse 9 by the
striking words concerning its active agents: "they turned not
when they went; they went every one straight forward"!
God's purposes cannot be avoided or diverted. The folly of
a mere man holding up his hand and commanding God to
stop is as ludicrous as my aunt's command to the sea. God
does not detour around men's plans. No wall can be built
that can stop the irresistible forward movement of His
throne's purpose. Like a mighty bulldozer, He takes before
Him all that would stand in His way. Like a tremendous
steamroller, He flattens every Pharaoh, Haman, or Hitler,
who foolishly tries to stand in His way.

Not only do God's purposes move straight forward, in the
sense that resistance is futile, but God's ways are not devious.
He "turns not" when He goes straight forward. He again
and again announces His plans. He does not deceive nor
stoop to subtlety. His ways are truth. Men are forewarned
and they have no reason to be surprised when the throne
of God moves straight forward toward them. They can never
cry out in accusation that they did not have a chance to make
a right decision. The words of Scripture apply not only to the

individual but to nations: "So that they are without excuse" (Ro 1:20). To resist Him is futile and disastrous. He is the irresistible God!

8. God's Counterforces of Checks and Balances (v. 16)

Have you ever visited a factory where there were large numbers of belts running, seemingly, in all directions on larger and smaller wheels? It looks like utter confusion to the outsider who sees it for the first time. Yet, every one of those wheels propelling those belts, often in opposite directions, are all fulfilling a coherent purpose of the designer who engineered them.

So it is with the throne of God. We read: "The appearance of the wheels and their work(ing) was . . . as it were a wheel in the middle of a wheel" (v. 16). God does not always deal directly with a person or a nation. In the world there are all kinds of contrary purposes, as man views them. There is the extreme right of the ultraconservative and the extreme left of the permissive freewheeler in politics, economics, religious convictions, and other spheres. It often seems that everything is topsy-turvy. But with God, there is no confusion. His second, third, and fourth causes are fulfilling His purposes just as effectively as His more obvious primary interventions into human affairs.

God uses the diverse activities of men to act as checks and balances of group upon group. What seems chaos to us is being overruled in His wise design to work harmoniously in the ultimate accomplishment of His purposes. Not only to the individual, but in the affairs of corporate groups and nations: God "works all things together" for the good of His own and the carrying out of His plan. The wheels and belts are not . . . in His wisdom . . . working against each other, although where men's hates and stratagems are involved they may emanate from human nature with that intention. But God is wise enough and strong enough to make them complementary, even when they may seem to be going at cross purposes.

One of the great spirituals of our black brethren has caught the inner significance of this passage when it declares

> The little wheel moves by faith
> And the big wheel moves by the grace of God.

How perceptively true this is! Whatever our perplexity or evil men's machinations, God is causing the wheels which carry His throne to proceed toward that

> Long far-off, divine event
> Toward which the whole creation moves. (Tennyson)

To the eye of faith, the wheels are accomplishing God's purpose, however confusing they may outwardly appear to our limited knowledge.

9. The Multihued Throne of Grace (v. 28)

As the appearance of the bow that is in the cloud in the day of rain, so was the appearance of the brightness round about [the throne of v. 26]. This was the appearance of the likeness of the glory of the LORD.

Plainly we have a rainbow about the throne, as we later see it in Revelation 4:3. The rainbow was first called to our attention when God made His gracious promise that the earth would not again be judged with a flood (Gen 9:12-16).

If God judges, it is always with a gracious purpose. Like the surgeon who must cut and hurt in order to cleanse and heal, so God's judgments are to get at the causes of man's pains and provide sustaining grace for His own in the interim until a cleansed earth will be brought to pass by the personal return of the Lord Jesus Christ.

Thus the vision declares that all the purposes and activities of God's throne are consonant with His grace and mercy. There is a rainbow about the throne!

Hence, the cries of sinful and unbelieving men in accusation against God are both invalid and insolent. "Why does God allow Vietnam? Why does God allow hunger, poverty, degradation, and pain to stalk the earth? Why doesn't He just outlaw them, push a button, and cause them to stop, if he *is* God?" Such insulting mouthings, which ignore man's rebellious sin as the real cause, but demonstrate how blind is unbelief to the character of God and the stated sequences of God's program.

God is not callous to men's sufferings. He is pained, as are men, by the horrendous results of men's sins as they affect the whole world. But the rainbow about the throne portrays that throne as gracious now, as well as prophetic of a golden age shortly to come, when international gangsters will be removed with flaming fire; when righteousness will permeate the earth; when wars will cease; when little children will not go to bed hungry; when even the animal creation will become benign and the earth yield her bounty; when the earth shall be full of "the knowledge of the LORD, as the waters cover the sea" (Is 11:9). The throne of God is not cold like a stone; it is warm like a throbbing heart! God cares! He loves us!

10. THE AUTHORITATIVE THRONE (v. 24)

Finally, the vision asserts that the throne is characterized by "the voice of speech . . . as the voice of the Almighty . . . like the noise of great waters."

This is what we would expect from such a throne, the voice of authority. Only such a One has the right to rule and only such a throne can take over a bruised, battered, and bleeding world and nurse it back to health, sanity, and stability.

Even now, the ear of faith hears that authoritative voice. But one day, all men will hear its stentorian tones and, at long last, obey it!

The dreams of poets, the wistful hopes of philosophers, the agonized cries of the suffering and oppressed of earth cannot change things for man's good. Only this voice, like that of a trumpet, with no uncertain sound; only an authoritative voice from the unshaken throne, activated by Omnipotence, can fulfill the words He has spoken concerning the future and bring in earth's golden age, when

> Jesus shall reign where'er the sun
> Doth his successive journeys run
> His kingdom stretched from shore to shore
> Till moons shall wax and wane no more. (Isaac Watts)

How wonderful are these "visions of God" (v. 1) vouchsafed to Ezekiel and preserved for us in the great book bearing his name.

It is against such a background, with visions of such a throne, that we now proceed to examine the various prophetic themes included in the chapters of this book.

There are no more appropriate words to write over this perspective of God in prophecy than those of William Cowper's great hymn:

> God moves in a mysterious way
>   His wonders to perform;
> He plants His footsteps in the sea,
>   And rides upon the storm.
>
> Ye fearful saints, fresh courage take;
>   The clouds ye so much dread
> Are big with mercy, and shall break
>   In blessings on your head.
>
> Judge not the Lord by feeble sense,
>   But trust Him for His grace;
> Behind a frowning providence
>   He hides a smiling face.
>
> His purposes will ripen fast,
>   Unfolding every hour:
> The bud may have a bitter taste,
>   But sweet will be the flower.

Blind unbelief is sure to err,
    And scan His work in vain:
God is His own interpreter,
    And He will make it plain.

And let all the people of God reply, "Amen! So let it be!"

2

The Key Covenant

ALL PREMILLENNIALISTS properly insist that the validity of
the premillennial position depends heavily upon the unchanging character of the covenants of God with Abraham and with
David. It is, indeed, due to these covenants that we insist
upon the unchanging continuance of the promises of "a land,"
"a people," "a kingly line," with the view to the establishment
of a future kingdom ruled over by David's greater Son, the
Lord Jesus Christ, in a period of blessing to "all families of
the earth" (Gen 12:3). (The period is later identified as being a thousand years, Rev 20.)

The opponents of the premillennial position are just as
urgent in saying that the earthly aspects, at least, of the covenants of God with Abraham and David, were dependent for
their continuance upon the continued obedience of Abraham
and David and their respective descendants. Thus, Israel's
failure set aside any promised rights they had to the land,
to an earthly kingdom, and to any particular relationship to
Christ in a future kingdom on earth, say the amillennialists.
According to this view, Israel's failure has made them ineligi-
ble and has opened the door for the church to take over and
inherit the spiritual aspects of those covenants. Thus Christ
is king, but not king of the Jews. He reigns over the hearts
of His own in all the world, the church having superseded
Israel as "the seed of Abraham." Any earthly promises have
been set aside in favor of heavenly promises.

The premillennialist replies that there is, of course, a half truth in all of this. Israel is blind in part and is temporarily set aside during this age when God is taking out from the nations "a people for His name," Jew and Gentile. But Romans 9-11 is just as insistent that God will graft "the natural branches" back into their native "olive tree" when Israel repents. The Israel of God will be rescued by the returning "Deliverer out of Zion," and all God's kingdom promises to Israel, and through Israel to the world, will be fulfilled in accordance with the unchanged Old Testament Scripture. Thus Israel's failure requires discipline, but the covenants are not canceled, and the church does not take over permanently.

The most casual reading of amillennial and premillennial literature on this subject will make crystal clear that the real issue is the question of whether the Abrahamic and Davidic covenants are conditional or unconditional.

This is a crucial point and there is no cause for premillennialists to think that they have solved it by oversimplification and a wave of the hand. Mere asserting that the promise to Abraham was unconditional does not make it so. We shall proceed to an examination of this problem, but first let us refresh our minds with the wording of the first announcement of the covenant of God with Abraham as recorded in Genesis 12:1-3:

> Now the LORD had said unto Abram, Get thee out of thy country, and from thy kindred, and from thy father's house, unto a land that I will shew thee: and I will make thee a great nation, and I will bless thee, and make thy name great; and thou shalt be a blessing; and I will bless them that bless thee, and curse him that curseth thee: and in thee shall all families of the earth be blessed.

The usual approach of the premillennialists to this passage declares that Abraham had to leave Ur in order to activate this covenant. Perhaps one of the best and clearest statements of this approach is given by my good friend, Dr. J.

Dwight Pentecost, in his excellent book, *Things to Come*. Dr. Pentecost, as well as Dr. John F. Walvoord whom he quotes, is thoroughly committed to the unconditional character of the Abrahamic covenant, just as much as I am. Yet the following selection from his book (pp. 74-75, italics added) reveals that he places a condition to be fulfilled by Abraham between the promise of God to him in Ur and the actual establishment of the covenant. He says,

> While Abraham was living in the home of Terah, an idolator (Josh. 24:2), God spoke to him and commanded him to leave the land of Ur, even though it entailed a journey to a strange land he did not know (Heb. 11:8), and made certain specific promises to him that *depended* on this act of obedience. Abraham, in partial obedience, inasmuch as he did not separate himself from his kindred, journeyed to Haran (Gen. 11:31). He did not realize any of the promises there. It was not until after the death of his father (Gen. 11:32) that Abraham begins to realize anything of the promise God had given him, for only after his father's death does God take him into the land (Gen. 12:4) and there reaffirm the original promise to him (Gen. 12:7). It is important to observe the relation of *obedience* to this covenant program. Whether God would institute a covenant program with Abraham or not depended upon Abraham's act of *obedience* in leaving the land. When once this act was accomplished, and Abraham did obey God, God instituted an irrevocable, unconditional program. This *obedience*, which became the basis of the institution of the program, is referred to in Genesis 22:18, where the offering of Isaac is just one more evidence of Abraham's attitude toward God. Walvoord clearly states this fact when he writes:
>
> > "As given in the Scriptures, the Abrahamic Covenant is hinged upon *only one condition*. This is given in Genesis 12:1. . . . The original covenant was based upon Abraham's obedience in leaving his homeland and going to the land of promise. No further revelation is given him until he was obedient to this com-

mand after the death of his father. Upon entering Canaan, the Lord immediately gave Abraham the promise of ultimate possession of the land (Gen. 12:7), and subsequently enlarged and reiterated the original promises.

"The *one condition* having been met, no further conditions are laid upon Abraham; the covenant having been solemnly established is now dependent upon divine veracity for its fulfillment." ["Millennial Series," *Bibliotheca Sacra* 109:37]

Whether there would be a covenant program with Abraham depended upon Abraham's act of obedience. When once he obeyed, the covenant that was instituted depended, not upon Abraham's continued obedience, but upon the promise of the One who instituted it. The *fact* of the covenant depended upon obedience; the *kind* of covenant inaugurated was totally unrelated to the continuing obedience of either Abraham or his seed.

It is with this position that I disagree, namely, that a condition had to be fulfilled by Abraham in order to activate the covenant. It appears to me that we concede the very thing around which the question of conditional or unconditional hinges, as witness the quotation from Dr. Walvoord, "the Abrahamic Covenant hinged upon only one condition." This concession, in my judgment, plays into the hands of those who insist that Abraham's continued obedience was necessary to the fulfillment of the covenant.

May I suggest that you look above and read again the truth referred to in Genesis 22:18, where the offering of Isaac is just one more evidence of Abraham's attitude toward God. I submit that if the Abrahamic covenant had been conditioned upon Abraham's obedience (Gen 12:1), then that obedience was not completed in the act of Abraham's leaving Ur, for his father's house was with him (11:31) even though he had left his kindred and his country. Nor was his obedience completed by indirection in the release afforded him by his father's death (11:32), nor by his going into a land that God would show him (12:1), nor by his separation from Lot (13:9). Abraham's obedience on the occasion of his willingness to offer up Isaac is accompanied with the same basic language formula in Genesis 22:16-18 as God had used in Genesis 12:1-3. If it be argued that the obedience of Abraham would have been necessary to the establishment of the Abrahamic covenant in the first instance, then it might likewise be affirmed just as surely that his obedience in the willingness to offer up Isaac would of necessity have to take place before the covenant could be established.

This reasoning is fatal to the thesis of an *un*conditional covenant, for it requires the continued and cumulative obedience of Abraham as the basis for the establishment of the Abrahamic covenant. And however loudly we may protest that the covenant when once given becomes an unconditional covenant, if one espouses this theory the Scripture plainly indicates a shifting of the obedience-condition:

from Genesis 11:31 (leaving "country" and "kindred")

to 11:32—12:6 (death of father and entrance into the "land" that God would "shew" him)

to 13:9 (the final break with his father's house by separation from Lot)

to 15:1-7 (the promise of Isaac because Abraham ignored the king of Sodom and honored God through Melchizedek)

to chapter 22, especially verse 16 (because he did not withhold Isaac)

This constant shifting of Abraham's fulfillment of the condition of obedience (from 11:31 to 22:16) plays into the hands of amillennialists who insist that the covenant was always conditioned upon obedience. This presents us with the added hazard of proving that the covenant was really and finally established in Genesis 15. If we argue that Abraham had to perform even one act of obedience before the covenant could be established, our opponents have a dangerous wedge and precedent offered them as basis for their insisting that other and further acts of obedience continued to condition the covenant.

It appears to me that the basic hermeneutical cue to the solution of the passage is the recognition that the sequence of the oft-repeated word "and" merely connects the clauses of Genesis 12:1 with those of 12:2 and 12:3. Thus, rather than urging that obedience to the command of verse 1 established the covenant of verses 2 and 3, the better solution is that the "and" which opens verse 2 is not one which implies any condition, but simply the first of a series of "ands" which describe *a sequence of events.*

God did not say to Abraham, "When you get out and because you get out of Ur" (i.e., leave your "kindred" and "father's house," v. 1) and get to "a land that I will show you," (v. 1), "I will *then* make a covenant with you." Nor did He say, "I will then make this covenant valid which I am preannouncing to you, subject to your obedience." The verses are simply stating the sequence of events which will necessarily occur as God works out His unconditional covenant already announced to Abraham *before* he left Ur.

Thus Abraham will *first* leave Ur ("country" and "kindred") for the very good reason that God has commanded it, and that Abraham believes God and will therefore exercise the obedience that is the hallmark of true faith. This is not the basis for God then making a covenant. The covenant was given *before* he left Ur, not *because* he left Ur!

Unfortunately for the condition-of-obedience theory, Abraham would not and did not leave his father's house. Abraham's obedience was not complete and God had to wait until Abraham's father, Terah, died. Further, it is obvious that his obedience to this command concerning his "father's house" was not complete until after entering the land, for Lot was still with him. Abraham made no move to separate from Lot. He did it only because their herdsmen could not get along together (Gen 13:5-9). This demonstrates that these things were not primarily steps in obedience on the basis of which God's covenant hinged. Indeed, some of them were apart from Abraham's action entirely, as for example his father's death. They are rather a sequence in which things naturally occurred in the implementation of God's already announced unconditional covenant.

The next event after the completion of Genesis 12:1 in accordance with God's announcement was that God would make of him "a great nation" (v. 2). Necessarily this required the birth of Isaac and the extended growth in numbers of his descendants, first in Palestine and finally in Egypt. Then God made his "name great" (v. 2) through Israel's exaltation of it as being the name of their nation's founding father. Finally, through his own experiences and those of his descendants, the rest of verses 2 and 3 were fulfilled in the history which grew out of Genesis 12, with an overriding climactic central thought that "all the families of the earth" would be eventually "blessed" through Abraham's Seed—the Lord Jesus Christ!

Hence, verses 2 and 3 are no more conditioned upon verse 1 by the "and" which introduces verse 2, than any other statement of these three verses is conditioned upon the material that precedes it, introduced by the recurring "ands."

The proper interpretation of the "ands," therefore, is that they are simple conjunctions, binding together, and making as one whole, a list of related statements. At no point is it said that any one of these statements depends upon a previous statement. It is simply the sensible and reasonable order in which the story would unfold, and the events transpire as an all-knowing God foresaw and foretold them. God gave the covenant to Abraham *before* he left Ur of the Chaldees. He did not predicate the covenant on Abraham's obedience but upon His own unconditional purpose. He announced that He would do these things for Abraham and through him to his descendants, to the nation Israel, and to the world, with all its ultimates fulfilled through Abraham's Seed, the Lord Jesus Christ.

Thus the proper viewpoint is that the giving of the covenant was not conditioned upon Abraham's obedience, whether it be in chapters 11, 12, 13, 15, or 22, but that the covenant was unconditionally given in Ur to one who God knew would obey Him because he believed Him and loved Him. The key passage in substantiation of this thesis is recorded in Genesis 18:17-19, where we read,

> And the LORD said, Shall I hide from Abraham that thing which I do; seeing that Abraham shall surely become a great and mighty nation, and all the nations of the earth shall be blessed in him? For I know him, that he will command his children and his household after him, and they shall keep the way of the LORD, to do justice and judgment; that the LORD may bring upon Abraham that which he hath spoken of him.

Observe that this was said before the great climactic act of obedience in Genesis 22, and it presents the better explanation of what God subsequently said in Genesis 22:16-18:

> By myself have I sworn, saith the LORD, for because thou hast done this thing, and hast not withheld thy son, thine only son: that in blessing I will bless thee, and in multiplying I will multiply thy seed as the stars of the heaven, and as the sand which is upon the sea shore; and thy seed shall possess the gate of his enemies; and in thy seed shall all the nations of the earth be blessed; because thou hast obeyed my voice.

This solution avoids the peril of making the institution of the Abrahamic covenant dependent upon the obedience of Abraham, which all admit was at first very incomplete. The peril is all the more apparent when it is remembered that his obedience was not declared by God to be complete until he demonstrated his willingness to slay Isaac in sacrifice (Gen 22). Thus the solution avoids the peril of starting an obedience aspect of the covenant, demanded by amillennialists as being continuous, but which the usual premillennial view wishes to break off arbitrarily somewhere along the line between chapter 11 and chapter 22. If we start with obedience as a prerequisite to the covenant, the amillennialist has a right to claim we are inconsistent and have no warrant to stop with Abraham's leaving Ur, for who can confidently declare at what point his obedience would be sufficiently complete to cause God to establish the covenant? If Genesis 22 be urged as the completion of his obedience, then the covenant was not made in Genesis 12 or 15, but only after Isaac was offered in Genesis 22. This would work against and not for premillennialists in our disagreement with the amillennialists.

The discussion concerning the Abrahamic covenant above may well lead to a broader inquiry than this one covenant. To be specific, what do we mean by an unconditional covenant? And what do we mean by a conditional covenant? And, perhaps more basic, what is a covenant? Here are my suggested definitions:

1. A covenant is a sovereign pronouncement of God by which He establishes a relationship of responsibility (*a*) between Himself and an individual (e.g., Adam in the Edenic covenant), (*b*) between Himself and mankind in general (e.g., in the promise of the Noahic covenant never again to destroy all flesh with a flood), (*c*) between Himself and a nation (e.g., Israel in the Mosaic covenant, Ex 19:3ff.), or (*d*) between Himself and a specific human family (e.g., the house of David in the promise of a kingly line in perpetuity through the Davidic covenant). A covenant of one category may overlap with other categories, as in the case of the Davidic covenant where the promise of a continuing kingly house to David has tremendous results (*c*) to the nation Israel and (*b*) to the whole world of men in the eventual reign of Jesus Christ.

2. The covenants are normally unconditional in the sense that God obligates Himself in grace (by the unrestricted declaration, "I will") to accomplish certain announced purposes, despite any failure on the part of the person or group with whom He covenants. The human response to the divinely announced purpose is always important, leading as it does to blessing for obedience and discipline for disobedience. But human failure is never permitted by God to abrogate the covenant nor block its ultimate fulfillment.

3. A covenant is conditional when its establishment is made dependent upon man's acceptance of the terms of the contract, as for example in the case of Israel's acceptance of the terms of the Mosaic covenant, as evidenced by the words in Exodus 19:5, 8: "if ye will obey . . . ye shall be" (i.e., God's offer which compact Israel accepted as expressed in v. 8) and "all the people answered, . . . All that the LORD hath spoken we will do" (i.e., man's response).

In the light of these definitions, it will be helpful to summarize our discussion of the Abrahamic covenant in respect to what makes a covenant conditional or unconditional.

It is regrettable that many definitions of a conditional covenant hinge around the idea that God commits Himself to bless a person or group so long as obedience is forthcoming, and warns that He will of necessity discipline him or them if disobedience should later result.

It will be found from the definitions above that this is not that which makes a covenant conditional. It was seen that all of God's great unconditional covenants are not dependent upon the human response to keep them in force. God proposes to see to it that they are kept in force. That is what makes them unconditional. But it must also be borne in mind that in the case of every one of God's *un*conditional covenants, "the human response to the divinely announced purpose is always important, leading as it does to blessing for obedience and discipline for disobedience. But human failure is never permitted by God to abrogate the covenant nor block its ultimate fulfillment."

And, on the contrary, we saw that the better solution as to what constitutes a conditional covenant is to observe, as in our definition, that the condition is something which *precedes* the establishment of the covenant. Once the condition is accepted by man, then the covenant is ratified. Further, the conditional covenant is to be distinguished from the unconditional covenant in the fact that a conditional covenant is not permanent, since man's failure not only brings discipline, as in the unconditional covenant, but it can in God's time lead to the dissolution or voiding of the terms of the contract. This is something which could never occur in an *un*conditional covenant.

To return to our discussion of the Abrahamic covenant in the light of the above, it should be carefully borne in mind that we should avoid confusing an act of obedience as being necessary to the institution of an *un*conditional covenant. Indeed, the fulfillment of a condition before a covenant is ratified would, according to my definition, make that covenant a *conditional* one, whereas Abraham's various acts of obedience (or his regrettable failures) would not in any way condition the validity of the making or continuance of an unconditional covenant.

If one argues that the covenant of God with Abraham was tentative until Abraham obeyed some condition upon which the establishment of the covenant would hinge, one has laid the foundation for the argument that the covenant was not unconditional, but conditional in its institution, as well as in its continuance.

In addition, Abraham's failures (as well as those of his descendants) would have long since abrogated the covenant, if its continuance were contingent upon continual obedience (e.g., Ro 4:13-16). Any one of the following disobediences would have abrogated the covenant:

1. Abraham's lack of faith and his lie in Genesis 12:10-20

2. His failure to separate from Lot previous to Genesis 13

3. His failure to trust God to give him Isaac instead of Ish-mael (Gen 16)

4. His failure to trust God for the renewal of Sarah's body (Gen 17:17-19)

5. Sarah's failure to believe God's promise of a son (Gen 18:12ff.)

The same thesis would apply to the disobediences of Isaac, Jacob, and their many descendants. Because this was not the case and because the covenant was not established upon the condition of Abraham's obedience, it is therefore improper for the amillennialist to bring in a condition then or later (and especially in the case of Israel's failure involved in the rejection of their Messiah) and urge that this is the basis for God's abrogation of that part of the Abrahamic covenant which refers to the land of Palestine, while also urging that Israel's failure permits only certain spiritual promises to remain to those in Christ, the Seed, namely the church. All the covenant was unconditional in its institution and from the time of its institution. An excellent proof of this may be found in the words of Hebrews 6:13ff., which reads in the Centenary Translation of the New Testament:

> For when God made the promise to Abraham, since he could swear by none greater, he swore by himself, saying: "Surely I will bless you, and bless you; I will increase you, and increase you" (Gen 22:16-17). And so by patiently waiting, Abraham obtained the promise. (I am referring to the oath) because men swear by what is greater than themselves, and in every dispute of theirs the oath is final for confirmation. On which principle God, wishing to show more convincingly to the heirs of the promise the immutability of his purpose, mediated with an oath; that by means of two immutable things—his promise and his oath—in which it is impossible for God to break faith, we refugees may have strong encouragement to grasp the hope set before us. This

hope we have as an anchor of the soul, secure and strong,
and passing into the sanctuary which is beyond the veil;
whither Jesus himself is entered as a forerunner on our behalf, having become a priest forever, after the order of Mel-
chisedek.

It is plainly stated that God made a unilateral covenant,
imposing upon Himself alone the responsibility for the orig-
ination and culmination of the covenant ("he swore by himself"). Abraham entered into the blessing benefits by obedi-
ently waiting in faith, but it is just as clear that only Abraham's subjective enjoyment and encouragement were affected by his response. The covenant itself was as firm, un-
changeable, and inviolate as the character of God Himself.
Because God is unchanging, Abraham could know how sure
the covenant was. It is on the basis of His immutability that
Abraham was encouraged to rest in sure confidence.

This is in harmony with the great scene in Genesis 15.[1]

1. Some have insisted that the oral statement of Genesis 12:1-3 does not
constitute a covenant because the word *covenant* does not appear. I reply
that an unqualified promise by God to a person or group constitutes a contract or covenant in which He has put Himself on record as requiring Himself to do certain things. (Obviously, there are minor covenants of which
we are not speaking here. We are referring to what Scofield rightly calls
"The Major Covenants of Scripture.")
It is understood by practically all dispensationalists that the first two
such covenants are the *Edenic* and the *Adamic covenants*. If Pentecost,
Walvoord, and others are right in passing over Genesis 12 to Genesis 15
before the *Abrahamic covenant* is enacted and in force, then logically they
must discard the Edenic and Adamic covenants, because the word *covenant* is not used by God in either of these cases (Gen 1:26-30; 2:15-17; 3:
14-19). Why would God have to use a particular word or formula? Is not
His unequivocal statement of purpose enough?
The proposition they make that there is no Abrahamic covenant until
Genesis 15 is based upon the misconception that the words "In the same
day the LORD made a covenant with Abram, saying" (v. 18) proves that
position. However, in addition to my previous objection, that the word
covenant is not a technical requirement, I offer further objection. The verses
preceding the words "made a covenant" do not rehearse the *details* of what
God already had said to Abraham in 12:1-3; 12:7; or 13:14-17. The only
tie-in is the statement that He previously had given him "this land" (15:7).
All the other provisions are omitted. Hence, at this point, it is simply
expanding His previous promise and making clear what He includes in
"this land." On that "same day" God formally makes a covenant about the
exact delineation of land area affected, namely, "from the river of Egypt
unto . . . the river Euphrates." There is not the slightest suggestion that
God had not previously said a number of other things as binding on Him

Customarily in a blood covenant, the carcasses were divided and both covenanters passed together between the carcasses in confirmation of the solemn covenant. But in Genesis 15 Abraham is in "a deep sleep" (v. 12) and cannot pass through the carcasses with God. God passed through alone (v. 17), since the covenant was entirely dependent upon Him. He pledged Himself to fulfill all that He had said before to Abraham, as well as such details as He added here (15:18-21) and later (e.g., 22:16-18). All these things were announced sovereignly by God to Abraham, as being His unconditional good pleasure. He knew Abraham's faith and love would implement the beginning of that sequence of events described progressively in Genesis 12:1-3 and enlarged and reaffirmed in such passages as Genesis 12:7; 13:14-17; 15:1-21; 17:1-8, 15-21; 18:17-19; 22:15-18; 26:2-5, 24; 28:12-15; 35:9-12; 46:3-4; 48:14-16, 19-20. God's purpose did not rest upon Abraham's faithfulness, but God encouraged and assisted him to grow little by little from the partial

as the promise of "this land," which was not previously explained specifically. So this phrase, "made a covenant," is circumscribed as being a fuller addition to an already given covenant. It is simply an addition to the corpus, much like that when a father might put a child down for $5,000 in a will but later add "and the house and the lot" at a certain address.

The additions of chapter 15 no more imply nothing was promised, contracted, covenanted before chapter 15 than they imply nothing was covenanted after chapter 15. Both premises are false. Much was said before and much was added later, but it is all one basic covenant! Chapter 12 is the basic original announcement of the covenant. Numerous reiterations, confirmations, and additions followed: 12:7; 13:14-17; 15:7-21; 17:1-21; 18:17-19; 22:15-18. But, in addition to these statements to Abraham, there are later confirmations to Isaac (Gen 26:2-5, 24), to Jacob (Gen 28:12-15; 35:9-12; 46:3-4), and—strange as it may seem—to David (Ps 72:8) where the land grant is expanded to read "He [Christ] shall have dominion also from sea to sea, and from the river [i.e., the Euphrates—the previous extent of Gen 15] unto the ends of the earth"!

It is absurd to try to place the beginning of the Abrahamic covenant at anything but the beginning, Genesis 12:1-3. Otherwise, language is bereft of meaning. Anything else is defective semantics. When God says something, He means it. He does not deal in trick formulas. Ultimate confusion is added to confusion when it is insisted that Abraham had to leave Ur or do anything to make God's plain promises and covenant valid. Such a premise destroys the distinctiveness of *unconditional.*

If it would make anyone feel more secure, we might say that the covenant is first announced and enacted in Genesis 12, formally confirmed in Genesis 15, then confirmed and expanded many times—not only to Abraham but also to Isaac, Jacob, and even David!

step of obedience in leaving Ur, to the full climax of his obedience in offering Isaac, a sacrifice supernaturally interrupted by God Himself.

Thus by the viewpoint suggested in this chapter, certain advantages are attendant: (1) the unconditional character of the Abrahamic covenant is not jeopardized through the admission of even one condition as essential to the establishment of the covenant with Abraham; (2) the unconditional character of the covenant is clearly demonstrated; (3) the amillennial viewpoint is shown to be totally out of keeping with the facts of the case and thus totally incorrect; (4) the establishment of the covenant is shown to be an act of God's own will which is to be carefully distinguished from subsequent blessing or discipline for obedience or disobedience, respectively.

To summarize, therefore, the basis for God's making the covenant with Abraham was not the fact of his leaving Ur or any other act of obedience. The covenant was given to him *before* he left Ur, *not because* he left Ur, and rested upon the unconditional purpose of God to do something in grace, not only for Abraham but ultimately for all the world through the greater Son and Seed, the Lord Jesus Christ.

It is maintained that the following points have been established:

1. It is urged that the usual definitions of a conditional covenant be re-examined to conform to the thesis expressed in this article, namely, that the condition is offered by God and accepted by man *before* the covenant is ratified and is not the issue *after* the ratification.

2. It is held that blessing and discipline after a covenant is established are an inevitable and inherent part of God's way of dealing with men and their response to Him; and that, in the case of the unconditional covenant, there is no effect whatever on the validity or continuance of the covenant.

3. It is claimed that a clarification of our thinking, as emphasized here, as to what constitutes a conditional or an unconditional covenant, will warn us against the fallacy of permitting any condition as a prelude to an unconditional covenant, such as the Abrahamic covenant which has been under consideration here.

4. It is declared that no concession or comfort be given the amillennial position by the fallacy of requiring Abraham to leave Ur, or perform any other act of obedience, in order to pave the way for the instituting of the Abrahamic covenant. Rather, God announced this covenant of His own free will, apart from any condition, because He had the wisdom, power, and grace to carry out His purpose, for He "worketh all things after the counsel of his own will" (Eph 1:11).

3

The Virgin Prophecy

I. INTRODUCTION

ON SEPTEMBER 30, 1952, the *Revised Standard Version* Old Testament was released to the public, along with the already published New Testament (1946). Almost immediately there was a roar of protest from the fundamentalist camp when it was discovered that Isaiah 7:14 was rendered that it was a "young woman" who would conceive and bare a son who would be named Immanuel.

Some of the extreme things that were said and written at that time, as well as since, obviously were motivated by the notion—which I consider to be erroneous—that such a wording was incapable of acceptance by any sincere Bible believer because it made impossible the acceptance and security of the doctrine of the virgin birth of our Lord Jesus Christ. Perhaps this great fear led to the emotional intemperance of many statements made in written and oral public pronouncements. Indeed, some of the hysteria would have been ludicrous, if it had not been so painfully tragic. Instead of "they have taken away my Lord and I know not where they have laid Him," the terror-stricken voices cried, "they have taken away my Lord and I know not where they have begotten Him."

II. NO REASON FOR HYSTERIA

I take second place to no one in strong adherence to the

43

plainly stated biblical fact that Jesus' begetting was of the
Holy Spirit of God, and that His birth was therefore of
Mary, while still a virgin, since Joseph had no copulation
with her until *after* "she had brought forth her firstborn
son" (Mt 1:25). Both Matthew 1 and Luke 1 make it un-
mistakably clear that our Lord, as to His humanity, was supernaturally begotten by the Holy Spirit in the virgin womb
of Mary. Matthew goes out of his way to show that the
genealogy of chapter 1 establishes Jesus' legal title to the
throne of David; that Joseph was only the foster father of
Jesus; but that Joseph's marriage to Mary was absolutely
essential for the very good reason that Jesus would have
been legally classified as a bastard, if Joseph had not married
her. And no bastard could have a pure and clear status before the law or to the throne of the Jews. Thus, if another
translation than "virgin" in Isaiah 7:14 could possibly negate
the history of Matthew 1 and Luke 1, there would be good
cause for deep concern, and perhaps some concession to the
extremity of the statements made against such a translation.

But that is not the case. Whatever may be the solution
to the proper translation of Isaiah 7:14, a historic fact is established by historic statements, such as are brought before
us in the historical accounts of Matthew and Luke. It is utterly improper hermeneutics to urge a problem translation of
a prophecy as negating or diluting a bona fide, unequivocal
statement of a historical document. Perhaps this is the place
to say, once and for all, the fact that Jesus was supernaturally
born is firmly rooted in *historical* fact and does not rest upon
some interpretation of prophecy.

The strange thing about this whole furore over the Isaiah
translation in the *Revised Standard Version* implies that
something new or unusual had occurred. It is simply a matter of fact that, despite the plain statements of Matthew 1
and Luke 1, many had previously doubted or denied the
virgin birth. Indeed, this unbelief goes clear back to our

Lord's day. Did not members of the Sanhedrin sneeringly say to Jesus' face, "We were not born of fornication" (Jn 8:41)? They blatantly blasted Him as a bastard! And some of the magnitude of Mary's wonderful submission to, and trust in, the heavenly Father becomes more pointed up in her words, "Behold, I am the handmaid of the Lord; let it be to me according to your word" (Lk 1:38). Mary was painfully aware that the old "hens" of camel-crossroads Nazareth, dirty-minded as it was (Jn 1:46), would piously cluck around about "that hypocritical young woman" who posed as pure, when "everyone" knew that, when she came back from her visit to Elizabeth in Judea, she was already pregnant before she went to live with Joseph. Mary counted the cost and bowed her head in noble submission to God! So, even if it could be proven that the translators of the *Revised Standard Version* were seeking to deny the virgin birth, a thing that is by no means automatic in the translation, this should not be thought of as a novel or modern idea.

Further, that the Hebrew should be so translated is nothing new. Are the objectors to this translation not aware that the Greek translations of Aquila, Symmachus, and Theodotian in ancient times (to name a few) rendered the word *neanis*, "young woman" or "maid"? Indeed, in more modern times, when the earlier rationalists argued that the virgin birth of Jesus was not historical but had been suggested by the words of Isaiah 7:14, conservatives were quick to point out that the word used in Isaiah's prophecy did not specifically mean "virgin".[1] It is strange that, with the advent of the *Revised Standard Version* Old Testament, the argument was completely turned around by numerous conservatives, evidently from fear that the doctrine of the virgin birth was now, at long last, in mortal danger.

1. See statements in International Standard Bible Encyclopaedia, 3:1458(b), 5:3051(b), and 3052(b), among others.

III. Rejection of Virgin Birth, not a Matter of Scholarship but of Unbelief

Objection to the virgin birth is not new. It is not only a flat rejection of historical accounts of Matthew and Luke, but comes from an overriding doctrinal bias against the whole position of the Scripture that Jesus was "God manifest in the flesh" (1 Ti 3:16), and that "all the *pleroma* (fullness) of the Godhead" was in our Lord's human body ("in bodily form," Col 2:9). Only people with a compulsion for unbelief doctrinally would have the audacity to defy all laws of historical evidence in Matthew and Luke that Jesus was indeed uniquely gestated, born without a human father, and thus constituted a once-forever, only one-of-his-kind person. Now, having said that, it might well be argued, "Why the amazement? Was not the first man Adam produced without either a human father or a human mother? Was not Eve produced without a human mother? Why should it be thought out of keeping with the previous activity of a miracle-working God that Jesus should be gestated and born without a human father?"

So, rejection of the virgin birth is not a matter of scholarly interpretation, but of unbelief. Since with God there is neither past nor future, only the eternal present, there is no problem to Him who sees everything as a present related unit. With our limited comprehension, we sometimes have problems, but we should not; for when God says a thing, it is true, even if we fail to catch all the nuances. This makes important the absolutely essential fact that God can only be understood in an atmosphere of faith, as we read: "Through faith we understand . . . without faith it is impossible to please him: for he that cometh to God must believe . . ." (Heb 11:3, 6).

IV. The Matthew Method of Identifying Fulfillments

There is another connected aspect to our discussion, a matter that will be labored later, namely, the scriptural practice in prophecy of what is called the law or principle of double fulfillment. This is an important and oft-neglected clue to proper interpretation.

If anyone has any problem about the double fulfillment position that I am taking in this chapter, I challenge him with Hosea 11:1. It reads: "When Israel was a child, then I loved him, and called my son out of Egypt." I categorically deny that anyone would have ever come up with the idea that this passage had an ultimate, far-view fulfillment in Jesus Christ, unless he had the words of the Holy Spirit through Matthew in 2:19-21 before him. I shall not even urge a consideration of the rather oblique prophecy, stated as fulfilled in Matthew 2:23, "And he came and dwelt in . . . Nazareth: that it might be fulfilled which was spoken by the prophets, He shall be called a Nazarene." But I will remind the reader that the same Holy Spirit through Matthew in the same book records the fulfillment of Isaiah 7:14 in the chapter immediately preceding these rather unique statements of fulfillments in chapter 2, verses 20 and 23.

If the Holy Spirit feels at ease to adopt this free method of fulfillment interpretation in the two instances in chapter 2, what right has anyone in the name of hermeneutics to insist upon a cast-iron, inflexible interpretation of His statement of fulfillment in the virgin passage of 1:22-23? It would seem to me that, at the least, restraint would be appropriate in their criticism of anyone who, equally devoutly believing in the virgin birth, sees flexibility as legitimate in the interpretation of Isaiah 7:14 as having a double fulfillment, a near and a far view.

No biblically-oriented, conservative believer in the fundamentals of the Christian faith could hold any other view than that our Lord was virgin born and that the Matthew 1 quotation provides the ultimate (or far-view) interpretation of the Isaiah passage. But to use Matthew 1:22-23 to cast doubt upon, or obdurately deny, any possible near-view interpretation of Isaiah 7:14 is not only not in harmony with some of Matthew's other statements of fulfillment, as cited above on Matthew 2, but is both unbrotherly and invalid. If we must take up the weapons of truth, let us use them against the enemies of the truth, rather than against those who hold to the truth as doggedly as ourselves!

One is tempted at this point to launch into a direct analysis of Isaiah 7:14. But for many reasons I feel this examination will be much more profitable if we would first look at the background of the whole great prophecy of Immanuel and the Assyrian, recorded by Isaiah in 7:1—9:7.

V. THE OVERALL MESSAGE OF ISAIAH (7:1—9:7)

In chapters 1-12 of Isaiah, we have the Holy One of Israel rebuking a people who drew near with their lips, but whose heart was far from Him (cp. Mt 15:8). There are five prophetic discourses with chapter 6, Isaiah's call, inserted parenthetically. Our section is the fourth prophetic discourse (7:1—9:7), discussing the near and far view of Immanuel and the Assyrian (the literal historic Assyrians in the near view and the king of the north of the end-time in the far view, Dan 11:40).

There is a crisis situation. As Isaiah 7:1-2 opens, war clouds threaten because of a plot of Syria and the northern ten tribe kingdom of Israel to remove Ahaz and put a puppet on the throne, subject to them. This man is so inconsequential that he isn't even named (v. 6)! Godly Uzziah is dead (Is 6:1). His weak son and successor, Jotham, has either been overlapped or superseded by Ahaz, a poor excuse for a descendant of David (7:13).

In this crisis situation, Isaiah is told to take his son Shearjashub and go to meet Ahaz with the good news that God is going to intervene in behalf of Judah and cause the plot to abort (vv. 3-9). This he does. God categorically says Judah will not be overcome. Isaiah's very name is played upon, in accord with 8:18, and by his very presence God is saying to Ahaz, "Jehovah will deliver you," and, by the same token, this is the only sensible reason for God's order to Isaiah to take his son along with him to meet Ahaz, for *Shear-jashub* means "A remnant shall return." God is saying, "This confederacy will fail; I will see to it; I am going to deliver (save) Judah (i.e., *Isaiah*). But even if you find that hard to believe, be assured that if an invasion seems successful, that is not the end of David's house. A remnant shall return (i.e., *Shear-jashub*). No one can overcome My word and purpose. So accept My word, Ahaz, in order that you—personally—may be established (v. 9b). But whether you personally believe or not, the attempt to overthrow Judah's throne will come to naught. I have spoken!"

One would have thought that Ahaz would have rejoiced at this good news, but like so many of those who profess to believe God today, he trusted his unbelieving feelings rather than the comforting word of God. Thus, seeing unbelief written all over his face, Isaiah further pleads for Ahaz to believe the peremptory challenge which Jehovah now authorizes: "Ask a sign. Any kind of sign in heaven above or earth beneath. Make it hard. Make it spectacular. Come on; let Me show you by a miracle that I mean the plot will fail and Judah will not be overcome" (v. 11).

It is amazing that people can be so adroit at using religious words to cover their unbelief with a cloak of piety! Ahaz says, "Oh, I wouldn't need anything like that to make me believe. I will not put God to a test" (v. 12). Isaiah sees through this thin gauze of hypocritical unbelief, and reprimands Ahaz for his unbelief, not simply as a man, but as the titular head of God's covenant people and as David's successor (v. 13). Isaiah responds: "So, you won't seek a sign when Jehovah commands you, you hypocrite? I'll tell you something. Adonai (i.e., Lord—master) Himself has therefore chosen an unmistakable sign which I am hereby announcing to you. A child will be born, who will be called 'God with us' (*Immanuel*). And things are going to happen just like I said. Judah is going to be delivered. The plot is going to fail. It is going to happen fast, for before the child comes to the age of moral responsibility (v. 16), the threat will have come to naught. And if you were to choose the name of the child yourself, you would have to say, 'God did this. God was with us. This is His deliverance!'

"However, due to your unbelief, God is going to discipline you and your land (vv. 17ff.). Assyria, not Syria and Samaria, is going to invade. Their army will overflow the land, like the Euphrates overflows its banks in the rainy season (8:5-8). Judah will be all but drowned—will be like a man keeping his nose above water by standing on tiptoe. The land will be horribly decimated, thanks to your unbelief (7:17-25). The fields will not be able to be tilled, because of invading armies. Men will have to live off of that which nature provides (7:21-22). Even this child, of whom I have spoken, will have to survive like the rest of conquered Judeans. 'Butter and honey shall he eat' (7:15; cp. 21-22). But delivered they shall be (*Isaiah*)! I will see to that (8:9-14), though many—like yourself—will fall because of unbelief (8:15). This is my word; do not seek the message of the lying spirits; seek me" (8:16-20).

In confirmation, we have the strange scene in 8:1-4. Is this simply pre-naming the near-view child to be born of his first wife, mother of Shear-jashub; or is this a pre-naming with the suggestion that he is now taking a second wife (with the presumption that the first wife has died, though polygamy was not forbidden in Israel)? I do not know. I suggest it is the first wife, with flexibility being given to the *almah* of 7:14 (later to be discussed). But plainly the message in its first and primary force is given to Ahaz and the people then in Judah, whatever may be its ultimate fulfillment. If not, the language becomes heavily pointless as an answer to Ahaz's unbelief and as an appeal to belief on the part of the people of Judah who were then being called upon to seek God's shelter and accept His word, however dark the days (8:13-20). This, I am convinced, is the main thrust of the message God is giving through Isaiah to Ahaz and the people of Judah in that day. Of course, I hasten to add: it is my thesis that there is a double fulfillment, and the future application is undoubtedly to the Lord Jesus Christ, both in 7:14 and in 9:1-7. This law of double fulfillment runs constantly through Old Testament Scriptures and should be understood as divinely purposed and revealed that way.

(Perhaps, as an aside, it should be said that "Maher-shalal-hash-baz" may best be translated "Speed to the spoil; haste to the prey," picturing the ravenous conquest of the Assyrians who would have completely overthrown Jerusalem and Judah, had it not been for the miraculous intervention of God as described in Isaiah 36-37, especially 37:7, 30-37.)

With this background, it is hoped that the whole problem of the virgin passage has been brought into clearer focus. It is now appropriate that we return to the linguistic and theological details which have loomed large in the historical debate on the meaning of Isaiah 7:14 and its surrounding context.

As previously stated, the mid-twentieth century is not the first occasion for serious disagreement on the "virgin" sign to Ahaz, as recorded in the two inextricably overlapping prophecies of Isaiah 7:14-16 and 8:1-8. It will be helpful to delineate.

VI. THE FOUR VIEWPOINTS ON THE ISAIAH PASSAGE CONCERNING THE VIRGIN

(Isaiah 7:14-16; cp. 8:1-8)

These may be classified under two headings: the unorthodox view and orthodox views—as follows:

UNORTHODOX (near view *only*):

(1) That the whole passage (7:14-16) refers to Isaiah's time only.

52   *Prophetic Problems*

ORTHODOX:

(2) That the whole passage (7:14-16) refers to the future only.

(3) That 7:14-15 refer to Christ only (far view) and that 7:16 refers to someone else and was fulfilled in Isaiah's time, either by Shear-jashub (as per William Kelly, translating "child" by "lad"), or by some other child (e.g., Maher-shalal-hash-baz, 8:3-4). A few commentators say verse 14 is entirely future and verses 15-16 are near view only.

(4) That 7:14 refers to Isaiah's time (near view) and to Christ (far view) and thus has a double application, and that 7:15-16 refer to the near view only. This is the view I hold and will give evidence for so holding as we proceed with the chapter.

VII. THREE REASONS FOR BELIEVING THERE IS A NEAR VIEW APPLICATION (to Isaiah's time)

(Observe: This rules out view (2) under VI above; i.e., applies to future only.)

A. Because the passage is primarily concerned with an event soon to occur (7:15-16).

B. Because the cowed king could not be calmed in his panic over the immediate disaster of an impending invasion by a prophecy of value only in the distant future.

C. Because 8:1-4, 8, 10, 18 speak of the prophet's child Maher-shalal-hash-baz in a way favorable to a near view application (cp. 7:15-16).

VIII. FIVE REASONS FOR BELIEVING THERE IS ALSO A FAR-VIEW APPLICATION TO A FUTURE MESSIAH (CHRIST)

(Observe: This rules out view (1) under VI above; i.e., a near view only.)

A. The familiar "law of double fulfillment" applies here. Even George Adam Smith, who cannot be accused of being prejudiced toward conservative views, says there must be a sign of a future Messiah here or words are diluted of any real meaning.

B. In Matthew 1:22-23, we find the complete fulfillment. No personality has ever lived, except the Lord Jesus, who has or could fill out the prophecy in full measure.

C. It is of no inconsiderable value to remember that this identification of the *complete* fulfillment with Christ has been the mind of the Christian church from apostolic times till rather recently. It is significant to note that until the relatively recent surge of rationalism, only infidels and Jews challenged the view.

D. This interpretation agrees with the teaching of Isaiah all through this prophecy (cp. 8:4, 8; 9:1-7; 11:1, etc.).

E. There is a prophecy of striking similarity in Micah 5: 1-3. And Matthew 2:6 identifies this passage as fulfilling a prophecy concerning Christ. Micah was contemporaneous with Isaiah, and he was so similar in thrust to Isaiah that many call him "the little Isaiah."

I have already pointed out that view (1) has been disposed of by VIII, and that view (2) has been answered by VII. This brings us to views (3) and (4), as the only remaining options. I now propose to show why view (3) is untenable.

IX. Five Reasons for Rejecting View Three Urged by Kelly

(that 7:14-15 refer to Christ and verse 16 to a "lad"— Shear-jashub)

Evidently William Kelly feels that a failure to limit verse 14 to Christ would weaken the evidence for the virgin birth of Christ. Recognizing there is a problem he seeks to avoid it by assigning both 7:14 and 15 to Christ, but assigning verse 16 to another than Christ. He seeks to accomplish this by laboring the fact that the word "child" can be translated "lad." I don't consider this as crucial as he does. Obviously a "lad" would be a male "child," but he wishes to push the word's force to indicate not a child *to be* born, after the prophecy of 7:14-15 is announced, but a child *already* born, who is now old enough to be called a "lad." Because Shear-jashub is old enough to accompany his father Isaiah, at God's direction (7:3), therefore, the "lad" is Shear-jashub. Kelly imagines that Isaiah announces verses 14-15 as the sign of Messiah (only) and then motions with his hand to Shear-jashub, by his side, closing the interview thus: "For before this lad (Shear-jashub—by my side) grows up (i.e., in a short while), the land that thou abhorrest shall be forsaken of both her kings (i.e., 7:1) as I have just told you" (7:7-10).

This is an earnest and interesting attempt to assist in solving the proper interpretation of this important passage, but it is subject to some very pertinent objections. I shall list five.

A. To change so abruptly, from "the child" of 7:14-15 to another "child"—"the lad"—Shear-jashub in 7:16, is most unlikely. It is difficult to suppose that God intends us to see the motion of an invisible hand, Isaiah's, pointing to Shear-jashub, when He is very aware that none of us were there and nothing is said about such a motion of Isaiah's hand. If God intended to make this striking change by contrast with the child He had been causing Isaiah to announce, He could have simply substituted the name Shear-jashub for "this child" or "this lad." To argue that He meant this but did not make it clear, but left us to guess He meant it, is gratuitous reasoning. We have no right to assume the thing requiring proof.

B. Comparing 7:16 with 8:4, the child would have to be younger than Shear-jashub.

C. Further, 7:15 cannot be applied legitimately either to Shear-jashub or to Christ, because

D. 7:15 is indissolubly linked with verse 16 by the "for" of verse 16.

E. And language does not mean anything if there is not

some close connection between verses 14 and 15 or 16 (already seen to be connected by the "for").

X. Thus, Remaining View (4) Is the Only Viable View that Fulfills All Conditions Delineated Under Objections to Views (1), (2), and (3) Above

The whole passage of 7:14-16 would then have a near view application. And, yet, arising out of this near view setting is a far view application in verse 14 that could be completed by Christ alone, and to Mary His mother—a virgin both when Christ was gestated as well as when He was born ("sign-virgin-Immanuel"). Thus, 7:15-16 are in no way essential details of the sign in the *far* view (indeed, I feel they have no application; for instance, when did sinless Jesus have to learn to refuse evil and choose good, and when is He ever said to have been sustained on only "butter and honey"?). Finally, 7:15-16, vitally connected as they are, refer *only* to the immediate events of the *near* view (e.g., 7:21-22 and 8:4), as proof to Ahaz of God's power and purpose to perform His word speedily (7:6-7; cp. 8:4).

XI. The Word Translated "Virgin" (almah) in the King James Version of 7:14

We cannot properly proceed to other considerations until we turn aside to discuss the much debated key word which is at the root of the discussion of the problem. As indicated, the Hebrew word is *ha-almah*, with the definite article.[2]

It should be pointed out that the word is extremely rare

---

2. I am sure that the reader is aware of the fact that, originally, the Hebrew text did not have what we call vowels (technically, "pointings"). It was composed only of consonants (technically, "radicals"). The vowels were memorized by the "scribes" because Hebrew had become a dead language. These men found it increasingly difficult to pass on the correct word without error, so in the seventh century A.D. they inserted these pointings amid the consonants of the text. Many godly scholars, therefore, recognize that there are some situations in which either the inserted vowels or the combination of the consonants may lead to a problem as to which of two possible "roots" the word in the particular instance is to be taken as derived.

in Hebrew and rare in cognate languages. It is used only seven times in the Old Testament. The King James Version translates it with "virgin" four times (Gen 24:43; Song 1:3; 6:8; and Is 7:14). It is rendered "maid" twice (Ex 2:8; Pr 30:19), and "damsel" once (Ps 68:25). An alternate word *alamoth* is used twice (1 Ch 15:20 and in the title of Ps 46, where the translators refuse to decide whether *alamoth* meant "sopranos" or some high-pitched musical instrument like a woman's voice).

Thus, the word *almah* would naturally suggest the idea of "virgin," or certainly permit it, if there were no presuppositions of unbelief. But that it means "virgin" everywhere is an argument from inference, not sustained by facts, as will be seen next.

XII. How almah Is Translated in Other Greek Versions

It is simply a matter of fact that *Jewish* translators of the Septuagint, to name the most important Greek translation of the Old Testament, did not render the word uniformly by the strict Greek word for "virgin" (*parthenos*). They translated *almah* as follows:

> *neanis*—young woman, 4 times,
> *nestis*—youth, 1 time,
> *parthenos*—virgin, 2 times,
> *krupsian*—secret things, 1 time.
>
> (They merely transliterated *alamoth*.)

Thus, it will be seen that the Greek word *parthenos* is chosen only twice out of eight usages. (The unequivocal Hebrew word for virgin is *bithula*.)

And, as already cited, the versions of Symmachus, Aquila, and Theodotian all render Isaiah 7:14's *almah* by *neanis*, "young woman."

Although many fine conservative scholars (e.g., Edward Young, Allan MacRae) state dogmatically that *almah* must be rendered "virgin" in the English translation of Isaiah 7:14 or we do violence to the word, it is nevertheless true that the general consensus of conservative scholarship favors flexibility here, understanding the word to mean "a young woman of marriageable age, whether married or unmarried, though usually used of one unmarried."

In further pursuit of evidence, expositors have often called attention to the fact that the Hebrew word most commonly used for the strict, technical sense of "virgin" is *bithula*. Formerly, enemies of the virgin birth used to say that if the writer had meant to convey the strict idea of virginity, he would have used *bithula* instead of *almah*. Conservatives formerly responded to that charge by saying that even the use of *bithula* would have not been without question, because of its use in Joel 1:8, where we read: "Lament like a virgin (*bithula*) for the husband of her youth."

However, this is the only exception to an absolutely unanimous and plentiful opportunity to examine the word *bithula* in Hebrew and in cognate languages as well. Does Joel 1:8, though only one exception, disqualify the universal usage elsewhere? It is suggested that the answer is "No." Indeed, emphatically "No" due to Hebrew marriage custom. In their culture, a marriage contract was signed some time before the marriage was consummated sexually. At a later date, the bridegroom went to the house of the bride's father to claim the bride as his and take her for himself. Only after this was sexual union permitted. This custom underlines the Jacob-Rachel story (Gen 29:20-21), the Joseph-Mary story (Mt 1:18-24), and probably the parable of the virgins (Mt 25:1-13).

It is crucial to note that both Rachel and Mary were called by the term "wife" before their marriages were consummated. It is therefore highly reasonable and a valid assumption that the "virgin" (*bithula*) of Joel 1:8 was actually still a virgin, because "the husband of her youth" died before claiming her, though she was espoused to him. The Joel prophecy pivots around an imminent invasion in which such a man might well be killed in battle before being able to consummate the marriage by taking her to himself from her father's house. Evidently, therefore, here as well as in all other usages, there is no legitimate debate about the technical use of *bithula*. For the significance of this fact, see the footnote of LaSor's discussion of the philological evidence for *almah*.[3]

In contrast to those conservative scholars who urge an inflexible use of *almah* as limited to the technical meaning of virgin, equally devout and scholarly men of undoubted conservative integrity have urged a flexible usage, determined by context. Among these are men like W. H. Griffith Thomas, W. Graham Scroggie, and A. B. Winchester (one of the founders of Dallas Theological Seminary and a Visiting Professor of Bible there in its early days).

They feel that it was an unwarranted fear of weakening the truth of our Lord's virgin birth that led to such adamancy

3. W. S. LaSor, who specialized in Ugaritic and other languages cognate with Hebrew, points out that when a particular word is under investigation, it is often profitable to check out that word in the cognate languages.

This stratagem led to a rather striking discovery by LaSor in the case of *almah*. He points out that the problem of the root of *almah* is complicated by the fact that the initial letter in Hebrew *ayin* may represent two different sounds, the one being preserved in the Arabic as *gain.* Thus, the Hebrew word might come from an original root of *g-l-m* (as paralleled in Arabic) or from *'-l-m*.

This latter word means "to conceal," thus "a virgin." However, the first root above (*g-l-m*) carries the thought "to be sexually ripe," i.e., a young woman of marriageable age.

LaSor categorically states that Semitic phonemes are never confused and that roots maintain their distinctions, even though the letters seem to confuse them. He then proceeds to cite evidence from such cognate languages as Arabic, Ugaritic, Aramaic, Syriac, Sabean, Nabatene, and Egyptian Aramaic (and possibly Akkadian), that in none of these languages can it be affirmed that the parallel word to *almah* must always mean "virgin."

The only conclusion, LaSor says, is that *bithula* unequivocally means "young woman." This would certainly permit the flexibility of *almah* to argue for the fourth view of this discussion. This flexibility would permit a near-view application to Ahaz's day but, by the same flexibility, makes both possible and mandatory the full and ultimate fulfillment of the *almah* prophecy in Mary as the "virgin" and Christ as the "child—Immanuel," according to Matthew 1 and Luke 1. By the same token, if the absolutely unequivocal idea of "virgin" had been used in 7:14 by the substitution of *bithula* for *almah,* there could not have possibly been a near-view application to the then tremendous crisis in Judah which faced Ahaz, to whom Isaiah is sent to pronounce a message both relevant and appropriate to the immediate future (e.g., 7:16; cp. v. 7). Evidently God knew what He was doing when He caused Isaiah to use the flexible *almah!*

on the part of many conservatives. But those conservatives who hold to the more flexible meaning of *almah* argue that to see only a far-view application of Isaiah 7:14 to Christ does violence both to the context and to the hermeneutics of the passage. Griffith Thomas and these others are just as insistent in saying there is no concession to unbelief in this alternate viewpoint. They fully believe that the final and complete fulfillment of 7:14 are seen in Mary and Christ as revealed in the historical gospels. By the same token, they are convinced that there is no real message that can meet the demands of the context for a sign to Ahaz's generation, unless a near view of *almah* is the correct interpretation. This takes the argument out of Isaiah 7:14 where it does not belong, and places it upon the historical narratives of Matthew 1 and Luke 1 and 2 where it does belong. This is a far more effective way to deal with unbelievers, in my judgment, than to let the matter bog down into a battle of philology, where "tis" and "tain't" could go on forever to no profit and to no solution. The alternative double application, near and far-view fulfillment, solves the problem, and gets us back on the track of straightforward exegesis, where Ahaz's day and God's purposes in Christ are equally and emphatically placed in their proper focus.

XIII. Who then Is the almah (Virgin) of Isaiah 7:14?

In the *near* view—the primary or partial fulfillment:

1. Modern Jewish commentators are generally agreed that the wife of Ahaz is referred to here and that the child is Hezekiah. However, this would be impossible with respect to the child, because Ahaz reigned in Jerusalem sixteen years (2 Ki 16:2), and Hezekiah was twenty-five years old when he began to reign (2 Ki 18:2). Hence, this child was at least nine years old when this prophecy was uttered.

2. Others have supposed that the prophet pointed the king

either to a specific young woman of the king's court, or some other young woman standing nearby, and that he was really saying, "By the time *that* virgin can conceive and bear a son, the danger you fear will be passed."

3. Still others have supposed that the virgin was not an actual but an imaginery one. Macarus paraphrases verse 14 thus: "By the time when one who is yet a virgin can bring forth a son (nine months), the present impending danger will have so completely passed away that if you yourself, Ahaz, were to name the child, you would call him Immanuel ('God with us')."

4. Others suppose that the virgin was the prophet's wife, to the objection that the prophet was already the father of a son (7:3). But this objection is made on the basis that the word *almah* must be limited to the strict sense of virginity, which would not be necessary if the more flexible meaning of *almah* were accepted.

XIV. Evaluation of the Four Views on *almah* in the Near View

The first suggestion above, that Hezekiah is the child, is impossible. The second suggestion is possible, but unlikely, as no women of the court, or other women, seem to have been present when Isaiah met Ahaz (7:1, 10). This leaves two possible solutions, 3 and 4 above, which are not only possible, but are also harmonious with the setting. Of these, however, 4 seems far more likely to me than 3. I say this because:

A. Deliverance is promised before the child is scarcely more than a babe. Note the striking similarity between 7:16 and what is said of Maher-shalal-hash-baz in 8:4.

B. The words of 7:15 agree with 7:22, which describes the poverty and desolation which will result from the invasion of the Assyrians which accomplishes the overthrow of Judah's enemies, Israel and Syria (7:4-9).

Also compare 7:16b and 8:4b with the meaning of Maher-shalal-hash-baz's name: "Speed to the spoil; haste to the prey."

C. The deliverance of Judah from the Assyrian yoke is so plainly accomplished by God that 8:8 and 10 use the word Immanuel ("God with us") right in the same context with the mention of Maher-shalal-hash-baz (8: 1, 4) and the definite statement concerning the symbolical significance of Isaiah and his children (8:18). Is it then true that Maher-shalal-hash-baz is not called Immanuel? No, he is! Anyone will see this if he reads 8:1-18 as a connected paragraph. There can be no objection to a double name. This was common in the Orient and, in the complete fulfillment, our Lord was called both "Jesus" and Immanuel" (Mt 1:21-23).

D. The word "sign" (7:14) is indissolubly linked with "sign" of 8:18 which, as we have already said, is spoken in a setting where Maher-shalal-hash-baz and the significance of his name are the subjects of the discussion.

E. Further, there is no difficulty with the word "virgin," if it be borne in mind that the word simply means "young woman of marriageable age." Whether she be married or not is to be determined by the context. That she is married, in the near view, is harmonious with 8:2-3.

F. But, even if all scholars agreed that *almah* must be taken in the strict technical sense of "virgin," there is absolutely nothing in the context to hinder the possibility that Isaiah's first wife died, and that he is here called upon by God to remarry, with a view to emphasizing the significance of the sign upon Ahaz and others (7:14; 8:1-3, 18). Certainly the whole circumstance of 8:2 is public enough to permit the idea of a marriage. And the probable time of this incident (between 734 B.C. and 726 B.C.—probably near 727 or 728; hence he

is over 40 years old) would be more favorable toward
this idea than that Maher-shalal-hash-baz was borne by
his first wife, unless, of course, as is entirely possible,
he married later in life and married a much younger
woman. At any event, Shear-jashub is still but a lad
(7:3).

Therefore, if *almah* is taken in the general sense of its use,
the context would indicate that the *almah* was probably
Isaiah's first wife, and the child, Maher-shalal-hash-baz. If,
however, someone fearing the weakening of our position insists (unnecessarily, I believe) upon the strict sense of *almah*,
then the woman could be Isaiah's second wife, and the child,
Maher-shalal-hash-baz; or as Macarus suggested above in
view 3, the *almah* could have been an imaginery one, any
one of Judah's women who was a virgin at the time of the
prophecy and who might have conceived and borne a son
by natural processes (having married after the statement was
made) by the time of the fulfillment of 7:16. It is a question
too deep for me as to just what is the point of all the similar
language used concerning Maher-shalal-hash-baz in chapter
8, if the Macarus's view is accepted. So, although admitting
the possibility of this view, it seems to me far more logical
and natural, and I am satisfied it is the correct view, to con-
nect the prophecy of 7:14-13 with Maher-shalal-hash-baz
in chapter 8. It certainly presents less difficulties than any
other view, while doing something supremely necessary;
namely, giving point and purpose to the Maher-shalal-hash-
baz incident.

XV. Who Is *almah* in the Far View?

The ultimate fulfillment of *almah* in the far view is, of
course, to be found in Mary. Matthew 1:23 and Luke 1:27
absolutely establish this and the Greek word *parthenos*
(which is there used to translate *almah*), as well as the carefully worded context, clearly establish that, in the ultimate
fulfillment, the word is used in the limited sense of strict vir-

ginity. It is important to observe, however, that it is a well established historical fact that the Jews were not expecting their Messiah to be supernaturally born. They were simply expecting a greater than Solomon, by natural generation. We do not prove the virgin birth by Isaiah 7:14. We prove it by Matthew 1 and Luke 1, where the evidence is conclusive. And from these passages we see that God had in mind the virgin birth all the time as the ultimate fulfillment of Isaiah 7:14 (Cp. Resurrection of Christ, Jn 20:9!)

XVI. The Reasoning of the Passage

It seems clear, therefore, that in the near view the sign is not in the supernatural conception of a child, the language being elastic enough to take care of a perfectly natural event (i.e., 8:3), but the sign in the near view is rather in God's supernatural deliverance of Judah from the Assyrians (7:7, 16; 8:8-10), of which the child of double name is just a symbol, i.e., "God is with us" (Immanuel), to help, to deliver, and "spoil" our enemies (Maher-shalal-hash-baz).

Whereas in the far view the sign is (1) a supernatural conception (Mt 1:18, 22-23, 25; Lk 1:31, 34-35, 37) *and* (2) a supernatural deliverance (Mt 1:21 with Lk 4:20-26) in a future day when He shall destroy Israel's enemy, "the Assyrian," "the king of the north," and all other enemies, by His glorious return (Eze 38:39; Is 9:1-7; 14:25; 30:31; Dan 8:21-26; 11:15; Zec 14:1-4).

The reasoning of the passage is: "Why fear these nations? All these will pass away. They cannot save, only destroy! But here is a sign of deliverance. Immanuel will fulfill all promises and effect Israel's deliverance. Ahaz, Manasseh, Jehoiakim, Zedekiah—all will fail, but David's great Son and Lord, *He* will save!"

XVII. A Final Quote of Note

Although I don't come to exactly the same conclusion, I feel W. Graham Scroggie has provided us with an outstanding and perceptive quotation. In a few lucid sentences, he states the matter very helpfully. Evidently Scroggie thinks that the *almah* in the near view is either Isaiah's second wife or he inclines to Macarus's view. But, be that as it may, here is the quotation:

> Faith secures fixity. Do you believe? Apparently Ahaz did not (v. 10), but the Lord gives him another chance, offering him a sign, which, however, he refuses (v. 12). Generally, to seek a sign is an evidence of weak faith, or of unbelief, but when God offered it, it was sinful presumption to refuse it! No one tempts the Lord who does what the Lord bids him do (v. 12).
>
> But the nation must be preserved from the folly of its king, and so a sign is given nevertheless (vv. 13-16). Verse 14 has a primary AND an ultimate fulfillment. The primary fulfillment must have been within two or three years, or it would not have been a sign at all to Ahaz (vv. 10, 16). In the near view, when the prophecy (a virgin shall conceive) was made, the girl was unmarried, but not when it was fulfilled. In the ultimate fulfillment, the girl (Mary) was unmarried at the time of fulfillment (a virgin shall conceive, cp. Matthew 1:22-23). Think about this.

4

Hosea's Heartbreak

"Was Hosea Commanded to Marry an Immoral Woman?"

I. INTRODUCTION (1:1)

THE PROPHETS have customarily been divided by one of two methods: (1) either by size into Major and Minor Prophets, or (2) by time areas into Pre-Exilic, Exilic, and Post-Exilic Prophets.

I do not find either of these methods to be as meaningful as a third method because: First, the contrast between Major and Minor almost inevitably suggests a second-class status to the "Minor" Prophets. Actually that is unfortunate. The words are intended to contrast the size of Isaiah, Jeremiah, and Ezekiel with the tendency toward much shorter books among the Minor Prophets. But immediately a difficulty should be obvious. Daniel is included with the so-called Major Prophets. But Daniel has less chapters than either Hosea or Zechariah, and the "Lamentations" (of Jeremiah) is not a prophet at all, though oftentimes one sees lists or charts showing five Major Prophets, with Lamentations counted as one of the five. Further, Lamentations has only five chapters. I presume the arrangement of the Hebrew canon was the basic occasion for making the split between what is now called Major and Minor Prophets, for in the "Latter Prophets" the Hebrews had: Isaiah, Jeremiah, Ezekiel, and the twelve remaining prophets counted as one book.

The old rabbis said they put these twelve on one scroll (counting them as one) "lest they should be lost for their littleness."

Second, although the pivoting of the prophets as three groups around the exile is preferable to dividing them into Major and Minor Prophets, because it recognizes the importance of when the prophet lived and ministered, I feel a better chronological approach is to group the writing prophets in relation to the three great enemies of Israel who succeeded one another and had so much to do with the way the prophets spoke to the people. If this method is followed, we not only have chronology and a gradually expanding message on what God tells them is going to happen, but we have messages pertinent to the particular crisis that faced the prophet and the people at the time of the messages of the book. Thus, I suggest the following classification and order:

> PROPHETS of the ASSYRIAN PERIOD: Joel, Jonah, Amos, Hosea, Isaiah, Micah, Nahum
>
> PROPHETS of the BABYLONIAN PERIOD: Zephaniah, Jeremiah, Habakkuk, Daniel, Ezekiel, Obadiah (some put Obadiah early)
>
> PROPHETS of the PERSIAN PERIOD: Haggai, Zechariah, Malachi

It will be seen that this places the prophet Hosea right in the midst of the Assyrian period. According to Whitcomb, Hosea may have overlapped Amos slightly, but the major contemporaries of his ministry were Isaiah and Micah. The text of Hosea 1:1 shows the extended time of his ministry: "The word of the LORD that came unto Hosea . . . in the days of Uzziah, Jotham, Ahaz, and Hezekiah, kings of Judah, and in the days of Jeroboam . . . king of Israel." Hosea ministered to both the Southern and Northern Kingdoms, but his messages were directed mainly to the Northern Kingdom. The Jeroboam involved is, of course, Jeroboam II, who reigned long, prosperously, and wickedly.

II. Solomon Brings on Apostasy

Before proceeding into the book of Hosea, a review of history is in order. Much earlier, Solomon had ground down the kingdom he inherited from his father David by crushing taxation and lavish display of wealth. His mother had admonished him to be sure to avoid strong drink and an undue emphasis upon his relationship with women (Pr 31:1-9). Who knew better than she the danger involved, particularly in the latter? Evidently he avoided the pitfall of becoming distorted in his judgment by drink (Ec 2:3). But, unfortunately, a normal expansion of treaty marriages as his kingdom grew was completely ignored and he multiplied his marriages beyond all reason, ending up with 1,000 wives and concubines. Treaty marriages were a custom of the time. A daughter (1 Ki 3:1), like Pharoah's, or some highborn girl was sent along as a wife with the treaty with the expectation that she would explain her father to her new husband and in general seek to improve relations between the two countries, thus helping to avoid war. Presumptively his lavish display of wealth had its roots in an unhealthy pride.

At any event, it is clear that these wives, largely pagan, drew away his heart from Jehovah (1 Ki 11:1-8), bringing the wrath of God (vv. 9ff.) and consequent discipline. Each girl would want a shrine to her god and one after the other put pressure on him. "You did it for her! You've got to do it for me. You don't love me, or you will make a shrine for my god!"

Well, most men have their hands full with one wife, but when a man has 1,000 wives on his back, vying with one another, he really has problems! One wonders at his courage and at his stupidity. For the wisest man of Old Testament times, he certainly became foolish (Ec 4:13; 7:25-28). And so, Jerusalem became cluttered with shrines to idols.

The book of Ecclesiastes fills us in on this large and wasted portion of Solomon's life when he left the revelation of God and reasoned "under the sun." He prostituted the wisdom that God had given him and went down any avenue of philosophical principles which attracted him. All he found was blind alleys, at the end of which he bloodied his head; and returned, bloodied but unbowed, to go down another blind alley. No one can see life in true perspective unless he views it from God's standpoint. So this sad book is put in our Bible with red lights of warning hanging at the head of these false theories, saying to the person about to go that way: "Don't do it! This is a blind alley. All you will get is pain and frustration. Keep on the King's highway. Follow God's main street!" I believe Solomon came back to the divine revelation in later life. I base this on the conclusion of Ecclesiastes: "Let us hear the conclusion of the whole matter: Fear God, and keep his commandments . . ." (12:13). Also, I believe this because it says that, as a result of his experiences, he "set in order many proverbs" (12:9-12).

III. Jeroboam Makes Apostasy Official

But the damage was done. The dam was broken. No sooner was Solomon dead than his very foolish son Rehoboam precipitated the rebellion of the ten tribes under Jeroboam I, as God had warned through the prophet Ahijah (1 Ki 11:29-40). In order to keep the people of the Northern Kingdom from going down to the temple at Jerusalem and having their heart turned toward the House of David, Jeroboam deliberately brought in official apostasy by placing golden sacred bulls at Dan and Bethel, proclaiming "Behold thy gods, O Israel, which brought thee up out of the land of Egypt" (1 Ki 12:28).

So his religious occasions were synchronized with those of the Jerusalem temple, and if among the pilgrims going south toward Bethel there were any who might be inclined to go on beyond Bethel to Jerusalem, people would say to them: "Why go clear down there? It's a long way. And in fact it isn't patriotic of you. Come on, stay with us at Bethel!" And, with a sly wink, "We have so much fun there." Yes, this was the worship of the sacred bull, brought out of Egypt in the hearts of the people, which almost destroyed the nation at Sinai, as we find recorded in Exodus 32. On that occasion, if it had not been for the swift and firm action of Moses, official apostasy would have resulted then. But under Jeroboam I it did take place and he is described in the Scripture by that infamous inscription: "Jeroboam, the son of Nebat, who made Israel to sin." What an awesome delineation!

Throughout the Old Testament, Israel is pictured as the wife of Jehovah. To take the affection which Jehovah alone deserves, and to give it to a pagan god was called spiritual adultery by God. It is just like a wife turning her back on her husband and having an affair with another man. God doesn't mince words (Is 50:1). Even in the New Testament, the equivalent relation of the Church with Christ carries this same analogy. James says flatly: "Ye . . . adulteresses, know ye not that friendship of the world is enmity with God?" (Ja 4:4). This whole picture language must be kept in mind for any proper understanding of the book of Hosea, as we now open it.

IV. DID GOD COMMAND HOSEA TO SIN? (1:2)

As we open verse 2, we read: "The word of the LORD by Hosea. And the LORD said to Hosea, Go, take unto thee a wife of harlotry and children of harlotry; for the land hath committed harlotry, departing from the LORD. So he went and took Gomer . . ."

It is strange that many pastors and teachers and many in the pew assume that this means Gomer was an immoral woman at the time Hosea was commanded to take a wife. Evidently they confuse this occasion with the later fact that she became immoral (3:1). The commentators are far more careful. They, almost without exception, state that she was not immoral when Jehovah commanded Hosea to take a wife. This is because we have here a very real ethical and theological problem. Since when did God command anyone to sin?

Name an instance! Paul is scandalized in Galatians 2:17-18 that Peter, by ceasing to eat with the Gentiles, makes it look as though he should not have given up keeping the ritual of the law. Yet it was precisely at Christ's command that Peter had done so. Hence, if Peter was wrong in having done so, it placed Christ in the position of being "the minister of sin"! Paul recoils from this awful thought, and his rebuke of Peter is so effective that Peter does not and cannot answer Paul's logic. No, it is utterly untenable that God could have commanded Hosea to take an immoral woman and thus sin.

What, then, is the explanation or is there one? There is. And it is so easy and so obvious that one wonders why there should have ever been any misunderstanding here. Look at the passage again. Who or what has committed harlotry? It is not the woman. It is the *land:* "the land hath committed great harlotry." How? By "departing from the LORD"; by going after false gods instead of their husband, Jehovah (1:9; 2:5-13; 3:1, 3b; 4:12-13, 15-17).

Idolatry is called spiritual adultery. Hosea marries a girl from the land of Israel, the northern ten tribe kingdom. We have already seen how that kingdom officially apostatized, with the golden bulls at Dan and Bethel. Hence, to a person of the Southern Kingdom, serving the Lord as Hosea was, any person of the Northern Kingdom would be *ceremonially unclean,* for it was a land that had committed harlotry by idolatry, "departing from the LORD." As further proof that it is not a personal sin of the woman but the official apostasy of the land God is speaking about, we read: "take . . . children of harlotry." Why, the children have not even been born when this is said. Until ceremonially cleansed, both the woman and her children would be ceremonially unclean. Thus Gomer becomes a double illustration of Israel's relation to Jehovah: Her association with the land of harlotry (idolatry) made her (like Israel) ceremonially unclean. Gomer's *later* betrayal of Hosea becomes an apt illustration of Israel's betrayal of Jehovah. A further amazing analogy develops when Hosea is commanded to love Gomer, even after she had sinned, and to take her back, illustrating the "undying love" of Jehovah for Israel, as Campbell Morgan designated it!

V. God's Names for Hosea's Children Teach Great Lessons (1:3-9)

(1) Jezreel, a Son (1:3-5)

God proposes to use Hosea, Gomer, and the children for dramatic illustrations of truths He wished to convey. This is nothing new. He often did this. Jeremiah is commanded *not* to marry, a very strange thing in the context of the Middle East. But, God has been saying Judah is going to fall; Babylon is going to conquer. If this is true, his suffering would be greatly increased if Jeremiah would have to see a wife and little children starving before his eyes in the coming siege of Jerusalem. So Jeremiah is to become a graphic object lesson to emphasize that the nation's usual pattern of life is going to be upset. God believes His own prophecy and Jeremiah illustrates its validity by not marrying. On the other hand, Ezekiel marries, because he was to be taken captive earlier. However, when his wife dies, he is not permitted to weep for her. By this, he is to picture that when the temple is destroyed (described as "the desire of thine eyes"), Judah would have wept so long and so copiously through the long siege, that there are no more tears left for weeping when that terrible climactic event occurs.

So, God proposes to take complete charge and make this experience of Hosea an object lesson, attesting important truths. He names the children Himself. The first child is a son, and God says, "Call him Jezreel!" Now watch, "for yet a little while, and I will cause to cease the kingdom of the house of Israel" (the Northern Kingdom). "And it shall come to pass at that day, that I will break the bow of Israel in the valley of Jezreel" (1:4-5).

This valley, also called Esdraelon and Megiddo, is a triangle of 15 by 15 by 20 miles. It was frequently used as a battleground. It will therefore be in this very place that Israel will be defeated and cease to be a nation. We know that she deserved it because of forsaking Jehovah, but why there? The answer is given in verses 4-5: "I will avenge the blood of Jezreel upon the house of Jehu . . . in the valley of Jezreel." What is the significance of this?

The Bible presupposes that you have read the other books. Jehoram was wounded and was recovering in his summer house in Jezreel. The city cousins from Jerusalem came up to cheer him with "get well" cards, as it were. In the meantime God had given Jehu command to take over the Northern Kingdom, which he did. But in fulfilling the command to execute the seed-royal of Israel, he exceeded God's orders and was guilty of overkill. He came across the seed-royal of Judah on their way to see the king of Israel and slew them. (We can only conclude that one of the princes of Judah was sick and couldn't make the trip.)

No doubt he cried his eyes out. But there must always be a man to sit on David's throne; so at least one was spared, just as in the time when Athaliah plotted the destruction of David's line, but little Joash was hidden in the temple and spared.

So all this innocent blood of the seed-royal of Judah had been shed and by God's righteous decree it must be avenged (v. 4). And God says that it will be avenged when Israel falls in the very place where it was shed, the valley of Jezreel (v. 5). This is what is called poetic justice. The very meaning of the name Jezreel is also instructive. It means "scatter." So Israel is going to be taken captive and scattered.

(2) Lo-ruhamah, a Daughter (1:6-7)

The second child is born. "It's a girl!" God says, "Name her Lo-ruhamah" (1:6). "Lo" in Hebrew is negative, so the name means "not pitied," or "not having obtained mercy."

"Call her this because I will no more have pity on the Northern Kingdom, but I will utterly take them away."

"But I will have pity on Judah," because of David (e.g., 2 Ki 8:19). "I will save (deliver) Judah by the Lord their God," not by the usual means of armies with bows and swords and horses and horsemen (1:7). "I will do it by my own intervention."

And so God did. You have the story in Isaiah 36 and 37. As Lord Byron described it:

> The Assyrian came down like the wolf on the fold
> And his cohorts were gleaming with purple and gold!

Twenty years previously (722 or 721 B.C.) the Northern Kingdom had fallen to the Assyrians in fulfillment of verses 4-6. Now, Sennacherib has overrun the land of Judah (Is 8: 5-8). Every walled city had fallen except Lachish and Jerusalem, and Lachish was about to fall. At this crucial juncture, Sennacherib sent his Rabshakeh (captain) with an ultimatum to Jerusalem, who proceeded to blaspheme the God of Israel and called upon the people of Jerusalem to forsake King Hezekiah and peacefully surrender.

Hezekiah had done his homework. Having given tribute on a previous occasion, he saw that one cannot bargain with gangsters. He told the men on the wall to listen and not to answer back. Having finished his impious speech, the Rabshakeh placed the ultimatum on an arrow and his bowman shot it into the city. Hastily it was taken to Hezekiah who wisely went into the temple, fell on his knees, and opened it. In essence he said: "Lord, You know you are our only hope. Just look at these insulting things they say about Your being unable to resist them and keep Jerusalem. Lord, show them who's running things! Lord, You answer them!"

And God sent word to Hezekiah through Isaiah saying He would defend Jerusalem. There were three things in the prophet's message. (1) Sennacherib would hear a rumor—which he did, namely that Tirhakah king of Ethiopia was

coming up against him. (2) There would be a blast; and
there was: 185,000 of the Assyrian's veteran troops were slain
in one night by Ha-Malak Jehovah (the Angel of Jehovah,
the Lord Jesus in pre-incarnate form, as many Bible teachers
understand). And (3) He "shall return to his own land; and
I will cause him to fall by the sword in his own land" (Is 37:
7). This was gruesomely fulfilled when his two sons slew him
in the act of worship in the house of his god (Is 37:38). This
is all the more remarkable, because one outstanding custom
of the Middle East was that a person is inviolate of attack
while he is worshiping and, in most cases, while he is on the
way to worship. What sort of gods are they that cause two
sons to flaunt this well-established custom and murder their
own father while in the act of worship? So God did spare
Judah in this remarkable way, as He said He would through
Hosea.

(3) Lo-ammi, a Son (1:8-9)

The third child now arrives. It is a son whom God names
Lo-ammi. *Am* means "people." *Lo* is the negative, and
the *i* has the same force as our personal pronoun. Call him,
"not-my-people; for ye are not my people, and I will not be
your God" (v. 9). Thus the message of judgment is reiterated in these names and fulfilled in these events. The Northern Kingdom is to be defeated, the innocent blood shed by
Jehu avenged in the Valley of Jezreel. God will not have
mercy on the ten tribes any more and they are to be "scattered" (*Jezreel*). They are repudiated (*Lo-ammi*) because
they have repudiated God, having deliberately apostatized
from Him by giving their affection to false gods, like a treacherous wife who became an adulteress. But Judah is to be
spared for now, for David's sake.

VI. THE PROMISE OF RESTORATION (1:10—2:1)

Someone has said that there is a certain stratagem employed by the masters in most of their great paintings. As I

watched for this in the Florentine galleries and those of Rome and Paris (the Louvre) and elsewhere, I kept thinking about it. The masters often put a dark background on the canvas, so that they might make more prominent the bright colors of their subjects and their scenes. It would seem that God, that Skilled Artist, has employed this method in the passage before us. Against the dark colors of rejection and judgment, war and suffering, He paints the luminous colors of His gracious purposes. Look at these verses:

> Yet the number of the children of Israel shall be as the sand of the sea, which cannot be measured nor numbered; and it shall come to pass, that in the place where it was said unto them, Ye are not my people, there it shall be said unto them, Ye are the sons of the living God. Then shall the children of Judah and the children of Israel be gathered together, and appoint themselves one head, and they shall come up out of the land: for great shall be the day of Jezreel. Say ye unto your brethren, Ammi; and to your sisters, Ruhamah (1:10, 11; 2:1).

There are seven main things prophesied here:

(1) "Yet"—not destruction but preservation! Although the Northern Kingdom is going to be "scattered," yet Judah is going to be retained. "I yet have a purpose for my people as I promised Abraham and as I promised David."

(2) There is to be an increase in numbers, despite invasions, despite persecutions, despite scatterings, despite even Hamans and Hitlers. No one looking at what Israel has gone through in this century, not to mention the past, can be other than amazed at the increase of Israel, especially the number back in their land: "As the sand of the sea."

(3) They are one day going to be converted in substantial numbers. They who were "not my people" (*lo-ammi*) are going to have the negative reversed. They are to become *ammi*, "my people"; indeed, "the sons of the living God"!

(4) They are to be regathered . . . to "come up out of the

land," sometimes pictured as coming out of the wilderness of the nations into Palestine, previously a "wilderness" in the midst of the nations (cp. 2:14). Against all reasonable expectation, the land of Israel has grown to nearly three million people, as against less than a million when the State of Israel was formed in May, 1948. In 1878 there were 24,000 Jews in Palestine; in 1914, 85,000; in 1918, it had slipped back to 56,000. In 1948, 483,000 Jews entered, bringing the Jewish population to 650,000 by mid-1948. By 1951, 684,000 more Jews immigrated. And so it has gone, upward and onward.

(5) They are to be regathered as a united people, "gathered together." Which of the people in Israel today, or for that matter anywhere in the world, are of the ten tribes and which are of the two tribes? They are all one. God never recognized the division of the kingdom, though He permitted it. A godly remnant seceded when Rehoboam foolishly brought about the division into north and south kingdoms. From time to time, especially during revivals, others from the ten tribe kingdom joined the two tribe kingdom, when kings of Judah invited repentant Jews to come back to Jehovah and His temple. Thus all twelve tribes were ministered to by our Lord Jesus in accord with His words in Matthew 10:6 and Paul's words before Agrippa in Acts 26:7. Thus, in God's view, there are no "ten lost tribes," as is often unfortunately said. With the destruction of the temple in A.D. 70, with its genealogical records, this fact became more final than perhaps earlier realized. There is only one Israel in the world today. God recognized the whole of continuing Israel as being in the Southern Kingdom, just as the twelve stones covered by the returning Jordan were seen by God if not by man (Jos 4:6-9, particularly 9).

(6) They will have one head, one king. Of course ultimately and fully, this is the Lord Jesus Christ. But many of us believe that David, to whom the kingdom promises were made, will be honored by Christ's appointing him as His re-

gent to rule over Israel in the millennial age. Christ is not the only king, but King of kings. Thus, the words of 3:5 may actually refer to David personally, not merely spiritually to his greater son, the Lord Jesus, as most commentators have assumed.

(7) They will be "sown," "planted," in the land, never to be plucked up. This is the clear prophecy of Amos 9:15. And here in Hosea 1:10, the same thought is hidden to the English reader in the play on words, unless one is especially alert as he reads that verse and 2:21-23. The negatives are dropped. It is no longer "*Lo*-ammi," "not my people," but "Ammi," "my people." No longer "*Lo*-ruhamah," "not having obtained mercy or unpitied," but "Ruhamah," "pitied or having obtained mercy." It is not therefore surprising to find that the Hebrew word meaning "scatter" (Jezreel) has a secondary meaning. Suppose a farmer scatters (Jezreels) seed. What do we call that? We call it "sowing" seed. So this is the secondary meaning. Thus, God says in 1:11, "for great shall be the day of Jezreel," i.e., the day of sowing in the land.

That this is the correct interpretation is affirmed by the wording of 2:21-23. Let me transliterate it:

> And it shall come to pass in that day, I will hear, saith the LORD, I will hear the heavens, and they shall hear the earth; and the earth shall hear the grain, and the wine, and the oil; and they shall hear the sowing (Jezreel!), and I will Jezreel (sow) her unto me in the earth (i.e., eretz Israel—land of Israel); and I will Ruhamah (have mercy) upon her who was Lo-rumahah (had not obtained mercy); and I will say to them which were Lo-ammi (not my people), Thou art Ammi (my people); and they shall say, Thou art our God!

What a tremendous prophecy and how graphic is this play on words, these very names that God chose to give to Hosea's actual, literal children, with their prophetic and symbolic overtones concerning the then present and future of Israel in His dealings with them.

Of course, putting all Scripture together, the complete fulfillment of this prophecy is yet future to us and is associated with the glorious return of Israel's Messiah to establish His kingdom in Jerusalem over the whole world (e.g., Mic 4:1-7).

VII. THE APPEAL TO PRODIGAL ISRAEL (2:2-13)

Obviously the pleading of verses 2ff. is not with Hosea's wife Gomer but with Israel, the unfaithful, adulterous wife of Jehovah, the Northern Kingdom in particular. God's message goes like this:

> I am going to chasten you people of the Northern Kingdom. Your mother (nation) has played the harlot (v. 5) and you children (citizens) should use your influence to plead for a change, for repentance and a return to Jehovah, your mother's legitimate Husband!
>
> I am going to expose her for the apostate that she is (vv. 3, 10). I will withdraw the rain (announced in the Palestinian covenant as the first discipline for disobedience to God). I will not have mercy upon her or you, her children, for she is guilty of harlotry and you are ceremonially unclean children (vv. 4-5).
>
> I am going to hedge her in with painful pressure from nations about her, digging into her like thorns (v. 6). She wants to be like these nations and follow their gods, instead of following Me (v. 7). She takes *My* gifts (v. 8) and has the audacity of crediting them to false gods (her lovers), as though they had supplied them (v. 9). She prostitutes My gifts by offering them to her lovers! What an awful thing is this; how perverted! So, I will tell you what I will do. I will take My crops—My gifts to her—and take the smile off her face (vv. 9, 11; Lev 26:3-10). I will spoil her crops and vines. I will retribute upon her the days of Baalim, when she dressed and primped like a harlot, and went out after lovers and forgot Me, her real Husband (vv. 12-13).

This is that spiritual adultery of the Northern Kingdom

of which we spoke in 1:2, where it has so grossly been misin-
terpreted by some who stumble over words while missing the
whole context, namely, Jehovah's message to idolatrous Israel, the *nation*, not the woman.

This God did. Enemies increased. In due time the Jews
were taken captive and the land which had been described
as "flowing with milk and honey" became a desolation. Mark
Twain once wrote of a portion of what was the Northern
Kingdom:

> There is not a solitary village throughout the whole extent
> of this area, nor for thirty miles in either direction. There
> are two or three clusters of Bedouin tents, but not a single
> permanent habitation. One may ride ten miles hereabouts
> without seeing ten human beings. To this region one of the
> prophecies is applied, "I will bring the land into desola-
> tion. . . ." No man can stand here by deserted Ain Mellahah
> and say the prophecy has not been fulfilled!

With Israel's return to the land, with irrigation, replanting
of forests—much of this is changing. But the prophecy of
Hosea was painfully fulfilled during the centuries in between judgment and restoration.

VIII. ISRAEL'S RESCUE AND RESTORATION (2:14-23)

Our Lord made it perfectly clear in His messages in Matthew 13 that He was, for the first time, revealing things
"kept secret from the foundation of the world" (vv. 16-17,
34-35). Thus, in reading the Old Testament we must be
prepared for no mention of the church and therefore for the
fact that messages concerning judgment and restoration co-
alesce, leaving no notice of, or suggestion that, the church
age is an intercalation, known to God from eternity but not
revealed, which He inserted into the succession of the ages.
The classic example is our Lord's sermon in His hometown
synagogue at Nazareth where, quoting Isaiah 61:1-2, He
stops dead in the midst of a sentence's flow, dramatically

closing the "book," and says, "This day is this scripture fulfilled in your ears." He was, of course, absolutely correct, but He would not have been if He had continued quoting the verse which reads, "and the day of vengeance of our God." That will yet take place in the future in the tribulation and in connection with His second coming to earth. Thus, our Lord emphasized this gap between two clauses of one sentence, a gap which has now extended nearly 2,000 years. On the basis of our Lord's own hermeneutics, we may therefore categorically say that there is a major gap of perhaps 2,700 years (at least the eighth century B.C. to the present) between verses 13 and 14 of our chapter, for plainly verses 14ff. are yet future to us at this point of time in the church age.

When one reads verse 14, he is reminded of Isaiah 40, where Jehovah cries, "Comfort ye, comfort ye my people!" Despite Israel's awesome sins, God has yet purposed in grace to bring her to the end of herself, and bring her back to Himself, where she rightfully belongs. This is all in harmony with the Abrahamic and Davidic covenants. As already mentioned, the picture language has God speaking tenderly to her ("allure her") to bring her back to Palestine (the wilderness amid the nations to which the earlier settlers of modern Israel returned), where He speaks "comfortably unto her." She will again be the vine of the Lord's planting (Is 5:1-2), and be placed in a situation which will be anything but comforting—"the valley of Achor." This word means "trouble" or, perfectly naturally, "tribulation," the word we are more familiar with in respect to Israel's future. This could of course include the trials Israel has passed through in seeking to be re-established in the land, particularly the war of independence which brought her to statehood (1948), and the two subsequent wars of 1956 and 1967. And these may be only the prelude to more such assaults, culminating in the massive assaults predicted in Daniel, Ezekiel, Zechariah and elsewhere, when kings of south and north and east zero in on her.

There is no good reason why Israel should have won in 1948, 1956, or 1967, with the massive outnumbering she faced. In the tribulation, she will be successfully invaded by the king of the north (Gog/Magog) and Jerusalem conquered (Zec 14:2), but then the Lord of battles shall "go forth and fight against those nations" (v. 3). Zechariah 14:4 gives the climax which follows Armageddon, the personal return of Jesus Christ to the Mount of Olives and "the Lord shall be king over all the earth" (Zec 14:9). This will be comfort indeed, as Hosea promises (2:14). The valley of tribulation (Achor) will become "a door of hope."

One of the most tender descriptions in the Bible now follows. The nation has disgraced and sullied herself, and brazenly mistreated Jehovah, as we have seen. Yet, in tender love, He says "I will betroth thee unto me." The word betroth is unique for this situation: it means "to woo as a virgin!" After all her defilement, God brings a repentant remnant to such a cleansed condition that she is pictured as a virgin, rather than—as she is—a sordid harlot! What grace! She shall be brought back to Him, and the honeymoon days, as when she came with the Lord out of Egypt, will be restored (vv. 15, 19-20). The very names and memory of the false gods will be removed. Though the word "Baali" means "my lord," it is too fraught with the painful past of idolatry. Israel will call her Husband "Ishi—my man." Some German-speaking friends have told me that they use this term "my man" for "my husband." At any event, that is the force of the word "Ishi" here. The curse of Genesis 3 will be removed (v. 18). Crops will spring forth (vv. 21-23). And the wonderful restoration, already exposited previously with 1:10—2:1, is brought before us in the close of the chapter, where the play on the meaning of the names God gave the children are now applied to the bright blessings He plans for the nation's future, the negatives (*Lo*) having been removed.

This brings us to

IX. THE SHORTEST CLASSIC SUMMARY OF ISRAEL'S CAREER ANYWHERE IN THE BIBLE (3)

Chapter 3 is a gem of condensation. In a few swift strokes of the pen, God's prophet tells the whole story of Israel, past, present, and future. Let us look at it carefully. Verse 1 gives us her tragic past. Verses 2-4 tell of her age-long displacement. Verse 5 epitomizes the glorious consummation of God's plan for her.

(1) ISRAEL'S TRAGIC PAST (v. 1)

"Go yet, love a woman beloved of her friend [!], yet an adulteress." What have we here? We do not know just how it happened, but it did. Gomer became unfaithful. Let us use a sanctified imagination. It must have been a real shock to this girl from the Northern Kingdom to be uprooted from all she was used to and brought into the inhospitable Southern Kingdom. War was often the order of the day between the kingdoms and hatred (or at least suspicion and fear) were all too common emotions. Thus, she is brought into a neighborhood of "enemies." Add to that the unusual experience of being the wife of a prophet. Ask any pastor's wife how strangely some people treat her! This would be difficult for a girl of the Southern Kingdom, but what would it be for one of the Northern Kingdom to be in the territory of an "enemy" kingdom? Extremely tense!

Undoubtedly Hosea loved her, for he was a good man. But how much communication and sense of union in mind and soul would a holy prophet have with a girl from an idolatrous background? More importantly, turn it around. How much communication would she feel she had with Hosea? Now add to this the absence of Hosea as he went away on preaching tours. Here she is, a foreigner, very ill-at-ease, perhaps looked upon with suspicion by the people of the neighborhood. Then, baby followed baby. She was tired and certainly very lonely.

One day, when she was hanging out diapers, the national flag of motherhood, feeling very lonely because Hosea was away, the wife next door was watching her and saw the sadness in her face and the evidence in her puffed eyelids that she had been crying. Her human sympathy egged her on. She leaned over the fence and spoke kindly to Gomer: "Say, I feel I owe you an apology. I haven't been very neighborly. And I see how sad you look today, with your husband away and those three young kids to care for. I don't think we have treated you very nicely. Tonight some of the girls are coming over to my house. I'll send my teenage daughter to care for your kids, if you would like to come over. You need a change. Wouldn't you like to relax and come over for a while?" Would she! Almost too eagerly she accepted and her heart sang all day. That night, with just "the girls," she talked and laughed and relaxed and it was so much fun. Life had been pretty real and earnest! What a welcome change. She felt like a girl again!

Not too much later, when Hosea was away again, she was invited. Now the strange situation and the strain of the care of the children seemed to melt away. How good it was!

But there were other nights, subsequently. She was not told, but some men were there. Eventually the drinks flowed and illicit approaches took place. She recoiled from it. But there was such release in being there. One night she was compromised. And other occasions followed. Perhaps, because of the very spartan atmosphere of her life with Hosea, she went farther, faster. At any event, one day when Hosea came home from a preaching tour, he found, to his horror, three children crying and no Gomer. Naively he inquired around. People's eyes narrowed; they tried to keep incredulity from showing on their faces. Could he be so dumb that he had not suspicioned anything? Everybody else knew it!

Finally, one man half-sheepishly suggested he go down to the edge of town. "Last I heard, she was there." He went, and the further he trudged, his heart sank. But God had already given him orders. "Love her and take her back, like I love wayward, idolatrous, adulterous Israel." What a yardstick: "according as I love Israel"!

He found her and at first he wished he hadn't. He scarcely recognized her. As Kipling would say, she was "a rag, and a bone, and a hank of hair." She was in miserable condition and she shrank from his gaze.

(2) Israel's Painful Present (vv. 2-4)

According to the Law, she should be stoned. But God here contravened His own law for an object lesson in grace. Her surly master, for now she was merely a piece of abused property, struck a hard bargain: "Fifteen pieces of silver" (half the price of an able-bodied slave—she was pretty badly off), and seeing Hosea's condition of shock, he added "One and a half homers of barley." Hosea paid the price and took her home. There was a long silence; he did not blast her. She wondered why, and kept waiting for the furious word and the lash of a whip, or worse. He only said: "My dear, I have bought you back. You are mine. You will not play the harlot; you will not be for another man, not for anybody," he added earnestly. "Of course, I will not be, and I have not been, intimate with anyone else. But you and I cannot have marital relations. You must abide many days until the uncleanness is gone; until I can take you fully as my wife again. That day will come, I promise you." And, so he kept her separate, but he *kept* her. The days passed and finally she was restored.

What an object lesson! Israel, like Gomer, went astray after other "lovers" (false gods). Yet her Lover sought her and bought her! He was sold for thirty pieces of silver, the price of a slave. But with His own precious life blood, He bought Israel back.

So Israel, bought at Calvary, has persisted, and has not yet been restored. Yet she has continued "many days" without anything that would commonly keep a people together. For centuries they have had no homeland, until recently. They have had no king or prince or government to hold them together (v. 4). They have had no sacrifice, since the temple was destroyed in A.D. 70. Since they repudiated idolatry at Babylon, during the 70-year captivity, they have not even had a common worship of idols to keep them together!

The survival of the Jew is incredible and unique in the annals of mankind's history. When unbelieving rationalism began making itself felt in the court of Frederick the Great of Germany, a particular vitriolic enemy of the dependability of the Bible pressed this point with the emperor. Rattled and concerned, unable to answer the man, Frederick turned to his court chaplain and demanded: "Sir, give me one reason for believing the Bible is inspired!" In that tense moment there was given the chaplain wisdom to reply: "Your Majesty, the Jew!" The answer was both forceful and convincing. How else could the Jew be explained and who should know better than those in a Germany with ghettos? There is no natural explanation for Israel's survival. It has been a supernatural act of God.

(3) Israel's Glorious Future (v. 5)

But "afterward," God proposes to do something. He will, through the sufferings of the tribulation and the wooing of the Holy Spirit, bring a substantial number of the nation to repentance, as a remnant according to the election of grace. They will look on the Messiah, whom they have pierced, and mourn in agonized repentance over their sin of rejecting Him. They will "seek the Lord their God," and shall be found! They will seek the kingship of Christ and "David their king," as I have previously suggested. "They will fear the Lord . . . in the latter days."

What a glorious day that will be, the day of the gladness

of His heart. He has waited so long for His dear Israel to repent. Restored, a nation born in a day, they shall rejoice together in millennial blessedness. Hosea was used as a painful but graphic object lesson of how God plans to bring to repentance, and to forgive and to restore Israel. What a wonderful God we serve!

And now, heavenly Father, seal to our heart these words from Thy Word. May we realize that these people in the Bible were real people who walked on two legs and had heartaches and problems just like us. May this not just be a book in the Old Testament but a very real life experience from which we enter into and, by illustration, get some conception of Thy great heart. May we see how brokenhearted Thou art over our sin, as well as that of Israel's. And yet Thou didst not cast her off but bought her with the price of Jesus' blood, and will yet restore her. We of the church have nothing to gloat over. We too have sinned and hang our heads in shame. We have failed. We thank Thee for Thy great personal message that is involved here. We thank Thee that Thy love has sought us, bought us, and kept us, in spite of ourselves. So, Lord, may our hearts thrill to these great truths. In Jesus' name. Amen.

5

Two Kingdoms in Matthew?

ONE OF THE GREATEST FALLACIES in reading one's Bible is to suppose that a given word, like "kingdom," always means the same thing throughout the same book. Or, conversely, to suppose that there would be no chance of synonymity if two or more different words were used in relation to the same subject.

Although words often have distinctive meaning to guide us in interpretation, it is also true that context often dictates two or more different meanings for the same word.

A common source of failure in reading Matthew intelligently is the assumption that the word "kingdom" means the same thing wherever it appears throughout the book, whether in chapter 3 or chapter 13. It is, therefore, my purpose to investigate how the word and thought of kingdom is used in Matthew, first of all, and then elsewhere in Scripture.

THE KINGDOM AS USED IN MATTHEW 1–10: THE KINGDOM IN MANIFESTATION

It is significant that no one is recorded as ever having asked John the Baptist what he meant by the kingdom of heaven when he came upon the scene proclaiming, "Repent, for the kingdom of heaven (*lit.* of the heavens) is at hand (i.e., imminent)" (Mt 3:2). Many people have wondered why he did not say, "Believe on the Lord Jesus Christ and thou shalt be saved"; or, at least, they mentally equate what John actually said with what they assume John meant.

Actually, it should be borne in mind that John was the last of the Old Testament prophets (Mt 11:7-13, esp. v. 13). Those who heard him were well aware of the Messianic prophecies that made clear David's greater Son would rule and reign, as covenanted in 2 Samuel 7. They knew that the throne of David was on earth in Jerusalem, not in heaven (Mic 4:2; Is 2:3); His *own* throne, not someone else's throne, in the skies (Lk 1:32; Rev 3:21; Mt 25:31).

They knew that the kingdom would not only be over Israel, as originally announced, but would extend to the ends of the earth (Mic 4:1-3, 5; Ps 72:1-11, esp. v. 8).

They knew the kingdom would be instituted by force (Mic 4:3; Zec 12:9; 14:1-9, 16; Dan 2:44-45). Upon its establishment, they knew the kingdom would be peaceful, righteous, and beneficent. Indeed, it would be more wonderful than all men's dreams of utopia—earth's golden age! Later the Bible informs that the kingdom age will extend for a thousand years (Rev 20:1-5), a millennium (the Latin word for a thousand).

That John was merely appealing to individuals for personal repentance only, with no regard to the nation's long-promised kingdom, is a preposterous position in the light of Gabriel's announcement to Mary (Lk 1:26-33), and dozens of Old and New Testament passages. Christ was crucified, not only as Saviour, but also as King of the Jews (Jn 19:10-22). The question of the apostles, as our Lord taught them during the forty days ministry between the resurrection and the ascension, becomes most pertinent at this very point: "Lord, wilt thou at this time restore again the kingdom to Israel?" (Ac 1:6). The kingdom had been disrupted by Israel's sin leading to the Babylonian captivity. Plainly, our Lord now offered Himself as Israel's King (Lk 19:35-40). But He—and with Him the kingdom—was rejected. Therefore, they were right in thinking that what had been interrupted and seemingly set aside by the cross might now be implemented as the logical next step in God's program. (See chapter 6 on "The Times of Restitution.")

Thus Matthew is led of the Spirit to present the claims of Jesus as King and tell the tragic story of the rejection of those claims. His book may be summarized thus:

I. The Kingdom OFFERED 1:1–11:1 (and His rights DISPLAYED)

II. The Kingdom REJECTED 11:2–12:45 (and Israel DISQUALIFIED)

III. The Kingdom POSTPONED 12:46–28:20 (and the church DISCLOSED)

Matthew presents five movements in his display of our Lord's kingly rights (1:1–11:1). His legal right is announced in chapters 1 and 2. He is *born* king of the Jews (2:2). Through His ancestor David, and as the legal foster son of Joseph, He is shown to have genealogical rights to the throne of David. Through His father Abraham, He has claim to the land (Gen 12:1-3; 15:18; Gal 3:16). Although He is Israel's king in the first instance, the visit of the Gentile magi (Mt 2) emphasizes that He will reign over all the earth on the throne of David.

Our Lord's second right to the kingship is His personal right (chapter 3). He is the Father's beloved Son, who ever delights in the Father's will. Thus, His Father finds His delight in Him (Mt 3:17; Heb 10:7).

In Matthew 4 we are shown His third right to be King, namely, His moral right. The trouble with all earthly rulers is this: no one has a moral right to rule others who cannot rule himself. Through the centuries men have proved they could not rule themselves. The best of kings have failed right here. But on the occasion of His temptation, Jesus defeats the devil, orders him off the premises with a "Get thee hence!" and shows us a man able to rule others because He is Himself ruled by heaven. As the chapter ends, He takes up the ministry of John, disrupted by imprisonment, and continues to announce the kingdom of the God of heaven, so eloquently explained by God through Daniel to Nebuchadnezzar: "The most High ruleth in the kingdom of men, and giveth it to whomsoever he will" (Dan 4:17, 25, 32).

The fourth right of our Lord Jesus to be King is His judicial right, recorded in the Sermon on the Mount of Matthew 5-7. This has been called the King's Inaugural Address and the Manifesto of the Kingdom. Christ announces those spiritual principles and precepts by which He will one day govern the earth when He reigns as the Great King in Jerusalem (5:35). Not only will He then rule by these principles, but those disciples who during His earthly ministry accepted His claims (as well as those who are anticipators of His kingdom during the tribulation period) are instructed in their proper conduct as "children of the kingdom." The truly spiritual and righteous character of His kingdom is prophesied in dozens of Old Testament passages (e.g., Is 11:1-5), and here expanded and heightened by our Lord Himself. Indeed, no one may enter the kingdom unless he has genuine righteousness; not outward but inward; not ceremonial but spiritual (Mt 5:20). As our Lord explained to Nicodemus, a member of the Sanhedrin, no one may enter or even "see" that kingdom, unless he has been born from heaven (lit. from above, Jn 3:3-8). This second birth excludes all unsaved and limits the entrants of the kingdom to regenerate people.

However properly or strongly the emphasis is placed upon the spiritual character of that kingdom that our Lord has pledged Himself to set up on earth, this can in no legitimate way be used to argue against a very literal kingdom on earth, ruled over by the Lord Jesus from Jerusalem, on the basis of these spiritual principles. Traditional Rabbinical misunderstandings concerning that kingdom must in no wise be allowed to change the facts concerning its earthly character, announced in extended prophetic passages, as well as by our Lord and His apostles.

Just as distortions of Scripture truth concerning baptism and the Lord's Supper constitute no argument against their genuineness, nor caricatures of marriage provide no basis for rejecting its validity, it is likewise unscientific, unscriptural, illogical, and absurd to argue against a literal kingdom on earth because of Jewish misunderstandings and distortions. So, whether it be the removal of the curse of Genesis 3 from the earth (e.g., Is 11:6-9; Amos 9:13-15; Ro 8:18-22), or the judgment of literal nations when He rules with a rod of iron (Zec 14:9-18; Ps 2:9; Rev 12:5), Christ's throne is *in* Jerusalem and the kingdom is *on the earth.* To spiritualize or allegorize these facts takes all context meaning out of Scripture. Thus, in the Sermon on the Mount, the people being instructed as to their proper duties are viewed as being on earth. There are earthly altars (5:23), earthly courts and judges (5:22, 25); earthly prisons and fines (5:25-26); and an earthly dump heap outside Jerusalem where judged criminals' bodies are thrown after execution (5:21-26).

Certainly a person thus summarily judged with capital punishment would also enter into God's eternal lake of fire, but "Gehenna" in this context must primarily refer to earthly punishment. In matters of eternal judgment, present bodies are not cast into the lake of fire, either in entirety or with missing parts (5:29-30). Bodies of sinners will be resurrected and completely changed to endure eternal fire (Rev 20:11-15). The bodies Christ referred to are of men who are still on earth. Of course, our Lord is not arguing for self-mutilation, but urging in the strongest hyperbolic language that anything would be better than yielding to sin which would bring capital punishment. The same warning accompanies sins of false accusation (5:22). Jerusalem's Valley of Hinnom (Ge-Hinnom or Gehenna) was where rubbish and bodies of animals (and sometimes criminals) were thrown. Since there were continual "burnings" going on, it became an apt symbol of eternal fire.

Although our Lord rejects and rebukes Rabbinical aberrations and distortions of the Mosaic law, it is just as clear in the Sermon on the Mount that, again and again, He indicates He is superseding and heightening the Mosaic law itself. This He does chiefly by going back of the overt act to the inner decision of spirit which leads to the overt act. Three classic examples are: Moses' law against murder (5:21-26; Ex 20: 13); the law against sexual impurity (5:27-30; Ex 20:14); and the law against divorce for every cause (Deu 24:3; Mt 5:31-32; cp. 19:9, 3-12).

This does not suggest that Christ is abrogating the Mosaic law; rather, He builds upon it. But He is making clear that with His first coming, as truth personified, more light demands higher requirements. Thus anticipators of the kingdom during His earthly ministry then, as well as those anticipating the kingdom during the tribulation period of Daniel's seventieth week, are made responsible for the standards that will be the laws of the kingdom when it is established at our Lord's second advent. As with all Scripture, not all Scripture is *to* us, though all is *for* us, because it is God's holy Word (2 Ti 3:16-17). Thus, there are properly many applications to Christians of the church age in the Sermon on the Mount. However, this must never be allowed to detract from the fact that, prior to the setting up of the millennial kingdom, the primary and direct application of the Sermon is not to the church, but to the anticipators of Christ's earthly 1,000-year kingdom.

The fifth and final right of our Lord to be King is His prophetic right (8:1—11:1). Without regard to chronology, Matthew is led by the Spirit to group together multiple miraculous incidents of our Lord's ministry. He is shown to do just what the prophets had foretold He would do (cp. 11:4-5). Somewhat as a salesman would open his sample case to demonstrate what his products are like, in His earth-life our Lord showed man a sample of what it will be like when, at long last, He rules and reigns on the earth. When Christ returns, the curse of Genesis 3 will be taken from the realm

of nature. Crop will follow crop in abundance, and the sav-
agery of beasts will be removed. Disease will vanish, the
blind will see, the deaf hear, the lame walk, and death will
be indefinitely postponed by longevity. A thousand wonderful things will happen in the thousand years reign (e.g., Is 11;
61; 62; 65:20, etc.).

Since Israel was born, nurtured, and sustained by miracle,
it is no wonder that Paul should, of all people, say "the Jews
require a sign" (1 Co 1:22). Thus, our Lord's Messianic
claims are authenticated in the very ways the Jewish mind
works. Indeed, in the letter to the Hebrews we are told these
were "signs of the coming age" (i.e., the millennium, Heb
2:3; 6:5). Heaven loudly testified to the identification of our
Lord as the heaven-sent King who has the right to rule on
earth (Eze 21:26-27).

These five proofs, marshalled by Matthew through the
Holy Spirit, provide indisputable evidence for our Lord's
qualifications to fill the office of King of Israel, or perhaps
better stated, that our Lord was and is the only valid Person
who can and does fulfill the Scriptures in respect to the Kingship. It is not immaterial to observe that He did not marry
and, though He died, He arose again and took back to heaven
with Him the title to the throne. No earlier person than our
Lord can claim the title, for they are dead. No later person
can claim the title, for "He ever liveth," and cannot be superseded. And, as I said, there are no heirs. The title rests with
Him alone. When He comes back, He will sit on His glorious
throne in Jerusalem and judge Jew and Gentile (Mt 25:31).

THE TRAGIC REJECTION—IN MATTHEW 11-12

At this point in his narrative, Matthew proceeds to tell the
story of Israel's rejection of her King through the authoritative action of her responsible leaders in blaspheming the Holy
Spirit (11:2—12:45). Trouble had been brewing (9:34). The
problem with these religious racketeers was not lack of light.

They knew full well who He was, but were unwilling to face up to what accepting those facts would mean.

They were furious that the people were impressed by Jesus. They would have had to admit their error, lose face, and change their ways, if they accepted Jesus' claims. Their enmity was therefore rooted in callous egotistical stubbornness. They rejected great light and we are told that Pilate later rightly diagnosed their motive when "he perceived that for envy they had delivered him up" (Mk 15:10; Mt 27:18).

Thus they kept challenging Jesus to discredit Him in the eyes of the people. Matthew 12 records four such instances. When Christ healed a deaf-and-dumb man and the amazed people cried, "Is not this the son of David?", they saw red and formally accused Him of being in league with Satan (Mt 12:22-24).

Our Lord responded with those awesome words of 12:25-37, flatly accusing them of blasphemy against the Holy Spirit, a sin which in their specific case would never be forgiven or forgivable, for apostasy is not forgivable. This should never be confused with persistent rejection of Christ as Saviour, which can be forgiven (v. 32a). Rather, this was a deliberate perversion of known truth into a lie. This was not a mere unbelief, but vicious apostasy.

So this sin, committed by these blaspheming leaders who later persuaded the people to crucify Christ, was one which our Lord declared could not be forgiven either in that age ("world" is a mistranslation), nor in "the age to come" (i.e., in future ages beginning with the church age).

However tragic as this scene was for those individual rejectors, there was far more involved here. They spoke and acted for the *nation*. However improper their decision, they were the responsible "powers that be." Individual Jews could personally repudiate their leaders' action and personally be forgiven, but the nation was committed to official rejection of Christ as King. The cross was an inevitable aftermath.

Thus it was that Jesus recognized His rejection in those

poignant words of Matthew 11:20-27, but significantly turned to individuals who would receive His message and seek to be delivered from the load of sins which burdened their consciences (Mt 11:28-30). Having refused to accede to the leaders' impious demand for simply another sign, our Lord bluntly announced that no further sign would be given but the sign of Jonah, that is, the sign of His resurrection from the dead (Mt 12:38-39).

A Tremendous Transition: the Kingdom in "Mystery"—Chapter 13

Right at this point our Lord made it evident that a watershed had been reached and a tremendous transition was taking place. The occasion was a strange reaction (seemingly) to a visit from His mother, accompanied in Mid-Eastern filial courtesy by His unbelieving brothers (Mt 12:46-50; Jn 7:5). Our Lord seizes this "natural" to act out a dramatic audio-visual revelation. Word comes through the crowd to Jesus "in the house" that His mother and brothers desire to see Him. To the consternation of all present, our Lord appears to brush off with discourtesy the expected response of going out to greet them. His amazed hearers see Him stay right there and point to His disciples, exclaiming: "Who is My mother? . . . who My brothers? . . Behold My mother and brothers. . . . For whoever shall do My Father's will . . . he is My brother, My sister, My mother!"

Certainly our Lord, ever warm toward His mother, would not have done this seemingly brutally discourteous thing, unless a great truth were involved. What was our Lord saying? Very definitely this: Having been rejected by the responsible leaders of Israel, He is acting out the fact that He is now turning from natural fleshly ties ("family" and "house" of Israel) to spiritual ties ("whosoever" . . . "multitudes by the seaside" of Gentiles). That is, He foretells that there will be believers from all nations, as symbolized by the word *sea* in Isaiah 60:5 and explained in Revelation 17:15. Now, for the first time, Jesus, the Great Prophet foretold by Moses, declared that "the field is the world" (Mt 13:38), no longer just Palestine and the Jews. So something important is happening. What is it?

With a crowd like this, the apostles are scandalized that Jesus resorts to parables (13:10). Here is a chance to use scorching truth, such as He gave in the Sermon on the Mount. So they challenge the Lord with "Why?" Our Lord patiently explains that He is deliberately veiling what He is saying from those who "have not" faith; He is revealing something tremendously important to those who "have" faith (vv. 11-12). He quotes the Isaiah apostasy passage (vv. 14-15; Is 6:9-10). He says that only the spiritually-minded will understand. He wants and expects them to do so.

Something further is here, though. These great truths which He is now revealing in these parables were never before revealed: "I will open my mouth in parables; I will utter things which have been kept secret from the foundation of the world" (v. 35). This is why even spiritually-minded prophets never knew these things (vv. 16-17). It was not yet the proper *time* to reveal them. But he indicates it is *now* the proper time for Him to tell these things, and His disciples are the privileged hearers!

Considerable light is thrown on this crucial event by the words of First Peter 1:10-12:

> Of which salvation the prophets have inquired and searched diligently, who prophesied of the grace that should come unto you: searching what, or what manner of time the Spirit of Christ which was in them did signify, when [he] testified beforehand the sufferings of Christ, and the glory that should follow. Unto whom it was revealed, that not unto themselves, but unto us they did minister the things, which are now reported unto you by them that have preached the gospel unto you with the Holy Ghost sent down from heaven; which things the angels desire to look into.

This passage makes it clear that Old Testament prophets prophesied better than they knew. They knew that Jesus was going to come into the world and suffer. They knew He was to have a glorious reign. However, they could not see how these two things could happen to Jesus. How could He both suffer and be glorified? This deeply puzzled them, and no wonder. They lacked the clarifying time element, so they searched for it (v. 11), but to no avail. In fact, some rabbis imagined two Messiahs; Messiah ben Judah, the suffering servant of Jehovah, and Messiah ben Joseph, the glorious king.

Though a solution was not granted them, God mercifully informed them that they had not written wrongly. Indeed, says Peter, in so many words: "God does not intend for you to know now; you are ministering to a people of a future generation who will understand." So God hid the time areas in His own counsel until it was the proper time to reveal and clarify them. Until Jesus was rejected, no one could piece the time elements together. It was at this point our Lord reveals the secret. As the Great Prophet He is the first to reveal it (Mt 13:11, 17, 34-35). Further detail was given later through His New Testament prophets and apostles (Col 1:25-26; Eph 3:1-5, esp. v. 5).

To have revealed the coming church age in the Old Testament, or before abundant opportunity had been given for the leaders of Israel to render their verdict, would have made a genuine offer of a literal kingdom ethically invalid. To conceal and leave somewhat vague what would happen, so that the prophets could not solve the puzzle, was entirely in keeping with God's method and plan of dealing with people, which might be summarized: full warning and full responsibility.

So our Lord now, for the first time, announces basic details concerning what will happen during the period between His rejection by Israel's responsible leaders (Mt 12), and the time when He will return to earth (upon Israel's repentance) to establish the kingdom they had previously rejected in rejecting Him. The two mountain peaks of His first and second advents were plainly seen by the prophets, but they could not see the valley in between, either in detail or in extent. The fact that a period of time, now 2,000 years, would intervene between the two comings was never dreamed of by the Old Testament prophets. *This* was its first announcement by our Lord Himself. No wonder He thought it important. No wonder He congratulated them that they were the first to be told things that even the holy prophets had not been told (Mt 13:16-17). We can now understand the prophets' perplexity. It was not their lack of perception but God's timing that hid these things from their eyes, things which provoked the holy curiosity of even the angels (1 Pe 1:12)!

It is not the purpose of this chapter to exposit the parables of Matthew 13 in detail. It is rather to provide a proper background for their interpretation and especially to emphasize their uniqueness. "The kingdom in manifestation," the glorious kingdom over which our Lord will reign on earth from Jerusalem, had been amply revealed by the prophets and by our Lord Himself. But now He is talking about something *entirely new*. This has been called "The kingdom in mystery," that is, a form of the kingdom which had been hidden in the counsels of God from ages and generations past, but is now for the first time revealed.

The word "mystery" could be misleading. In fact, it is generally misunderstood. It is not a translation. It is simply the Greek word brought over into English letters. The Greek word did not emphasize mysteriousness, but simply something which had not before been revealed. The classic example is the secrets of the secret societies. Outsiders did not know them. But once the neophyte was initiated, he knew them. The aura of mystery was not there. It was rather the fact of secrecy.

So, Jesus took things, which God had seen fit to keep secret until Jesus' firm rejection by Israel's leaders, and now

explained what would take place between the time of His
rejection (Mt 12), prior to the cross, until the time of His
return to take the kingdom for which He holds the title and
throne rights. Though the period includes the church age,
the period of the "mystery" form of the kingdom must not
be equated with the church era. Indeed, the church had not
yet been announced; that remains for Christ to do in Matthew
16:18. In the full light of New Testament truth, we see many
things in the parables of Matthew 13 which explicate what is
happening in the church era, but Matthew 13 traces a longer
period than is involved in the church era. Perhaps a simple
chart will help:

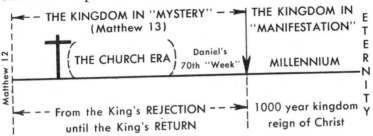

What, in summary, did Jesus reveal in the parables of Matthew 13? He revealed that old Jewish boundaries were now
to be ignored; that the seed of the Word was to be sown in all
the world (v. 38). That some would take root and some
would not (parable 1). That there would be true and false
in the sphere of profession (parables 2 and 7). That Satan
would constantly oppose (parables 1, 2, 3, and 4). That
Satan's buzzards would be in the branches of that which outwardly constituted the testimony for God upon the earth
(parable 3). That false doctrine would be mixed with the
true (parable 4). That He (our Lord) would "buy" the field
of the world to get the treasure, at that time hidden but
known to Him (parable 5). That out of the sea of nations
a pearl of great price would be obtained (parable 6). That
at the end of the era of our Lord's rejection, He would come
back to earth to judge the wicked, repudiate the phony, and

rescue and reward the righteous (parables 2 and 7). That the righteous would rule and reign with Him in the glorious kingdom instituted by His fiery return (vv. 40-43; 49-50). That eternal destiny was also at stake. Some would be consigned to eternal fire (vv. 42, 50). Some would be gathered by the angels into the Father's eternal care (vv. 43, 49).

Since truth is truth whatever the era, one can easily recognize principles that were true during the Old Testament and during the ministry of our Lord up till the time of His rejection by the Pharisees' blasphemy of the Holy Spirit. The setting, the details and distinctives of the era described by our Lord, and the dramatic consummation of that era, constitute a body of truth never before revealed. Our Lord recognized both aspects when He instructed the apostles that they were now stewards of what they had heard; that it was now their duty to bring forth from their treasures "things new and old," that is, truth they knew from the Old Testament and this entirely new truth. The Bible is not dichotomized. Truth is cumulative, however much the interpretation of truth may be specific and distinctive in a given era and a given context.

Thus, to confuse the kingdom announced by the Old Testament prophets, by John the Baptist (Mt 3), and by our Lord and His apostles (Mt 4-10), with the aspect of the kingdom that our Lord introduced in Matthew 13 is to ignore completely the distinctions our Lord went out of His way to make. Particularly does it ignore His statement that He, for the first time, is revealing these things (Mt 13:34-35, 11, 16-17).

Tremendous damage has been done to the sequence of events of our Lord's life and ministry when our Lord's appeal to the whole nation, calling on them to repudiate their past and receive Him as their King (Mt 1-10), is confused with and/or equated with the appeal to individuals within the nation (during the "mystery" period of the kingdom, Mt 13)

to repent and repudiate the formal rejection of Christ as King
by the representative leaders of Israel (Mt 12).

THE KINGDOM OF HEAVEN AND THE KINGDOM OF GOD: DISTINCT OR EQUATED?

This major distinction is also accompanied by a corollary
interpretation which, though less crucial and more debatable,
is nonetheless of greater importance than it first seems to be.
I refer to the question as to whether the descriptive Matthew
phrases, "kingdom of heaven" and "kingdom of God," are to
be equated or to be distinguished from each other. In my
judgment, although less rides at stake, earnest students of the
Word want to be right in their interpretations and there are
sometimes accompanying hidden dangers. For instance, one
writer has tried, unsuccessfully, to insist that if one can establish the two terms are synonymous, then it can be asserted
that Jesus did not actually offer Himself as a King and thus
did not offer a literal kingdom to Israel on the occasion of
His first advent. I refer to Dr. George E. Ladd's *Crucial
Questions Concerning the Kingdom of God.*

This is not the place, nor is there space, for an evaluation
of Ladd's thesis, but the point is important. In essence, my
reply might be summarized: The truth or falsity of the kind
of kingdom our Lord offered, whether literal or spiritual, does
not hinge on some special, distinctive meaning of each of
these phrases. It depends upon the exegesis, in context, of
all our Lord said about His kingdom, using these phrases, not
only as recorded in Matthew's gospel, but in the other three
gospels as well. Ladd is both right and wrong—right in asserting the two phrases are properly equated, and very, very
wrong in saying that the argument for the postponed kingdom hinges upon the distinction some early premillennial
writers, like Scofield, made between the two phrases, "kingdom of heaven" and "kingdom of God."

In fact, in rebuttal, it can be pointed out that Dr. George
N. H. Peters equates the two phrases in his 2,200-page classic,

The Theocratic Kingdom of Our Lord Jesus, the Christ, probably the strongest book in favor of the *literal* kingdom. Thus, Peters ignores any relevance to Ladd's thesis, and presents crushing evidence that the literal, Messianic, 1,000-year kingdom of our Lord, yet to be set up on earth at His second advent, is the same kingdom He genuinely offered Israel in Matthew 1-10.

Since Scofield has widely popularized a careful distinction between the two phrases, kingdom of heaven and kingdom of God, at Matthew 6:33 (page 1003) of his well-known *Reference Bible* of 1909 and 1917 (somewhat softened in the *New Scofield Reference Bible* of 1967), it seems appropriate that this chapter should include an evaluation of his views on the subject. Let me preface my comments by saying that my parents were among the first to purchase the 1909 edition and, like multitudes of others, were greatly helped by its valuable notes. Having been born just five years before, from earliest remembrance I was made aware of Scofield's views and quite naturally received them. In due time I became acquainted with the technical distinction he made between the two phrases.

Scofield's close friend and successor, Lewis Sperry Chafer (and others), carefully instructed our first class at Dallas Theological Seminary (1924-27) in these distinctions, using the analogy that Dallas was in Texas but Dallas was not all of Texas. The larger sphere (kingdom of heaven), like Texas, included the smaller sphere (kingdom of God), i.e., Dallas. The kingdom of God was supposed to refer to the true-believer core within the larger sphere of profession, the kingdom of heaven, but the two were not to be equated. There usually was also a corollary idea that, in the ultimate, the kingdom of heaven was the rule of Jesus Christ on the earth during His 1,000-year reign.

However, some forty years ago, I came to the conclusion that this distinction, which has brought enormous comfort to Scofield's enemies while baffling many of his friends, is not a valid distinction. Indeed, not only is the supposed distinction confusing; it brings with it certain unnecessary problems of interpretation.

I therefore urge the following reasons for recognizing *no distinction* between the two phrases:

(1) The verbal inspiration argument

Jesus said something about a new form of the kingdom when He gave the parables of Matthew 13 (Lk 13; Mk 4). What did He say on that day? Matthew records He said "kingdom of heaven." Mark and Luke record He said "kingdom of God." If the two things mean different things, then plainly Matthew misquotes our Lord, or Mark and Luke misquote Him. If this be true, then the Bible is in error and verbal inspiration is disproved. To imagine that our Lord said approximately the same things on another day to another crowd, but with another meaning, is wishful thinking or, at least, assuming the thing to be proved. Also see uses of "kingdom of God" by Matthew in 6:33; 12:28; 19:24; and 21:31, 43.

(2) The argument from Daniel's use of the words

The two phrases come to us right out of the book of Daniel, where the Holy Spirit directs him to write a great deal about the "kingdom" of "the God of heaven" (Dan 2:37). God "rules in the kingdom of men and gives it to whomever He wills"; "the heavens do rule" (Dan 4:17, 25-26, 32; 5:21); "Lord of heaven" (5:23; 7:18, 25, 27; 7:13-14). Note that "God" . . . "the Lord" . . . "the Most High" . . . and "the heavens" are said to rule. Hence, His rule might be called "the kingdom of (the) God of (or) heaven."

Since God's dwelling place is the third heaven (2 Co 12:2), by metonymy "heaven" is often used as a synonym for "God," just as, e.g., Jesus used "the cup" in instituting the Lord's Supper as a metonym of that which the cup contains—"the blood" of Christ (Mt 26:

27; Lk 22:20). No one stumbles over the alternate use of "cup" for its contents, "blood" or "wine." Why should we stumble over the use of the word "heaven" (in the phrase "kingdom of heaven") as a metonym for "God," who dwells there?

(3) The argument from Jesus' use of "heaven" as a synonym for "God"

As a matter of fact, the Hebrews used the two terms as synonyms, as witness the occasion when the prodigal came to his senses and proposed to return to his father. He planned to say: "Father, I have sinned against heaven, and before thee" (Lk 15:18). It is absolutely certain that he meant "I have sinned against God." Any other idea would make nonsense.

(4) Scofield's arguments invalid

The arguments for the supposed distinctions between "kingdom of heaven" and "kingdom of God" given by the Scofield note on page 1003 of the 1909/1917 edition at Matthew 6:33 are not valid:

    a. Scofield's argument from silence concerning the omission of the parables of the wheat and tares and the dragnet is gratuitous. No gospel writer includes everything. This is the point of the Holy Spirit's guidance in the selection of materials (Jn 21:25). Matthew omits Mark's "Parable of Gradual Growth" (Mk 4:26-29), not because it says "kingdom of God" (for Luke omits it also), but because it is not pertinent to his purpose in writing (nor that of Luke).

    b. As to the parable of the leaven, how could Pharisees, Sadducees, and Herodians be representatives of error, if "kingdom of God" means *only* the good and the true? Since both Luke and Matthew cite the parable, they must be recording what our Lord said about the same thing, not two different things. If not, which recorder is wrong?

(5) The elaborate attempt to show a distinction between the

two kingdom phrases ("of God" and "of heaven") is proved false and artificial by the use of *both* phrases by our Lord, speaking to the same men in the same context of two succeeding verses (Mt 19:23-24). Luke, recording the same incident, uses "kingdom of God" for the two statements (Lk 18:24-25). Likewise, Matthew records that one must be converted to enter "the kingdom of heaven" (Mt 18:3; cp. "kingdom of God," Jn 3:3, 5)!

(6) In the light of the above, it seems to me that the simpler and better solution is to recognize that the terms are synonymous and that the variation is due to context, not the variant word. The "kingdom of God" is not always good, nor the "kingdom of heaven" both good and bad, as Scofield urges. As the following chart shows, there is flexibility (determined by context) to cover three possible meanings—true and false; true only; false only. Note the evidence:

The constituency of the kingdom:	"Kingdom of heaven" used in:	"Kingdom of God" used in:
a. Both true and false together		
the parable of the soils	Matthew 13	Mark 4 and Luke 13
the parable of wheat and tares	Matthew 13	
the parable of the dragnet	Matthew 13	
b. The true only		
the parable of gradual growth		Mark 4
the parable of hid treasure	Matthew 13	
the parable of the pearl	Matthew 13	
c. The false only		
the parable of the mustard tree	Matthew 13	Mark 4 and Luke 13
the parable of the leaven	Matthew 13	Luke 13

It will be observed that Matthew uses "kingdom of heaven" of all three combinations, and that likewise "the kingdom of God" is used of all three combinations by Mark and/or Luke. Thus, each of these two phrases is used in the same way as the other with three different meanings, determined by context.

(7) Lest this should be thought confusing or strange, let it be remembered—for example—that we use the word "church" in different contexts to mean these three different things:

    a. We use "church" to mean Christendom, the true and the false in the whole professing body of Christ or in any given local area or local church.

    b. We use "church" to mean only true believers, those who have been baptized into the body of Christ, whether we consider the whole period of the church age from Pentecost to the rapture, or whether we mean all true believers at any one point of time on earth.

    c. We use "church" of a false heretical group who claim to belong to Christ, e.g., The Church of the Latter-day Saints, Jehovah's Witnesses, or the Church of Christ, Scientist!

Thus it is perfectly true that sometimes our Lord is talking about the *whole* group (of true and false), or one *part* of the group (either good or bad). But He does this regardless of whether He is using the phrase "kingdom of heaven" or the phrase "kingdom of God." The difference is not in a distinction between the *words* "heaven" and "God," but it is a distinction of *thought* while using the same words, or using the different words interchangeably.

David Baron, the great Hebrew Christian scholar, sponsors this view, suggesting that Matthew in writing to the Jews is aware of their reticence to use the name of Deity, because of which sensitivity they very often substituted the word "heaven," used by metonymy for "God." Thus, as our Lord spoke, He used both terms freely as synonyms, but each writer selected the word best suited to his readers: Matthew using "heaven" (for Jews); Mark, "God" (for Romans); and Luke "God" (for Greeks).

It is interesting that in the first ten chapters of the gospels: Matthew uses "God" only 18 times while Mark uses it 29 times, Luke 55 times, and John 53 times. Matthew, on the contrary, uses "Father" for "God" over 40 times; Luke less than 20 times; and Mark less than 4 times. This tends to support a disposition on the part of Matthew to avoid overuse of "God."

It is submitted, therefore, that by making the two phrases, "kingdom of heaven" and "kingdom of God" synonymous and flexible, we avoid awkward problems of inspiration and interpretation. But, more important, proper emphasis is placed upon the oft-neglected fact that context rather than trick phrases is the chief guide to accurate interpretation of the text of Scripture.

THE MULTIPLE USES OF THE IDEA (OR WORD "KINGDOM") IN THE BIBLE

Perhaps it will expand our concept of the uses of the word or idea of "kingdom" or "dominion" to list the many ways it is used or viewed in the Bible. It is used of:

1. "Dominion" of mankind over nature, Genesis 1:28; Psalm 8; Hebrews 2:5-8.

2. God's rule over nature—the physical universe, including the animal realm, Psalm 103:19; cp. 19:1-6.

3. God's rule over the spiritual universe (i.e., universe of spirits), whether holy or unholy angels, Satan, demons, human beings (e.g., 1 Pe 3:22; Col 1:16; Phil 2:9-11; Dan 7:9-10; Rev 20:1-2, 7, 10).

4. God's rule over the kingdom of men in providence over nations and history, (e.g., Ac 17:24-28; Dan 4:25, 32, 35).

5. God's rule in *direct* theocracy (using Moses, priesthood,

Law) through religious leaders, instituted at Sinai, Exodus 19ff.

6. God's rule through *indirect* theocracy (using human kings of Israel, beginning with Saul, 1 Sa 8:6-7, 19-22; 1 Sa 9ff.).

7. The ordinary rule of God over the kingdoms or nations of men through "the powers that be," during the "times of the Gentiles," beginning with Nebuchadnezzar (Dan 2:36-38ff.; Ro 13:1-7; 1 Pe 2:11-17).

8. The eschatological kingdom of 1,000 years, Christ's kingdom over and on the earth from Jerusalem, instituted at His second advent (Rev 19:11—20:6; 2:26-27; 3:21; 11:15-18; Mic 4:1-5, etc.). This kingdom was announced by the Old Testament prophets; by the angel Gabriel (Lk 1:30-33); by John the Baptist (Mt 3:1-2; Mk 1:1-8; Lk 3:1-18, etc.); by our Lord (Mk 1:14-15; Mt 4: 12, 17; Lk 4:16-21, etc.); by His apostles (Mt 10:5-15). This kingdom, because of Jewish rejection (Mt 12) is now in abeyance until there is national repentance (Mt 23:37-39; Zec 12:10; Ro 11:11-12, 22-23, 25-27). Note: God never counted the *physical* seed of Israel as "God's Israel," the *spiritual* seed. "God's Israel" will repent and be rescued by Christ at His return to earth. This is carefully explained in Romans 11:1-6.

9. The rule of God over individual hearts of men, voluntarily subject to Him in every age of God's dealing with man. This is the kingdom we are "born" into by believing the gospel (Jn 3:3-7). "The kingdom of God is not food and drink, but righteousness, peace and joy in the Holy Spirit" (Ro 14:17).

10. The "mystery" aspect of the kingdom (sacred secret now revealed), exposited by our Lord Himself for the first time in Matthew 13. This is the sphere of both true and false—the sphere of profession—during the extended

period of the King's rejection by Israel until their repentance and acceptance of Christ as "God's Israel" on the occasion of His second advent when He returns to set up the kingdom in manifestation (i.e., His eschatological kingdom—see No. 8 with references).

11. The eternal kingdom, 2 Peter 1:11 and numerous passages. The mediatorial, millennial kingdom of Christ proceeds into the eternal kingdom, in which the Godhead—Father, Son, and Spirit—co-equal in nature and attributes will reign together eternally (1 Co 15:24-28).

    It would not be out of order to mention two other aspects of "kingdom" or "rule."

12. Satan's well-ordered kingdom (Mt 12:26, 22-30; Jn 14:30; 2 Co 4:4).

13. The literal translation of Romans 6:12-14, "Let not Sin (the old ego, the old Adam, the old nature) reign as king in your mortal body, that you should obey its dictates and desires; neither keep on yielding your bodily members as weapons of unrighteousness unto Sin (the old nature), but once for all yield yourselves unto God . . . and your members as weapons of righteousness unto God, for Sin shall not have dominion over you."

6

The Times of Restitution

I. The Meaning of the Text

In examining this passage together, it seems appropriate that we should first of all investigate the true meaning of the text. This will enable us to proceed to our discussion with a clear understanding of just what was said by the apostle Peter to his audience on that tremendously significant afternoon when the healing of the lame man led to this second of his great sermons as recorded by Luke in the book of Acts. To do this we shall deal with meanings of words and phrases and suggest a free translation of some of the portions involved.

Perhaps it would be well to start with verse 17 of Acts 3, where the apostle says: "And now, brethren, I wot that through ignorance ye did it, as did also your rulers." The key phrase is *kata agnoian* and means literally, "according to ignorance." Thus the apostle is saying, "Now, brethren, I realize that the awful deed of slaying your Messiah is measured and interpreted by your ignorance."

On this point, Dean Alford remarks:

> There need be no difficulty in the application of the *agnoia* to even the rulers of the Jews. It admits of all degrees—from the unlearned, who were implicitly led by others and hated Him because others did—up to the most learned of the scribes, who knew and rightly interpreted the Messianic prophecies, but from moral blindness, or perverted expecta-

110

tions, did not recognize them in our Lord. *Some* degree of *agnoia* there must have been in them *all*.

Verse 18 then proceeds: "But those things, which God before had shewed by the mouth of all his prophets, that Christ should suffer, he hath so fulfilled." The paradox that their great conquering Messiah should also suffer this seeming contradiction, which the Jews could not understand (hence their *agnoia*), is here explained by Peter as being solved by the facts of our Lord's suffering for sin on the cross and His subsequent victorious resurrection. The statement that "all the prophets" told of these things is not exaggeration, for the prophets are here envisioned as being one body inspired of the Spirit of God to present one concerted message, the sum of which was that God's Christ should suffer.

That word "suffer" is interesting in that it is the aorist tense and thus emphasizes our Lord's passion as being a single definite act accomplished at a point of time past. Also, W. Robertson Nicoll points out that the word "fulfill" means more than that; it implies "to fill up to the full." Thus, "not only is our Lord the subject of direct predictions in the Old Testament, but His claims go to the full extent of affirming that all the truths which are imperfectly, and frequently very darkly shadowed forth in the pages, are realized in Him as the ideal to which they all pointed."[1]

"Repent ye therefore and be converted" should rather be read as active voice. "Repent ye therefore, and turn again that your sins may be blotted out." The next phrase is very misleading. It cannot properly be read "*when* the times of refreshing come." Rather, this particular construction is peculiar to Luke in the New Testament. It has a purpose or causal thought and should be rendered either "that so there may come" or "in order that there may come times (seasons) of refreshing from the presence of the Lord and (in order that) He (the Father) may send Jesus Christ . . ." The phrase "seasons of refreshing" indicates a definite arrival, not a

1. *Row, Bampton Lectures,* pp. 202-203.

mere occurrence, and v. 20 shows the Person sent to be the envoy or representative of the Sender, literally: *"so that He may send* the Christ who hath been appointed for you, *even* Jesus."

The Lord Jesus is here declared to be the One "whom heaven must receive until the times of restitution of all things." One might well freely transliterate the thought: "It behooves the heaven (which is His, obeying His will) to receive Him till the time appointed for earth to receive Him." He said after His resurrection, "All power (authority) is given me in heaven and in earth" (Mt 28:18). That authority ("power") is already being exercised by Him at His Father's right hand. This is however only until the time of His sending, which will be the "times of restitution of all things." God has spoken about these times of restitution "by the mouth of all His holy prophets since the world began," or literally "from of old"; certainly this goes back as far as Enoch, who foretold Christ's coming to judge sinful men (Jude 1:14-15).

"Until the times of restitution of all things" is the key phrase of the whole passage. What is the meaning of this word translated "restitution," *apokatastasis?* *Young* indicates it means literally "to place down again, hence to restore." *Thayer* says "to restore to its former state," and comments: "The restoration not only of the true theocracy but also of that more perfect state of (even physical) things which existed before the fall of man."

Vincent calls attention to the fact that the verb from which our noun comes is used as a technical medical term, "denoting complete restoration of health; the restoring to its place of a dislocated joint, etc." Is it not interesting that the passage before us was written by Luke, a doctor?

Moulton and *Milligan* give further illustrations of the uses of this word. It is used to describe "the repair of a public way"; "the restoration of estates to their rightful owners"; "a balancing of acounts." A most striking use is in astrology, where it is used to indicate "the final point of agreement of the world's cyclical periods, as, e.g., the Egyptian Apocatastasis Years." Certainly this indicates the rounding out of an appointed time and the arrival of a time of destiny.

Josephus uses the word to denote the restoration of the Jews to their own land from the Babylonian captivity, and *Philo* speaks of the restoration of inheritances at the Jubilee.

As we read our English version we are likely to think that the emphasis is "the restitution of all things which the prophets said would be restored." The emphasis is rather upon the fact that this great climax, called "the restitution of all things," is a theme concerning which all the prophets have spoken. There may be many things God proposes to do in addition to certain things He has had His prophets record. The term "restitution-of-all-things" might well be read as though it were a hyphenated word. Peter's aim is to show the unanimity of all the prophets in speaking of a great climax of God's dealings with men. This great climax is something to which the whole Bible has looked forward and, note carefully, it is dependent upon the sending of the Lord Jesus Christ back to earth, which we are told will take place when a true repentance has been made by Israel.

The remaining verses present no problem of translation, so we shall proceed to an examination of:

II. THE FORCE OF THE CONTEXT

It is a favorite interpretation among the traditional theologians that this passage is simply referring to the refreshing of heart and spirit which comes about when God sends Jesus into our hearts in response to our repentance toward God and faith toward Jesus Christ. That there is such refreshing is blessedly true and we would be both foolish and unscriptural if we failed to agree that God intends this to be the experience of every new convert. But that this is Peter's meaning, in the words he uses on this occasion, we respectfully deny. Consider the context.

Our Lord had been crucified. On the third day He arose. He ministered forty days to His disciples, "speaking of things pertaining to the kingdom of God" (Ac 1:3). What He said caused them to ask Him in Acts 1:6: "Wilt thou at this time restore (same verb) again the kingdom to Israel?" Contrary to the usual commentary interpretation, our Lord did not rebuke them for asking that question. One of the last major discourses of our Lord before His death was the Olivet Discourse in which He said a great deal about His coming again and setting things right on earth. No, our Lord did not rebuke His disciples because they asked about a restoration of the kingdom to Israel. He rather cautioned and instructed them that *the time* was in the Father's hand. Their job was to witness concerning Him, beginning at Jerusalem, and leave the time of the setting up of the kingdom to the Father.

Our Lord then ascended from Olivet and two men informed the watching disciples that He would come back again to earth as really and tangibly as they had just seen Him go to heaven.

On the day of Pentecost, Peter began this witnessing, explaining that the events of Jesus' life, death, and resurrection were the fulfillment of the prophet's words. This being the case, they had with Roman help murdered their Messiah and should repent immediately and genuinely. At least 3,000 heeded his appeal. The believers met together for fellowship and encouragement, and others continued to be saved.

One afternoon shortly afterward, Peter and John were going to pray in the temple when they were asked by a lame man for a gift. Peter told him he did not have that kind of gift; instead, empowered of the Spirit, he gave him a greater gift. He was miraculously healed. In the joy of this wonderful experience he leaped up and down in the temple and praised God. The crowd gathered to watch and marvel. Peter seized the opportunity to preach to them. He said that they had made a tragic error; they had sinned against God in killing the Prince of Life. He said it was this risen Christ who had made this man well. He then called upon them to repent of their sin and turn to God.

If they would do this, he promised: (1) that times of refreshing, long prophesied by the prophets would be sent them; (2) that the Father would send Jesus back to earth in response to their repentance; and (3) that His return from heaven would inaugurate the period known as "the times of restitution of all things," a great and wonderful transformation to which all the prophets had looked forward throughout the whole Old Testament. He is the Great Prophet of whom Moses spake (Deu 18:15-19). He is the active agent in the fulfillment of the Abrahamic covenant (first announced in Gen 12:1-3).

What does this passage mean, therefore, couched in this context? Let Dean Alford speak,

> No other meaning, it seems to me, will suit these words, but that of the times of refreshment, the great season of joy and rest,which it was understood the coming of Messiah in His glory was to bring with it. That this was connected by the apostle with the conversion of the Jewish people, was not only according to the plain inference from prophecy, but doubtless was one of those things concerning the Kingdom of God which he had been taught by his Risen Master. . . . Even if the word "send" be nowhere else applied to the second coming of the Lord, there is no reason why it should not be here: the whole ground and standing point of Peter are peculiar.

Nicoll also comments:

> The words here refer not only to the fact that Jesus was the appointed Christ, inasmuch as the Covenant with Abraham was fulfilled in Him (v. 25), but also to the return of Jesus as the Christ, the Messianic King at His Parousia, in accordance with the voices of the Prophets. . . . The context certainly conceives of Christ as then enthroned in Heaven, where He must remain until His Second Coming, although

we may readily admit an application value of Christ's spiritual presence with the repentant.

Hence the force of the context is plainly suited to the proposition that Peter is making a re-offer of the kingdom (see addendum documenting this viewpoint at end of chapter), and if repentance was forthcoming, God would send His Son, their Messiah, back to them with seasons of refreshing and the setting right of all things, in accordance with the message of the prophets.

Therefore in the apostles' question of Acts 1:6: "Wilt thou at this time restore again the kingdom to Israel?" the words "at this time" indicate that the institution of the church is *not* the time of the restitution of all things.

It is a question concerning the re-establishment of Israel and her kingdom ruled over by Messiah. This re-establishment has nothing to do with the founding of the church, its current status, or its rapture, but is *solely dependent* on the repentance of Israel, so that the prophecies concerning them and the Messiah's kingdom may be fulfilled.

In addition to Acts 1:6, there are two other important passages which should be thought of in connection with Peter's message here. Let me quote them:

In Matthew 19:27 Peter asked our Lord what would be done for the apostles who had forsaken all for His sake. In verse 28 our Lord replied: "Ye (that) have followed me, in the regeneration (*palingenesis*, rebirth) when the Son of man shall sit in the throne of his glory, ye also shall sit upon twelve thrones, judging the twelve tribes of Israel."

The other passage is in Matthew 17:11: "Elijah truly shall first come and restore all things." The word "restore" is our verb, and the Septuagint uses the same word in Malachi 4:6 in prophesying concerning Elijah's ministry of "turning the hearts" of the people to God. Thus the rebirth of the world, the restoration of Jewish hearts to God, are tacitly connected by our Lord with the occasion of His coming back to earth. And now, let us evaluate.

III. The Significance of the Sermon

In thinking through the wonderful things which God intends to do when earth has her *palingenesis*, her new birth, when our Lord shall be sent from heaven a second time by the Father, I felt they could best be summed up by drawing an application from each of the various uses of the word as mentioned by Thayer, Vincent, and Moulton and Milligan. Certainly He will do this and more!

The Times of Restitution in Prophecy will mean:

1. To restore a thing to its former state

How aptly this phrase describes what will happen when Satan shall be overthrown and the curse of Genesis 3 removed. Our minds cannot help but turn to the exultant words of the apostle Paul in the eighth chapter of Romans, verses 15-23:

> For ye have not received the spirit of bondage again to fear; but ye have received the Spirit of adoption, whereby we cry, Abba, Father. The Spirit [himself] beareth witness with our spirit, that we are the children of God: and if children, then heirs; heirs of God, and joint-heirs with Christ; if so be that we suffer with him, that we may be also glorified together. For I reckon that the sufferings of this present time are not worthy to be compared with the glory which shall be revealed to us. For the earnest expectation of the [creation] waiteth for the manifestation of the sons of God. For the [creation] was made subject to vanity, not willingly, but by reason of him who hath subjected the same in hope. Because the [creation] itself also shall be delivered from the bondage of corruption into the glorious liberty of the children of God. For we know that the whole creation groaneth and travaileth in pain together until now. And not only they, but ourselves also, which have the firstfruits of the Spirit, even we ourselves groan within ourselves, waiting for the adoption, to wit, the redemption of our body.

The wonderful words of Isaiah also come to one's mind as

he thinks of the removal of the curse of Genesis 3 and the restoration of the earth to its former state. Listen to what God says:

> And the cow and the bear shall feed; their young ones shall lie down together: and the lion shall eat straw like the ox. And the sucking child shall play on the hole of the asp, and the weaned child shall put his hand on the cockatrice' den. They shall not hurt nor destroy in all my holy mountain: for the earth shall be full of the knowledge of the Lord, as the waters cover the sea (Is 11:7-9).

2. The repair of a public (high)way

One is immediately reminded again of the glorious words of Isaiah 40:3-5 and 11:16a:

> The voice of him that crieth in the wilderness, Prepare ye the way of the Lord, make straight in the desert a highway for our God. Every valley shall be exalted, and every mountain and hill shall be made low: and the crooked shall be made straight, and the rough places plain: And the glory of the Lord shall be revealed, and all flesh shall see it together: for the mouth of the Lord hath spoken it. . . . And there shall be an highway for the remnant of his people, which shall be left.

The day is coming when earth-usurping authorities, when greedy rulers ("every mountain . . . hill") shall be humbled ("made low"). When everything that is devious and crooked in political affairs shall be made straight, when the humble ("valley") shall be exalted, when the pilgrim feet of the redeemed from all the nations of the earth will walk God's highway to Jerusalem to worship the King of kings and Lord of lords. It will not be a broad way "that leadeth to destruction" (Mt 7:13), but a broad way which the redeemed shall tread as they go to see "the glory of the Lord."

3. The restoring to its place of a dislocated joint

The world is all out of joint. I am sure that I do not need

to prove that is so. It has often been said that nothing is in its rightful place: the church is out of place, it should be in heaven. The Lord is out of place, He should be on earth; He is now at the right hand of His Father's throne; He should be on His own throne in Jerusalem. Israel is out of place, she should be in her own land at the head of the nations and not the tail. The day is coming when she shall be, and when all that is out of joint shall be properly related.

When one thinks of a dislocated joint, and the pain and distress of it, one cannot help but remember Ezekiel's vision of the valley of dry bones (chapter 37). You will remember that Ezekiel was told to prophesy to those bones lying all disjointed on the ground. He did so and "there was a noise, and behold a shaking, and the bones came together, bone to his bone." Sinews and flesh came upon them and skin covered them. Finally the breath of God was breathed into them and "they lived, and stood up upon their feet, an exceeding great army."

The day is coming when God's DPs., His displaced persons, will not only be placed back in their land but properly restored to their true position with the Lord through repentance and conversion. Everything out of joint will be put in its proper place. Earth's racking pains will be relieved. Oh what a day that will be!

4. The restoration of estates to their rightful owners

This use of the word pointed out by Moulton and Milligan is in line with a basic theme of the Scriptures. In Genesis 1:26, 28 we read,

> And God said, Let us make man in our image, after our likeness: and let them have dominion over the fish of the sea, and over the fowl of the air, and over the cattle, and over all the earth, and over every creeping thing that creepeth upon the earth. . . . And God said . . . replenish (fill) the earth, and subdue it: and have dominion over . . . the earth.

There is a great mystery involved in Satan's eagerness and desire to obtain the scepter of sovereignty which Adam lost when he sinned. One old writer has suggested that when it slipped from Adam's hand Satan caught it before it hit the ground. Certainly he was not lying when he offered our Lord Jesus "the kingdoms of the world, and the glory of them" on the occasion of the temptation (Mt 4:8). He is called "the prince of this world" (Jn 14:30; 12:31) and "the god of this world" (2 Co 4:4).

Led by the Spirit of God, David reiterated God's purpose that man should have sovereignty over the earth in those wonderful words of Psalm 8:6, where he says "Thou madest him to have dominion over the works of thy hands; thou hast put all things under his feet."

However, the Spirit of God's commentary upon that psalm beginning at Hebrews 2:5 states poignantly the tragic fact that, although God intended that all things should be in subjection under mankind's feet, "now we see not yet all things put under him" (that is under mankind). Nevertheless, the writer goes on to say by the Spirit: "We see Jesus, who was made a little lower than the angels for the suffering of death, crowned with glory and honour" at the Father's right hand. The passage then proceeds to explain that He became man so that He could be our Kinsman-Redeemer, and as such is not ashamed to call us His brethren.

As the Captain of our salvation, the last Adam, He heads a new creation, made up of those taken out of the headship of the old Adam and now indissolubly related to the last Adam, Christ Jesus. Thus all that Adam lost and more is regained through Christ. The purpose of God that man shall have dominion, that "estates shall be restored to their rightful owners," will be wonderfully fulfilled when Jesus comes again to reign. As Ezekiel 21:26-27 makes it clear we are now in the period of the words "remove the diadem, and take off the crown. . . . I will overturn, overturn, overturn, it (the diadem): and it shall be no more, until he come whose right it is; and I will give it him." And the kingdoms of this world will indeed "become the kingdom of our Lord, and of his Christ" (Rev 11:15, *New Scofield*).

By virtue of our union with Him we read "thou . . . hast made us unto our God kings and priests: and we shall reign on the earth" (Rev 5:9-10).

Sometimes I take my family for a drive in the beautiful suburbs of Philadelphia. There are some lovely estates which are interesting to see. I suppose all of us have sometimes wondered about the people who live in such luxury; perhaps we have envied them without intending to. Some years ago I got an entirely new viewpoint on this whole thing. After all I am joint-heir with Christ and all that He possesses. As He went back to heaven He said: "All power (authority) is given unto me in heaven and in earth" (Mt 28:18). Therefore, these people do not own the estates in which they are living. They belong to Christ and to me! So actually, they are "squatters." One day the estates will be returned to their rightful owners, Christ and His own. Why should I then begrudge them the little pleasure they may have before they go out into an eternity of suffering? I can afford to wait for God to fulfill His promise of my reigning with Christ on earth. We therefore rightly sing:

> Jesus shall reign where'er the sun
>> Does his successive journeys run;
> His kingdom spread from shore to shore,
>> Till moons shall wax and wane no more.

5. Complete restoration of health

This use of the word as a technical medical term, as pointed out by Vincent, is also particularly fitting for Dr. Luke. One need only casually read the newspapers and magazines to know the world is terribly sick. But for the more serious student who has carefully studied the sociological and economic implications of the contemporary scene, the problems, if faced realistically, are insurmountable. The only optimists

are those with "misty optics," those self-deluded people who
have accepted the thesis that man will be able to solve the
ills of the world through the cooperative endeavors of the
United Nations and other man-made stratagems.

The facts are these: wars have increased rather than de-
creased, and the horror of war has increased. The world
does not have peace. It has only an uneasy truce between
wars. More than half the world will go to bed hungry tonight. Superstition and degradation are on every hand. The
world is sick and needs the Great Physician.

After the awful bloody centuries of the past, a kingdom of
righteousness and peace will be set up by the Prince of Peace.
Little children will not go hungry any more. Disease and
death will be stayed. As I understand the prophet Isaiah,
there is no good reason why anyone should die in the kingdom age except under the stroke of judgment: "the sinner
dying at a hundred years shall be but a child" (see Is 65:20).
That is, longevity shall be restored. The social, economic,
racial, and political problems which have harassed the world
will be solved. The infection of sin will be prevented from
contaminating the world when, in the providence of God,
man is finally tested by the release of Satan at the end of
the thousand years. His rebellion shall immediately be put
down (Rev 20:10). Christ will reign with a rod of iron.
Earth at long last will have her golden age. There shall be a
"complete restoration of health"!

The next of these meanings by which our word has been
translated is:

6. A balancing of accounts

Oh the inequities of the past! Think how the strong have
oppressed the weak! Think of *Israel* and her suffering. The
long centuries have been one continual record of injustice.
From Pharoah to Haman to Hitler the story has not improved
but become more gruesome. If there be a just God, and there
is, the accounts will have to be balanced. Besides the judg-

ments of God upon nations during the passing of the centuries, He will pour out His bowls of wrath during the judgments of the tribulation (Rev 15, 16). Christ will come with flaming fire taking vengeance (2 Th 1:8). He shall sit on the throne of His glory and judge the Gentiles with relation to His Israel, God's own of the seventieth week of Daniel (Mt 25:31-46).

Next, think of the *church* and her suffering as "God's minority." Despised and trodden down she has bled through the centuries. This has not only been at the hand of the political power but often at the hand of apostate Christendom. We too little realize that the precious treasures, our Bible and liberty of worship, come to us hallowed by the blood of martyrs.

Pause for a moment and consider the suffering of individual believers of all ages. Many scholars believe Job to be the first written book of the Bible. Is it not significant that it discusses the problem of the prosperity of the wicked and seeks an answer to the question, "Why do the righteous suffer in a wicked world?" The story of the world has been one of unbelievers continually mistaking meekness for weakness.

How many, many inequities will be righted when the accounts are finally balanced in the day of judgment. As Carlyle so strikingly said: "A final judgment! The universe demands it!!" How appropriately Paul speaks, "Know ye not that we shall judge the world . . . we shall judge angels?" (see 1 Co 6:2-3).

This brings us to the final use of the word:

7. The Apocatastasis years: the final point of agreement of the world's cyclical periods

This would certainly coincide with the thought of the rounding out of an appointed time, the arrival of the time of destiny, in accordance with Ephesians 1:10 "That in the dispensation of the fulness of times he might gather together in one all things in Christ, both which are in heaven, and which are on earth; even in him." God's purpose will reach its final hour and there shall come, as Tennyson has said, "That grand far-off divine event toward which the whole creation moves"!

There is a choice paragraph in a letter I received from my dear brother, The Rev. Herman B. Centz (of the American Association for Jewish Evangelism), which seems to me to exquisitely summarize this whole matter. Listen carefully to it:

> Ultimately, "the times of the setting right of all things" means the bringing to this habitable earth of a heavenly civilization, to take the place of all of man's civilization, his division of the earth, his culture, his cities, upon all of which God wrote "finis" when He called Abraham to become the father of a new race and begin life on new foundations. What God began with His friend Abraham will come to its full fruition only when heaven and earth reverberate with the announcement that "the kingdoms of this world have become the kingdoms of our Lord and of His Christ" (Rev 11:15).

To this I say a hearty Amen! and long to join my voice with the myriads of the redeemed and the holy angels as Revelation 5:9-14 describes:

> And they sung a new song, saying, Thou art worthy to take the book, and to open the seals thereof: for thou wast slain, and hast redeemed us to God by thy blood out of every kindred, and tongue, and people, and nation; and hast made us unto our God kings and priests: and we shall reign on the earth. And I beheld, and I heard the voice of many angels round about the throne and the beasts and the elders: and the number of them was ten thousand times ten thousand, and thousands of thousands; saying with a loud voice, Worthy is the Lamb that was slain to receive power, and riches, and wisdom, and strength, and honour, and glory, and blessing. And every creature which is in heaven, and on earth, and under the earth, and such as are in the sea, and all that are in them, heard I saying, Blessing, and honour, and

glory, and power, be unto him that sitteth upon the throne, and unto the Lamb for ever and ever. And the four beasts said, Amen. And the four and twenty elders fell down and worshipped him that liveth for ever and ever.

AND LET ALL GOD'S PEOPLE SAY
"Amen! Hallelujah!
The Lord God Omnipotent reigneth!"

ADDENDUM ON THE RE-OFFER OF THE KINGDOM TO ISRAEL

Even among dispensationalists, there has been a reticence to admit the possibility that we have in this situation a re-offer of the kingdom to Israel, either through fear of catering to the hyperdispensationalists' fantasies or, more probably, through fear of appearing to suggest something contrary to what turned out.

While fully recognizing that there is an obvious problem (namely, what would have happened to the church?), I am nevertheless convinced that we do violence to the plain meaning of language if we do not see that we have here a valid offer of the kingdom. I cannot see any other proper interpretation of the promise of Peter that if they repent, "God will send Jesus."

Send Him where? If not to earth, then to where? Let me be facetious—to Mars? I say this because plainly the sending would have to be to earth. If this be true, and it is, then the only question is, "When?" The answer is right in the text: when they repent, evidently in substantial enough number to reverse the decision of the nation which had been misled by their blind leaders into crying, "Crucify him"! But Peter plainly says that his hearers are not being considered as guilty of *willful* ignorance as their apostate leaders, but of *confused* ignorance, for which they are evidently not being held responsible, if they will but now repent.

Let me now retrace these important verses (chapter 3 of Acts) in this crucial interpretation. In verse 19 Peter pointedly emphasizes that repentance would lead to the return of

Christ (v. 20) to fulfill what the prophets had said God had in store for Israel. This offer hinged on the fact that it was through ignorance (v. 17) they crucified their Messiah. This *agnoia* (ignorance) was willful and unforgivable on the part of Israel's leaders (Mt 12:31-32). But it was forgiven on the part of the people, who had been deliberately misled by their leaders.

Spurgeon, who was not a dispensationalist, makes a strong case for the thesis that our Lord's words, "Father, forgive them, for they know not what they do," could not have been a prayer for individual forgiveness of the soldiers or others there at the cross. Spurgeon insists that God never forgives an individual unless he repents. He proposes that this is a general passing over of mankind's guilt in the sense of the general reconciling word of Christ as revealed in 2 Corinthians 5:19. Another writer has suggested that, in the light of Acts 3:17, the Father answered Christ's prayer on the cross ("Father, forgive") by forgiving the nation of Israel, giving them opportunity as individuals to repudiate and rectify the tragic mistake of their leaders in rejecting their own Messiah (acting as they did as representatives of the nation).

Thus, this prayer of Christ provided the moral basis for Peter's sermons at Pentecost (Ac 2) and in the temple (Ac 3; cp. v. 17 and 1 Co 2:8). In both of these sermons Peter calls on them to repent nationally. He did not proclaim, "Believe," but "Repent."

This, then, was evidently a re-offer of the kingdom, authenticated by multiple signs, for the Jews require signs (1 Co 1:22). The risen Christ's authority is authenticated by these signs and the apostle's message underlined as true, in the way Jews would best understand.

Though there were signs after this point in the book (i.e., Ac 7), it will be noted that most of them occur in connection with Jews or those closely acquainted with them. There is a tendency for signs to lessen as an instrument of witness as the book progresses. This harmonizes with our Lord's emphasis that once a miracle is recorded in Scripture, the record makes obsolete the need for or strategic value of other miracles (Jn 5:45-47; Lk 16:27-31).

All this would be in substantial agreement with Acts 1:6-7. The apostles asked, "Lord, wilt thou at this time restore again the kingdom to Israel?" Contrary to the traditional interpretation of non-dispensationalists, our Lord did not reply in rebuke, "Have I been so long time with you, and you do not yet know that I have not been talking about any crude Jewish political, earthly kingdom, but only of my rule over the hearts of men, my spiritual kingdom?" No, our Lord said no such thing. He did not rebuke them. Their question, in the light of Scripture, was perfectly proper and in order. Our Lord simply explained that the *time* elements are in the Father's hands. They should start witnessing (v. 8) and leave everything to the Father's time.

Thus this answer *allows full freedom* for the re-offer of "the kingdom again to Israel," but it does not pre-announce the result. To the silly question, "What would God have done about the church if Israel had repented?" we reply: "That problem is God's, not ours. All God's approaches to men leave flexibility for human reaction, but always within His plan. The method might vary, but the end-result is always sure." One might as well ask, "What would have happened if Adam had not sinned?" or "What would have happened if Israel had received and not crucified her Messiah?" These are things hidden in the counsels of God and present no problem to Him, even though we may not have the facts or ability to reach a solution. We should never ask, "What if?"

This viewpoint of a re-offered kingdom may also explain the strange statement of Stephen, who cried out (as he was being stoned) that he saw Christ "standing on the right hand of God" (7:55-56), whereas in all later New Testament instances He is said to be seated. The usual pious suggestion that Christ rose from the throne to honor His first martyr is gratuitous and sentimental. It would seem there should be a better suggestion more in keeping with all that is happening in Acts, especially in chapters 1-11. Could it not more likely be that by this graphic means God is emphasizing that a great transition is taking place, that God had been up to this point giving Israel *nationally* an opportunity to reverse their leaders' awful sin of rejecting Christ, and thus He—as it were—is seen standing, awaiting their decision?

It has been pointed out that each person of the Godhead had in turn been rejected by Israel. God the Father was rejected in Samuel's day when they refused the theocracy and clamored for a king (1 Sa 8:7-8). They rejected Christ as King and nailed the Son of God to a cross (Lk 19:11-14). And now they reject the Holy Spirit's miracle-studded testimony to the risen and ascended Christ (Ac 7:51-60), sealed their rejection in the blood of the first martyr, and closed the door of opportunity to Israel *nationally* "until the fulness of the Gentiles be come in" (Ro 11:25-26). So Jesus sat down, and the kingdom was indefinitely postponed. This action fulfills Jesus' warning that they would not believe "though one rose from the dead" (Lk 16:30-31; Mt 12:38-42). There is no national hope for Israel until they repent (Mt 23:39; Zec 12:10; Rev 1:7). Jesus sat down and withdrew the offer of the kingdom. The gospel was then sent forth to the Gentiles (Ac 8:5, 27; 10) to take out of them a people for His name during the intervening period (Ac 15:14-15).

7

What Kind of Body?

Resurrection! What a magic word.

It has always been the dream of man. In the artifacts of the tomb of Queen Shubad, at the University of Pennsylvania Museum, are the crushed skulls of her bodyguards and ladies-in-waiting. These servants were by this means presumptively sent along to accompany the queen from Abraham's hometown of Ur into the future life. That was about the third millennium before Christ.

Philosophers have conjectured and yearned. Rationalists have drawn a blank with their nihilism about the future. This is one area in which their writings show poignant despair.

The early church had a unique message. They preached "Jesus and the resurrection." Other religions had their salvation schemes, their lofty ethics, their colorful rites and ceremonies. They had their great men, saints, and alleged miracles, even including virgin births. They had their millions of devotees. Their founders were wreathed in extravagant claims.

But none of them claimed to have a resurrected founder who had come forth from the grave. In this, Christianity is unique among religions. It was this message that startled the philosophers on Mars Hill, accustomed though they were to hearing "some new thing." *This* was really new!

"I Am the Resurrection—An Integral Part of the Gospel (1 Co 15:1-11)

No one can be a Christian and deny the resurrection of the body, for no one can be saved without believing in the resurrection of Christ. We read in Romans 10:9: "If thou shalt confess with thy mouth the Lord Jesus, and shalt believe in thine heart that God hath raised him from the dead, thou shalt be saved." This is affirmed by the great resurrection passage in 1 Corinthians 15.

Although doctrine is scattered all through the Bible, God has been pleased to gather His great truths in special deposits. We call this a *textus classicus*. The *textus classicus* for love is 1 Corinthians 13; for faith, Hebrews 11; for the Holy Spirit, John 14 or Romans 8; for the rule of God, Daniel 4, where the God of heaven is shown to be sovereign. So the *textus classicus* for resurrection is 1 Corinthians 15.

Paul says the gospel is comprised of two essentials: (1) "Christ died for our sins" (v. 3)—and He was actually dead, for He was buried (v. 4). No one buries a loved one or a friend who is not assuredly dead, and it was Jesus' friends who buried Him, not soldiers or strangers. This forever gives the lie to those false cults who say that Jesus swooned on the cross or that His body was dematerialized there, but not buried. "Christ died" is a fact of history. "Christ died for our sins" is a fact of revelation.

But there is another fact, without which we do not have a gospel to believe and proclaim. It is that (2) Christ "rose again the third day according to the scriptures" (v. 4). And He was seen of at least 517 eyewitnesses. This is the kind of evidence that stands in a court of law. The resurrection has been called the best attested fact of history. Paul goes on to say that the universal testimony of the apostles and disciples forming this group of more than five hundred is that Jesus actually was seen by them in a body (vv. 5-8).

This is particularly noteworthy, for the old rationalist theory that Jesus was just projected by the minds of His followers, because they were anticipating His resurrection, is manifestly false. In the story in Luke 24 there were two tired, discouraged, disillusioned travelers walking from Jerusalem to Emmaus on the resurrection afternoon. Jesus Himself joined them, asking why they were sad. This gave them the opening for blurting out, "Are you a stranger? Don't you know what has just happened these last few days in Jerusalem? We had so much counted on the fact that the Messiah had come to redeem Israel. We were sure. But now He is dead and we are desolate. We had hoped it had been He. But it is all over. Our dream is exploded. We are going home disillusioned. Oh, there have been false rumors that some have seen Him, that the tomb is empty. But what does that prove? Evidently, His enemies have stolen His body, which makes us feel even worse."

Our Lord told them that Messiah had to suffer and enter into glory, but even then they did not recognize Him. They were crushed with grief. He was dead. Only later in their own home, as He gave thanks in the breaking of the bread, were their eyes opened. They hastened to Jerusalem to find the apostles and others in the upper room, the door bolted for fear of the Jews. Although it was reported that the Lord had appeared to Peter, obviously no one believed He was really alive; for when He appeared suddenly in their midst, they cried out in terror. They thought He was a spirit! But He assured them, "It is I!"

Even then He had to convince them of the reality of His bodily resurrection. "A spirit has not flesh and *bones* [notice, not blood] as you see me have." He proved the validity of His resurrection by eating fish and honey before them and by insisting that this was all predicted by the Scriptures (Lk 24:36-45). Jesus was the last person they ever expected to see that night. He had to prove to them who He was. Their fond hopes did not produce a phantom. He was actually there and they now knew it; but they had never expected to see Him.

It is instructive to note the constituency of that body—flesh and bones. Our bodies are kept alive by the life principle of blood, which circulates to every portion of our bodies. That, however, which keeps us alive ("the life of the flesh is in the blood," Lev 17:11) is the very thing that assures corruption at death, that is, when the spirit leaves the body (Ja 2:26). Thus, in the resurrection body a new principle of life will be the source of perennial life. This present body is constantly decomposing. We do not pay the doctors to give us life; we pay them to retard death. But the Bible has said that, as the result of sin in the race, "It is appointed unto man once to die" (Heb 9:27; cf. Ro 5:12). And, except for those who keep a prior appointment by meeting the Lord in the air at the rapture, none will fail to keep the appointment with death when He summons.

To Deny Bodily Resurrection Involves Denial of the Whole Structure of Our Christian Faith (1 Co 15:12-19)

How did death enter the world? It entered the world by sin. If Christ has, therefore, adequately taken care of the sin problem, He has taken care of the death problem. I am anticipating verses 19-21 for a moment, but the force of Paul's argument in verses 12-19 hangs on the fact that if everyone does not rise from the dead, no one has risen or will rise from the dead. It is a totality or it is nothing. For if Christ's death and resurrection were not the total defeat of sin, then His death and resurrection were not successful. If *one* body is left in the grave, Christ has been defeated in His own world. And if one sin had been left over, unjudged and unatoned, then Christ could not have risen from the grave. According to Hebrews, He took away sin. If one sin was left, He did not take away sin. It is as simple as that.

Thus Paul argues, with irresistible logic in this section, beginning with verse 12. Here is the sequence:

If no resurrection, Christ did not rise.

If Christ did not rise, our preaching is invalid.

If our preaching is invalid, we are bogus witnesses (liars).

If there is no resurrection and if Christ did not rise, your faith is inane; you are yet in your sins.

If Christ is not alive, your loved ones, whom you confidently believed were safe in Jesus' care, have actually perished!

If our message is not true, we are the most pitiable dupes in the world. We believed a lie, were deluded into false hopes, restricted ourselves within the bounds of a godly life, and it is all an exploded, fatuous dream! Who wants that?

No one!

THE VALIDITY OF CHRIST'S RESURRECTION AND THE SEQUENCE OF MAN'S (1 Co 15:20-28)

"But now is Christ risen." The words are extremely emphatic both in English and in Greek. Everything has been changed by that fact, and a whole new set of results follow in inevitable and logical sequence. The most obvious of these is the fact already declared in the last section; namely, sin which brought death came into the human scene through a man. His name was Adam. But, by the same token, the only way this problem can be solved is through a man. This man is the last Adam (v. 45). As sin and death have affected every member of the human race, the resurrection of Christ affects every member of the human race. Christ can only be demonstrated to be the total victor when the very last body of the totality of humanity is raised from the grave. This means the unsaved as well as the saved, all men of all ages. The "last enemy" is "death" (v. 26), and Christ "must reign until all enemies are put under His feet," including the last enemy, death (v. 25).

Too often Easter is simply made a glad announcement of the resurrection and bliss of the righteous. This is a partial truth which has in some quarters led to the view that only the righteous rise; the wicked will be annihilated, which is a distortion of the phrase *everlasting destruction*. This position undermines the foundation stones of the structure of truth. All must rise, and the resurrection of the unsaved is just as definitely taught in Scripture as the resurrection of the saved is. Hear Paul on Mars Hill: "Therefore having overlooked the times of ignorance, God is now declaring to men that all everywhere should repent, because He has fixed a day in which He will judge the world in righteousness through a Man whom He has appointed, having furnished proof to all men by raising Him from the dead" (Ac 17:30-31, NASB).

Judgment is coming upon the unsaved, and the resurrection constitutes God's guarantee of this fact. "Knowing therefore the terror of the Lord, we persuade men" (2 Co 5:11). God is not willing that any should perish; He has provided a Saviour and pleads with men to be reconciled; but if they do not repent, there is only judgment. The prelude to this judgment is the second resurrection, to damnation (Jn 5:28-29; Rev 20:11-15).

Thus, the sequence of resurrection, which begins with Christ (1 Co 15:20, 23), ends with the wicked (v. 24).

But what is the whole order of the sequences?

The key is found in the words: "But every man in his own order" (v. 23). The word *order* is a military term. In our language it might be translated "battalion" or "regiment." Everyone is going to be raised (Rev 20:4-6), but not all at the same time. This statement utterly repudiates the thesis of amillennialists who teach that there is a general resurrection, a general judgment, and then eternity. No, there are different battalions, or regiments.

In the days when it was not considered uncouth to be patriotic, there used to be more parades. In earlier days the general or commanding officer rode in front on a horse. Then there was a gap. Then followed various regiments, separated from each other by enough space to make them distinguishable. That is exactly the picture Paul gives us here. See

Christ, the captain of our salvation, as the first to be raised, long ago on the third day after His crucifixion. Look at Him and be thrilled with the conqueror of death! There is a considerable space of time between Him and the first regiments of the first resurrection. Putting verses 51-53 with 1 Thessalonians 4:16-17, we recognize that at Christ's coming "in the air" the saints of the church age are caught up to meet their Lord. By a comparison of scriptures we understand this to be before the tribulation period and to affect only the church, begun at Pentecost and fulfilled when, in God's providence, the last member is called out by the gospel from a godless world, thus completing the bride of Christ.

Pretribulationists understand there will be seven years (approximately) between the catching up of the church to meet her Lord in the air and the return of the Lord Jesus to earth at the end of the tribulation, to usher in the one thousand year kingdom of righteousness and peace. Of course, these battalions will certainly include tribulation martyrs (Rev 20:4, 6; notice the *second* resurrection comes after the thousand years, according to v. 5).

In recent years there has been an increasing number of prophetic teachers who feel that it is at the coming of the Lord to the *earth* that the Old Testament saints are raised, whether of Israel or the Gentiles. Others think that all the righteous dead to that time would go to meet Christ in the air. This would, of course, include Old Testament saints as well as the church. But holders of the latter idea have overlooked a basic principle of biblical interpretation: Resurrection closes God's dealing with any group of people. Plainly, Israel's age did not close with the sixty-ninth week, but—just as clearly—it closes with the seventieth week of Daniel 9. The only two Old Testament passages that clearly emphasize Israel's resurrection (Is 24:22; Dan 12:2) place it after a "time of trouble, such as never was since there was a nation" (Dan 12:1; cf. 11:36-45). This could be nothing else than the tribulation. If Israel is not to be raised at the translation of the church to meet the Lord in the air, why would Gentile believers before Abraham (or after Abraham) be given a different date? Thus, we place two separate sets of battalions as involved in the "at his coming" phrase; some at the coming to the air; some at the coming to the earth; but all are in the first resurrection, all who are Christ's, redeemed by His blood.

The next regiment, or battalion, is composed of those who are the unsaved at the end of the thousand years, as previously shown from a comparison of Revelation 20:5 and 20:11-15. This is the "end battalion," or "the end resurrection." It is an elipsis and either phrase would do because both are true.

THE ABSURDITY OF CHRISTIAN SERVICE, IF NO RESURRECTION
(1 Co 15:29-34, 58)

Many people have been puzzled by verse 29, and some false teaching has resulted. There is no problem if we keep the military figure in mind with which Paul has illustrated the orders or battalions of the resurrection. No army keeps the same personnel. Some are killed, some die, some get sick and leave, some have their enlistment expire. There is also a constant influx of new recruits or draftees. Every army runs this way, so the figure holds firm.

People of the first century (as well as now) enter the ranks of Christ's "army" by baptism. On the mission field no one pays much attention to a profession that one has become a Christian until the professed convert has submitted to Christian baptism. From that point on, pagans reckon the person to have joined the Christian ranks, but not before. Hence, Paul is saying here: "Why would anyone want to join the Christian army (by the induction process of baptism, a public witness) if there is no resurrection?" Naturally, such inductees would take the place in the ranks of those who have fallen in the fray (i.e., lit. rendering is "baptized in the place of the dead," or "to take the place of the dead"). Why would anyone place himself in jeopardy, being in constant danger of death because of his testimony, if there were no such thing as resurrection (vv. 30-32)? This would truly be foolish. If there is no afterlife, no judgment, no reward, no doom, let us eat, drink, and be merry. Why suffer? Why not live for time and sense, and let the appetites of the body take over!

"Evil companions corrupt good morals" (v. 33). Paul says, "You have evidently let Corinthian philosophy rub off on you. You are not thinking straight. So, awake to righteousness; and do not sin with such thoughts as these. Those pagans all around you should hear a trumpet with no uncertain sound (14:8). They do not know your God. But you do, and should be ashamed to be uncertain on so important a truth as the resurrection, with its implications for a holy life (15: 33, 58). Courage, brothers, and onward as good soldiers!"

"What Kind of Body Will We Have?" (1 Co 15:35-50)

Having heard so many strange questions about the resurrection body, one can sympathize with questions which must have often been asked Paul. Yet he brings the questioners up short: "Come now, think; you certainly know from nature more than you are showing by your question." The word *fool* here has the force of "Oh, unthinking one; if you thought a moment, you would see that is a foolish question!" (vv. 35-36).

When we drop a seed into the ground, that particular seed does not come up just as it was when we dropped it in the ground (v. 37). On the contrary, it disintegrates and comes up as something of the same *kind*, but not identical to the thing sown.

This establishes a first principle of the resurrection body, namely: The resurrection body has continuity with the old body, without exact duplication (v. 38). It is not the grain of wheat put into the ground that comes up; it is the beginning of a stalk of wheat, which will develop with many grains, but all wheat. But God authors life and gives it a body as it pleases Him.

This answers a number of questions often asked, such as, What about a person with a deformed body? What about a body emaciated by disease or old age? What about a body distorted by accident? What about a body that drops into a vat of acid, or into molten metal, or is disintegrated by an atomic blast? Or the old rationalist question, much like the Sadducees of Jesus' day: "What about the man who lost an arm in the Battle of Austerlitz and a leg at Waterloo, then decided to go to sea as a ship captain with a peg leg? In the South Seas his crew mutinied and threw him overboard where sharks consumed him and went in different directions. How will God collect *his* body and put it back together again?"

The analogy of the seed answers this. God does not have to reproduce or gather the exact molecules which constituted the old body. The body has continuity with the old body but is a *changed* body. We all want to look like Christ someday and we shall; for we shall be made like Christ. Here is comfort for all believers.

A second principle of the resurrection body is: There will be individuality in our new bodies without uniformity (vv. 39-41). Paul hastens to make it clear that, though the body will be changed, we shall not all be the same, like products coming off the assembly line, all the same shape and size. No, "God gives to every seed *his own* body" (v. 38). He cites different kinds of flesh and bodies (vv. 39-40) and emphasizes that even the stars differ. Individuality is God's pattern in His universe, whether it be people or leaves or snowflakes or stars. God is not limited, as men are, by molds or patterns from which a great number of the same thing are made.

Thus, by this passage God answers the oft-asked question, Shall we know each other in heaven? The answer is yes!

Certainly we shall know each other. If we know people here, shall we have less knowledge there? Indeed, in 1 Corinthians 13 we are told: "Now I know in part; but then shall I know even as also I am known" (v. 12). It is also not insignificant that on the Mount of Transfiguration, Peter, James, and John recognized Moses and Elijah whom they had never seen. And they were yet in their present bodies with limited knowledge!

Further, although there will be individuality, there are evidently other factors. A father dies when the child is two years old. The child lives to be eighty-one, then dies. Will the son be raised as an eighty-one-year-old man and would the father recognize his "child"? Such questions as these lead to the third important revelation concerning the resurrection body.

This third principle is: There will be a glorious perfection of the new body (vv. 42-50). Here the contrast is between the old and the new, with the growing emphasis on the perfection of the new. Our new bodies will be perfect; they will not grow old; they will not get sick; they will not feel pain; they will not change with the passage of time.

Their life principle is "spirit," not the "flesh and blood" (v. 50) emphasis on the body dominated by soul. As previously quoted from Luke 24, our Lord said His body was of "flesh and bones." There are some mysteries here, not revealed, but that is the force of verses 44-46: "It is sown a body dominated by soul (*psuchikos*, "soulish" body); it is raised a body dominated by spirit (*pneumatikos*, "spiritual" body)." We now have the former body. We shall have the latter body. "As we have borne the image of the earthy (not earth*ly*) body, we shall also bear the image of the heavenly body" (vv. 47-49). The corruption principle of blood is gone (v. 50*a*; cf. Lev 17:11). An entirely new kind of body will be ours, suited to our new estate. It is important to remember that the Lord Jesus could go through walls or appear and disappear. We now know that what we once thought to be "solids"—like walls—are not. They are whirling worlds of molecules. If one had the right molecular structure, he would have no more hindrance in walking through a wall than in walking through air. God knew this all the time. We have just attained this knowledge. Faith did not need this knowledge to believe, but faith is vindicated by this discovery of the constituency of so-called "solids."

Verses 45-47 bring us back to the contrast between Adam and Christ, the old body and the new body, the first man and the second man, the first Adam and the last Adam. According to Genesis 2, when God made Adam He fashioned him and, for all we know, laid him out on the grass. Then God gave him life. He "breathed into his nostrils the breath of life; and man became a living soul [lit., a soul of life]" (Gen 2:7).

It is striking that on the resurrection evening our Lord breathed on the disciples and said, "Receive ye the Holy Ghost" (Jn 20:22). This is the force of verse 45 in our chapter. The first Adam was breathed upon and became a *soul* of life. The last Adam breathed on the disciples and thus was a life-*giving spirit*.

This brings us back to the question of recognition involved in the appearance of the body in heaven. Certainly, we can get some light on the subject from the first man. Adam was not created as a baby, as a young lad, as an old man. He was a perfect physical specimen, mature, able to marry. So, evidently, will be our eternal bodies; bodies reconstituted at highest efficiency, best able to enjoy all the wonders of eternity with God. This also answers the well-intentioned but obviously sentimental question, Will I see my baby in heaven? The answer is, "Of course not! Mother, God loves you too much and loves that dear little one too much to have it go through eternity without being able to enjoy Him and heaven and you! How much could you communicate with a baby anyway?" No, God has planned the best for us so we can enjoy the most.

What a wonderful prospect this is for the believer. It is to be noted, however, that neither here nor elsewhere does God give any description of the unbeliever's resurrection body. However, certain principles we have already covered will apply. The body placed in the ground is not that body that is raised. There will be individuality in the resurrection, for God never gives us an IBM number, but treats us as distinct persons. And the body that God will give the unbeliever will be eternal, but suited to its eternal relation to the lake of fire (Mt 25:46; Rev 14:10; 20:14), as the believer's body will be suited to his eternal estate. It is interesting that when men developed a material that would not disintegrate in the flame, they selected the Greek word *asbestos*. This is the word which is used four times in the New Testament of "unquenchable fire" (Mt 3:12; Mk 9:43, 45; Lk 3:17). From this we are to understand that unquenchable fire does not destroy the body. The body is prepared by God to abide eternal fire. If men can develop a substance that will not disintegrate in flames, cannot God?

THE TIME OF THE RESURRECTION BODY (1 Co 15:51-58)

Since Paul is addressing the church, believers of this age, he now indicates when they will get these new bodies. Although he has covered the whole subject of resurrection, he now emphasizes how all this will affect believers of this age to whom he is writing. Thus, the next great event for them, and for us of the church, is the sacred secret, hidden in God but now revealed, that one generation of Christians will be caught up without death at the church's last trump to meet the Lord in the air (cf. 1 Th 4:16-17). The dead will be raised and changed; we in mortal bodies will be changed; and together we shall be caught up to meet Christ. What a glorious prospect!

Thus no believer's body will be the same but will be miraculously adapted to the eternal estate. The corruptible dead will inherit incorruption and the living will inherit immortality. For us this signalizes the final defeat of sin which issues in death (vv. 54-56). Some well-intentioned Christians claim the sting of death is passed, that Christians should not cry over loved ones. They are trying to be more holy than Christ, who wept at Lazarus' tomb. The Bible states clearly that death has a sting *until* the trumpet shout changes us, raises our dead loved ones, and takes us out of this vale of tears.

Since this is true, resurrection truth leads to steadfast service (v. 58).

8

The Day of the Lord Jesus Christ

THE WRITER is a great believer in free discussion among those of the premillennial, dispensational viewpoint and is of the conviction that much of our thrust has been blunted by arbitrary and stylized distinctions which are not a valid part of the view. In addition, there seems to be a hesitancy to debate such matters lest one be thought to be suspect in the house of his friends, if the result of his study should lead to the sacrifice of a sacred cow.

The writer places himself in the camp of the pro-Scofield teachers. Yet at the same time he finds himself—in some matters—appearing to be a member of the loyal opposition. An example will be found in chapter 2 discussing the terms and occasion of the institution of the Abrahamic covenant. Strong exception was taken to the thesis of many premillennialists that Abraham's leaving Ur was a condition to the establishment of that covenant.

A similar situation is found in the subject of the present chapter. The student of the Scriptures becomes increasingly aware as he goes through the Bible, and particularly as he gets into the epistles, that such phrases as "day of the Lord," "day of Jesus Christ," "day of the Lord Jesus," and "day of Christ" are prominently present.

Premillennialists especially have sought to ascertain from their usage the proper interpretation of the phrases. Considerable literature has been forthcoming and certain of the phrases have led to debate, often characterized by more heat than light.

143

The purpose of this chapter is to examine the evidence and suggest some conclusions as to usage. This would appear to be highly desirable in the light of the multiple forms in which the phrases occur. The following is a list of twenty different combinations in the New Testament of the word "day" with qualifying words which make a title or something similar to a title:

Various "Days" Mentioned by the New Testament

1. my day (i.e., Christ speaking, "Abraham . . . [saw] my day")—John 8:56 (cp. Gal 3:8)
2. man's day (lit.)—1 Corinthians 4:3
3. day of redemption—Ephesians 4:30
4. day of our Lord Jesus Christ—1 Corinthians 1:8 (cp. v. 7)
5. day of the Lord Jesus—1 Corinthians 5:5; 2 Corinthians 1:14
6. day of Jesus Christ—Philippians 1:6
7. day of Christ—Philippians 1:10; 2:16; (2 Th 2:2 probably should read as no. 8)
8. day of the Lord (cp. O.T. day of Jehovah)—1 Thessalonians 5:2; 2 Thessalonians 2:2; 2 Peter 3:10
9. the day—Luke 17:30; Romans 2:16; 13:12; 1 Corinthians 3:13
10. that day—Matthew 24:36; 26:29; Mark 13:32; 14:25; Luke 10:12; 17:31; 21:34; 1 Thessalonians 5:4; 2 Thessalonians 1:10; 2 Timothy 1:12, 18; 4:8
11. a day (when He shall judge the world)—Acts 17:31
12. last day—John 6:39, 40, 44, 54; 11:24; 12:48 (cp. no. 8); also last days—Acts 2:17; 2 Timothy 3:1; Hebrews 1:2; James 5:3; 2 Peter 3:3; last time—1 Peter 1:5
13. the great day—Jude 1:6 (cp. no. 8)
14. the day of judgment—Matthew 11:22, 24; 12:36; Mark 6:11; 2 Peter 2:9; 3:7; 1 John 4:17
15. his (i.e., Christ's) day—Luke 17:24
16. great and notable day of the Lord—Acts 2:20

17. great day of his wrath—Revelation 6:17
18. day of wrath and revelation—Romans 2:5
19. great day of God Almighty—Revelation 16:14
20. day of God—2 Peter 3:12

In the light of this wide diversity of phrases which include the word "day," it may seem rather strange to some readers that only four of them have been commonly accorded the status of titles among premillennialists. This becomes even more striking when it is noted that very distinctive and mutually exclusive meanings have customarily been attached to each of four, although in one classic passage two of the four are plainly used interchangeably within three verses (2 Pe 3:10-12).

The common premillennial usage of the four titles may be charted and explained as follows:

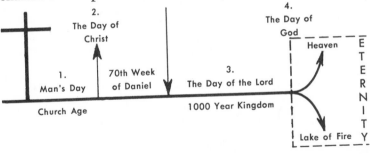

Man's Day is the literal translation of 1 Corinthians 4:3, rendered "man's judgment" in the King James Version. Evidently Paul is emphasizing that he is not greatly concerned with human judgment which is predicated on mankind's sense of self-satisfaction growing out of his lethal pride of achievement. Mankind is so drunk with his accomplishments that he feels no need for God or His salvation.

The day of Christ (Phil 2:16) is when Christ comes to the air and catches up the church to heaven, which is the occasion of the evaluation of believers' works at the judgment seat of Christ.[1]

1. Cp. *Scofield Reference Bible*, p. 1212, fn. 2.

The day of the Lord (or Jehovah) is the period which begins when Christ comes in judgment to the earth (2 Th 1:8-9) and reigns one thousand years with a rod of iron.[2]

The day of God (2 Pe 3:12) is at the end of the one thousand years when the heavens and earth will be purified by fire (2 Pe 3:7).

While being fully committed to the same order of events as charted above, for a number of reasons an increasing group of premillennial brethren have felt that the partitioning of time by mutually exclusive phrases is both arbitrary and unwarranted. Indeed, they are convinced that it leads to needless problems in exposition.

First, it can be shown that some of these terms are not mutually exclusive. For instance, as previously mentioned, within three consecutive verses (2 Pe 3:10-12) the same event is designated by both the terms *day of the Lord* and *day of God*. Certainly in that context both are used synonymously.

Second, the thesis is untenable that the term *day of Christ* is the official and only title used in the New Testament to describe the coming of the Lord to take His church to heaven, an event commonly called the rapture, or, perhaps more appropriately, the translation. Indeed, this title (*day of Christ*) is used by only one apostle in just one book and then only twice (Phil 1:10; 2:16), if the better reading of "day of the Lord" is adopted for 2 Thessalonians 2:2.

When one refers to the list of the various days previously cited, it is definitely demonstrable that at least eight different phrases from this list of twenty are used to designate the same event, namely, the translation of the church, as follows:

> day of redemption—Ephesians 4:30
> day of the Lord Jesus—1 Corinthians 5:5; 2 Corin
>   thians 1:14
> day of Jesus Christ—Philippians 1:6
> that day—2 Timothy 1:12, 18; 4:8

2. *Ibid.*, p. 1349.

the day—1 Corinthians 3:13; Romans 13:12
day of the Lord—1 Thessalonians 5:2
day of our Lord Jesus Christ—1 Corinthians 1:8
    (cp. v. 7)
day of Christ—Philippians 1:10; 2:16

The force of this argument is, therefore, that there is a well-defined event plainly taught, but that it is variously described and not limited to one title. This variety of expression for the same doctrine occurs often in Scripture.

Third, as suggested in the list of terms above, the phrase "day of Christ" (and its variants) and the phrase "day of the Lord" are not always describing a different time. Also, there are good reasons for suggesting that the day of the Lord must be seen as extending over a longer period than the old Scofield definition, and that it begins with the translation of the church, continues through both the seventieth week and the one thousand years, and finally culminates with the purgation of heaven and earth (2 Pe 3:10-12; cp. *New Scofield Reference Bible*, n. 5, p. 1372, at Rev 19:19).

Fourth, in this connection, the reader is requested to consider the term, "the day of our Lord Jesus Christ," used in 1 Corinthians 1:8. A comparison of this verse with verse 7 shows that on this occasion the title is used of the time of the catching up and rewarding of the church. May it not well be that this designation should be understood to be the full title which combines a number of different titles in itself, including most of those listed under the second point above, and particularly combining the terms "day of Christ" and "day of the Lord"? Why should not these terms be considered complementary rather than antithetical and mutually exclusive? Probably we have here the same situation as is involved in the varying wordings given in the four gospel accounts as to what constituted the title over the cross of Christ. Not one of the gospels gives the full title. All the gospel narratives must be combined to obtain that full title, which was: "This is (Matthew, Luke) Jesus (Matthew, John) of Nazareth (John), the King of the Jews" (all).

Would it not be foolish to argue that the titles above the cross were different or contradictory or that they meant various things? Is it not clear that all quoted that part of the title that was appropriate to their emphasis? Why should not the same analogy be pertinent to the eight variants of day cited above?

While generally "day of Christ" and its variants are used concerning the church's translation to heaven, and "the day of the Lord" comes into the New Testament with heavy overtones from the Old Testament concerning God's dealings with Israel and the nation (Zec 14:1-4, 9), the difference is not primarily one of time or of words but rather of emphasis. Very often any two of these terms may be used of things happening at the same time.

So the New Testament takes up all these terms and unites them in a full title, "The day of our Lord Jesus Christ" (who is God). This full title permits an interchange of various parts of the title without limiting any particular phrase to one fixed time or group. It remains for the context of a particular passage to determine the particular group of people, the particular event, and/or the particular point of time under consideration.

To make visual this suggested solution to the problem, the following chart is furnished:

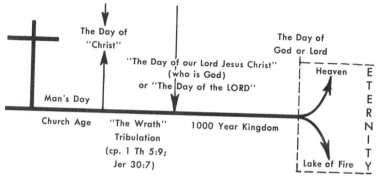

It will be seen in the chart that the coming of the Lord to take the church out of the earth is followed by an extended period known in Scripture as the day of the Lord, which is a condensation of the full title, "The day of our Lord Jesus Christ." This period extends from the translation of the church to the creation of the new heavens and new earth after the close of the millennial age, and includes the period of the tribulation, the whole millennium, and the judgments following the millennium.

The day of the Lord is always associated with judgment in Scripture. Beginning at Isaiah 2:11 the student may trace the related passages by following the references in the margin of the (old) *Scofield Reference Bible*. A fuller chain reference will be found beginning at Psalm 2:9 in the *New Scofield Reference Bible*.

The day of Christ, of the Lord Jesus, or the Lord (1 Co 1:8; 5:5; 2 Co 1:14; Phil 1:6, 10; 2:16; 2 Th 2:2, margin), is that portion within the day of our Lord Jesus Christ in which the Lord is particularly dealing with the church in heaven (e.g., judgment seat of Christ) while the judgments of the tribulation period are being poured out upon Gentiles and Jews on the earth. It also includes the glorious period of the reign of Christ upon the earth when He judges wickedness with a rod of iron (Is 2:2-4; Ps 2:9; Rev 12:5).

The day of God (2 Pe 3:12) is that portion of the day of our Lord Jesus Christ in which God is judging the heavens and the earth and removing the curse of sin from the universe.

Thus we see that the coming of Christ for the church releases all the judgments within that period known as "the day of the Lord," or "the day of our Lord Jesus Christ."

Perhaps the most appropriate way to demonstrate the value of the viewpoint suggested here would be through a practical demonstration of the application of the conclusion above to 1 Thessalonians 5 and 2 Thessalonians 2. In these passages a real problem of interpretation faces the pretribulationalist, if the old view of the day of the Lord is still retained.

Previously, in an exposition of 1 Thessalonians 5, it was difficult to make it appear that Paul was not contradicting in chapter 5 what he had just said in chapter 4. He closed chapter 4 with the revelation that Christ might come at any moment before the predicted events of Daniel's seventieth week, which are to be climaxed by the return of Christ to the earth, an event which, according to the old view, was called "the day of the Lord." Thus, if this view were correct, Paul is placed in the awkward posture of exhorting the saints in chapter 5 to be watchful, not to sleep, but to be ready for an event (v. 2, "the day of the Lord") which the old viewpoint said would occur seven years *after* the church had gone to heaven in the translation (rapture) of 4:16-17.

This did not make sense and played right into the hands of the posttribulation rapturists who said Christ would not come for His church until after the tribulation. But, if "the day of our Lord Jesus Christ" starts at the time the church is taken away from the earth *before* Daniel's seventieth week, then Paul enforces in chapter 5 that which closely harmonizes with what he has just taught in chapter 4. "Be ready for the rapture" is his exhortation.

Further, in 2 Thessalonians 2:2, the old view and the validity of our so interpreting it hung entirely on the insistence that the better textual reading was not "day of Christ" but "day of the Lord." If this reading were not sustained, then "the day of Christ" would be forced to cover the tribulation period conditions, which would invalidate the pretribulation rapture view. So all pretribulationalists became textual scholars and insisted upon the preferable text being "the day of the Lord."

But, if this study has proved its point, there is no problem whether the text reads "day of Christ" or "day of the Lord," if the flexibility of the terms is admitted and context left to determine *which part* of that extended day is intended.

In 2 Thessalonians 2, Paul is saying in essence, "The persecution and trouble through which you are now passing, though exceedingly severe, must not be mistaken for that unparalleled period of wrath and tribulation (the seventieth week) which is going to come on the earth after the church is translated. Let no one deceive you that you are now present in the day of the Lord (v. 2). That day cannot be asserted to be present until there come first 'the falling away' (or departing) and, second, the manifestation of the man of sin (v. 3). Since these events have not yet come, plainly you are not in the day of the Lord. The wicked one cannot and will not be revealed (v. 8) until the Hinderer (v. 7, the Holy Spirit and with Him the church) be taken out of the way (i.e., from earth to heaven). Ergo, since you are here and the Hinderer has not been removed, you are not in 'the day of the Lord,' the tribulation period."

The theory here expounded releases the tension from the interpretation of these passages and makes their interpretation easy and natural.

Other passages will occur to the reader and he is invited to check them out. It is devoutly hoped that the opportunity afforded here will prove helpful to many.

The writer firmly believes that premillennialists have given themselves a bad press by stylized interpretation of many such phrases as those cited in this chapter. He argues for more free discussion and a willingness to consider the possibility of greater flexibility in terminology within the boundaries of an agreed order of events. The nub of the matter is a renewed emphasis on the principles of interpretation rather than upon arbitrary words and pat phrases.

9

Are Names Significant?

WHAT'S IN A NAME? Names have been important from the beginning. God gave Adam a name. He even had Adam name the animals. Names accomplish many purposes. This being true, then the names which God attributes to Himself must be of great importance.

THE SIGNIFICANCE OF NAMES

First, a name identifies. Many of us are not happy about the growing tendency to give us numbers. The population explosion may require it, but it is degrading to the dignity of the individual. At an annual meeting of the Middle States Association of Colleges and Universities, during a panel discussion an amusing statement was made. It seems that a student came to the registrar's office and blurted out, "The only time this university knew I was a person was when I bent my IBM card!"

It has been said, "There is nothing sweeter to the ears of a man than the sound of his name." A name identifies the individual; it personalizes.

Second, in the Bible a name often attests to the attitude and faith of the parents of the child. One example is the occasion of the birth of Jacob's second son by his favorite wife. As Rachel was dying, she named him Benoni, "son of my sorrow." But his father called him Benjamin, "son of my right hand." One can see the reason why the parent called him what (s)he did; each name was appropriate. Modern parents, with their careless method of naming children, could learn much from the Hebrews.

Third, there is often a great significance in the giving of second names to Old Testament characters—for instance, Abram, Abraham; Sarai, Sarah; Jacob, Israel; and others.

The Importance of the Names of God in the Old Testament

There are a number of occasions when the use of a different name for God greatly enhances the meaning of a passage. Scofield did the church a service when he listed these in his notes, especially in the summary at the end of the Old Testament, in the *Scofield Reference Bible*.

For instance, in Isaiah 6, there is a play on the names of God in the shift from "Lord" in verse 1, to "Lord of hosts" in verses 3 and 5, and back to "Lord" in verse 8. It is the Master (Lord) who commissions him to service (v. 8) with "Go, and tell this people, . . . until the cities be wasted" (vv. 9, 11) and until the covenant God (Lord) disciplines them, in accordance with the Palestinian Covenant (see Deu 30:1-10), for disobedience (Is 6:12).

Some of the things said about the name of God in the Old Testament are especially helpful and instructive. Here are a few selections:

1. Genesis 32:29. Jacob is wrestling with an "angel" whom most of us identify with *the* Angel of Jehovah, our Lord Jesus in a preincarnate appearance. Jacob asks his name; and He replies, "Wherefore is it that thou dost ask after my name? And he blessed him," by changing his name from Jacob to Israel.

2. Manoah in Judges 13:17 similarly asks the name of the one who has appeared to him to announce that Samson is to be born and greatly used of the Lord. Evidently, this is again the Angel of Jehovah, for He responds, "Why askest thou thus after my name, seeing it is secret

[lit., wonderful]?" One is immediately reminded of Isaiah 9:6.

3. In Exodus 3:14, 15 God is instructing Moses as to His name in relation to his commission to call Israel out of Egypt. He says, "Thus shalt thou say unto the children of Israel, I AM hath sent me unto you. . . . this is my name for ever." This great covenant name is frequently used, and properly so, for throughout the Old Testament God is dealing primarily with Israel.

4. In Nehemiah 9:10, in his great prayer of repentance, Nehemiah is speaking to God about His activity in Egypt and says, "So didst thou get thee a name!" How important is the name of God! Moses appeals to this name when Israel is in trouble because of disobedience.

5. In the prophecy of Psalm 22:22, quoted concerning our Lord in Hebrews 2:12, it is recorded that in His resurrection song of victory, He says, "I will declare thy name: . . . in the midst of the congregation will I praise thee." The intelligent and proper use of the name(s) of God is one of the keys to scriptural worship. Christians today are entirely too careless in the use of names of deity.

6. Psalm 48:10 reads: "According to thy name, O God, so is thy praise unto the ends of the earth." The purpose of God is that all should know Him from the least to the greatest and none shall say "Know the Lord" (See Jer 31:34). This has not been accomplished through missionary work, but it will be fulfilled when the Lord returns.

7. In Psalm 111:9 is the statement, "Holy and reverend is his name." It is unfortunate that this verse has been used to claim that this "title" should not be used of a man. In this verse *reverend* is no more a title than *holy*. Both are adjectives. The force of the passage is to remind us that we should honor His name by holy living in

line with the exhortation, "Ye shall be holy, for I am holy" (Lev 11:44).

8. Isaiah 42:8 reads: "I am the LORD: that is my name: and my glory will I not give to another." Our God is a jealous God. His name expresses His character; when His character is understood, we will extol His name!

9. Jeremiah 10:6 gives another emphasis of the importance of God's name. It reads: "Forasmuch as there is none like unto thee, O LORD; thou art great, and thy name is great in might." Again and again the Scriptures emphasize the importance of God's name as an insignia of His majesty.

10. "Hallowed be thy name" was an emphatic point when our Lord was teaching His disciples the basic principles of praying (Mt 6:9; Lk 11:2). They were still men in the Mosaic age under the dispensation of law, thus it was Old Testament ground. The New Testament, however, does not abrogate but builds upon the foundation stones enunciated in the Old Testament about the person and program of God. Hence in this instruction to His disciples on our attitude toward God and toward our responsibility to Him, our Lord reached the high point in the teaching of Old Testament saints concerning the majesty and importance of the name of God.

THE DELINEATION OF CHRIST'S NAMES IN REVELATION

Having discussed the significance of names and shown the importance that God has placed upon His name(s), this study now turns to the book of Revelation to examine how many emphases concerning Christ's person and work are delineated by the uses of His various names.

1:1 JESUS

"The name of Jesus is so sweet, I love its music to repeat!" What Christian does not thrill to that name? *Jesus* is the Greek form of the Hebrew name *Joshua,* which is a contraction of *Jehoshua,* meaning "Jehovah saves." This is the human name of our Lord. It emphasizes His actual and genuine humanity, but it also emphasizes the major result of His coming. The angel instructed Joseph in Matthew 1:21: "Thou shalt call his name JESUS: for he shall save his people from their sins." Since only God could save, He had to devise a plan. God could not provide for our salvation in heaven; therefore, "This is a faithful saying, . . . that Christ Jesus came into the world to save sinners" (1 Ti 1:15). He had to come into the world to do it, for the blood of bulls and goats could never take away sin (Heb 10:4). Nothing less than the blood of Jesus was necessary to accomplish that (Heb 9:22; 10:8-10). When He came into the world, He told the Father, "a body hast thou prepared me" (v. 5); therefore, "Lo, I come to do thy will, O God" (v. 9), that is, take away sins once for all (v. 10).

1:1 CHRIST

Christ is more of a title than a name; but since it is so often used as a name, this list includes it. It is the Greek for the Hebrew *Messiah* which means "anointed one." Our Lord embodies and gathers up in Himself all that the Old Testament prophesied the Messiah would be and do. It is fitting that at a Jewish mission congress we should emphasize the majesty of His Messiahship.

1:5 THE FAITHFUL WITNESS
THE FIRST BEGOTTEN FROM AMONG THE DEAD
PRINCE OF THE KINGS OF THE EARTH

These three titles cluster together in this introductory verse and therefore are considered together. In verse 4 greeting comes to the seven churches from the Triune God. The Father is intended by the name "him which is, and which was, and which is to come." The Holy Spirit is then described as the sevenfold Spirit before the throne—the Spirit in His fullness and perfection. And then verse 5 completes the Trinity with a trio of names about Christ.

Interestingly, these three names emphasize time and mission.

1. As to the past, He was the *Prophet,* who gave men the words that the Father gave Him. He was the faithful and true Witness who fully declared the Father (Jn 1:18).

2. As to the present, He is the *Priest,* who, risen and ascended, ever intercedes and advocates for us at the Father's right hand. He is the firstfruits from the dead, the leader of resurrection. As such, He has the title deed to the earth.

3. As to the future, He is the Prince of the kings of the earth; for He will be *King,* when He comes again from heaven to take over from earth's inept rulers.

1:8 ALPHA AND OMEGA, THE BEGINNING AND THE ENDING

These two fit together. In Him are hid "all the treasures of wisdom and knowledge," as Colossians expresses it (2:3). *Alpha* and *Omega* are the first and last letters of the Greek alphabet. Language is made up of sounds which make words. To record them, man has developed writing; and, in most languages, writing is expressed in letters of an alphabet. So Christ comprehends and transcends all knowledge. And He "is made unto us wisdom" (1 Co 1:30).

Likewise, Christ is the One who was there when anything or anyone had a beginning, and He will be there when anything that has an ending ends . Thus He is the eternal One, who had no beginning and who has no ending. Indeed, He created all things, visible and invisible, and by Him all things cohere (Col 1:16-17).

1:8 WHICH IS, WHICH WAS, AND WHICH IS TO COME

Plainly this ascribes the name *Jehovah* to Jesus Christ, and rightly so. Some theologians have claimed the Jehovah of the Old Testament is the Jesus of the New Testament. The statement is true but not the whole truth. As with the name *God*, the Father is God; the Son is God; the Spirit is God. So with Jehovah.

1:8 THE LORD

Since we have just indicated that Christ is called Jehovah, the word *Lord* here would have been printed in the Old Testament as "Lord," not "Lord" (Jehovah). For some reason the well-established archeological fact about this word has not been made known properly to the public. This word *kurios* had a technical meaning in the first century Roman Empire. It does not simply mean "Master," as *Adonai* (Lord) meant in the Old Testament. When used religiously, it meant that the person so titled was worthy of divine honors. Only deified emperors were called *kurios*. Polycarp, the early Christian martyr, died rather than say Kurios (Lord) Caesar. He would only say Lord Jesus! Many have failed to recognize that the apostles and those to whom they preached knew very well what they meant when they declared Jesus was *kurios!*

1:8 THE ALMIGHTY

Undoubtedly, if this were the Old Testament, this would be *El Shaddai*. Jesus is *El Shaddai*, the God who is enough, the sufficient God, the almighty God. How thrilling to see these Old Testament names for God assigned to show New Testament readers the majesty of His person, as one with the Father and Spirit, God!

1:11 THE FIRST AND THE LAST

This is similar to "the beginning and the ending" (1:8), but it carries further emphasis of the uniqueness of Jesus Christ. He holds primacy as well as preeminence. And all things will be gathered up into Him; He is the goal of all of God's purposes in the universe.

1:13 SON OF MAN

This is a name made significant in John 5:27 by the fact that the Father has committed all judgment to Jesus Christ, "because he is the Son of man." Evidently, God wishes to assure men of a fair trial. In other words, He says, "My Son who was down there with you is the One to whom I have committed judgment. He can understand you; He can make every concession and adjustment that mercy can make without vitiating righteousness. So I have committed your judgment to Him."

1:18 HE THAT LIVETH

In a world where recently we heard the fatuous cry "God is dead," this is a heartwarming antidote. No, Christians serve a living God, a living Christ. This One has in His nail-pierced hand the key by which He opens and no one shuts, and He shuts and no one opens. What comfort to know that the key to death is in that nail-pierced hand of the Lord who was alive, became dead, and now is alive forevermore!

2:18 SON OF GOD

This is a familiar name for Christ, but its occurrence here is significant. It is believed that in these seven letters of chapters 2 and 3 our Lord stated things pertinent to seven actual churches in the Roman proconsular province of Asia. But many expositors are convinced that our Lord also has given here an authoritative preview of the spiritual characteristics of the various eras of church history. With the church of Thyatira we have the rise of the papacy. The papacy so emphasized Mary, and Jesus as the Son of Mary, that truth was out of balance. Thus it seems significant that to this particular church our Lord emphasizes Himself as Son of *God*, whose eyes are like a flame and his feet like fine brass, to judge those who in error exalt His human mother in a way never intended by God and thus detract from His uniqueness

as Son of God. All eyes should be on Him, not Mary or anyone else.

3:12 MY NEW NAME

Obviously, this is an unrevealed name; but it is a glorious
privilege to be so loved by Christ that He would honor His
own with a very special name of His, allowing them to be
called by it. As a wife shares her husband's name, so the
church, His bride, shall share in the new name that the
Father gives Him.

3:14 THE BEGINNING OF THE CREATION OF GOD

This probably refers to the right of primogeniture which is
our Lord's prerogative. A Greek or Roman father could have
many male children by many women: wives, mistresses, or
others. However, though all were children, none was a son
unless the father so designated him in a legal, formal cere-
mony. Only the one or two certified by the father would be
his heirs. This is one of the wonders in what Christ has done.
In the resurrection He stated: "All power is given unto me in
heaven and in earth" (Mt 28:18). This is the right of primogeniture, later seen in His taking the scroll from the Sitter
on the throne in Revelation 5:1-7. This scroll represents the
title deed to the universe. And we are coheirs with Him
(Ro 8:17)!

4:8 HOLY, HOLY, HOLY, LORD GOD ALMIGHTY

Father and Spirit are included in the two titles; and, as
member of the Trinity, Christ is also addressed. The fact of
His humanity is something for which we should be eternally
grateful, but it should never dim our view of Him as fully
God.

5:5 THE LION OF THE TRIBE OF JUDA
THE ROOT OF DAVID

It is plain from verse 6 of this passage that John saw a

Lamb, as though it had been freshly offered in sacrifice, in the midst of the throne; but our Lord is announced by the names in the heading. Thus by His blood (v. 9) His rights as Root of David (and thus the proper heir to the throne of David as Lion of the tribe of Judah) are heralded to those in heaven. God made a covenant with David involving a dynasty and throne rights. They have not been and cannot be abrogated, for God has given His Word, which ascribes these titles to Christ!

5:6 A LAMB
6:16 THE LAMB

This name, often used for Christ in this book, is seen in amazing contrast in these two verses. In the first instance we see His dying love in the sacrifice of His precious blood as payment for our redemption. But in the second verse we see the One who became the Saviour of men now appearing in retributive judgment. Having spurned the Lamb, men will indeed fear the Lamb when He sends judgment upon them. They call for the mountains to fall on them to hide them "from the face of him that sitteth on the throne, and from the wrath of the Lamb."

12:5 THE MAN CHILD

Though He came as a tiny babe, He was the Infinite Infant, as Spurgeon denominated Him. But Revelation 12 emphasizes the fact that it is as though He never was a babe. Inherent in His coming was the emphasis that He would grow to manhood and accomplish great and mighty things. Among these will be taking the rod of iron and ruling the nations with absolute authority. Here is a majestic picture of Christ as King of kings.

15:3 KING OF SAINTS

This is His right by creation, by blood purchase, by being the example to all saints of what saintliness really is!

17:14 LORD OF LORDS AND KING OF KINGS

19:16 KING OF KINGS AND LORD OF LORDS

This title summarizes many of those already mentioned, picturing the Lamb in His great role as supreme conqueror and ruler. In his first letter to Timothy, Paul uses this title also, further describing Him as "the blessed and only Potentate" (6:15).

22:16 THE BRIGHT AND MORNING STAR

It is fitting that this title should be given at the end of the book which closes "Even so, come, Lord Jesus." (22:20). There is so much of darkness now. As children of the day Christians are working on the night shift, waiting for the coming to the sky of the One who will pierce the darkness as the bright and morning star. How warmly we should love His appearing, for the One who is coming is our Bridegroom.

There are a few places where the Lord is described by other than a name or a title. The heart that loves Christ rejoices as it reads of Him in 21:22: "The Lamb [is] the temple." A temple is a place in which one worships an absent God. But when one is with that God, no temple is needed, for He is the temple. Also in 21:23 the Lamb is said to be the light, a familiar title in John and elsewhere. Actually, here it should be translated lamp. Now Christians walk in His light. The sun of righteousness shines on us and we reflect His light. But one day we shall be with Him and shall be in His light. As a lamp is not stared at, but the light is cherished, so we shall love Him the more, in whose light we will be forever.

Finally, there remains to make an observation of the names of Christ in Revelation 19 as they relate to the gospels.

There are four gospels: Matthew, Mark, Luke and John. Our Lord is so many-sided, so versatile in meeting human need, so infinite as a person, that one story could not possibly have shown Him as He is. All the writers, led of the Spirit, selected material suited to their particular purpose (Luke 1:1-4; John 21:24-25).

It is interesting that the camp of Israel had four insignia: north, east, south, west—one for each three tribes. They were the face of a lion, the face of an ox, the face of a man, the face of an eagle. The living creatures of Ezekiel 1 also have these faces. Long ago it was suggested that these aptly illustrate the four gospels:

1. The face of a lion—Matthew, who writes to Israel of their Messiah King, the Lion of the tribe of Judah;

2. The face of an ox—the faithful and true witness of Mark, who writes to meet the Romans' need;

3. The face of a man—Luke, who writes to meet the need of the Greeks who philosophize about the ideal man, the good, the true, the beautiful;

4. The face of an eagle—John is led to show the Word (the One who lives high above the world) becoming flesh to meet the church's need.

In Revelation 19:11-16 the four gospels are illustrated by the names of Christ: (1) "KING OF KINGS AND LORD OF LORDS"—Matthew; (2) "Faithful and True"—Mark; (3) "a name written, that no man knew, but he himself"—Luke; (4) "The Word of God"—John. Indeed, this last title is a name for Christ used exclusively by John in his gospel and Apocalypse.

Thus we see the wide spectrum of the names of our wonderful Lord in the book of Revelation.

10

The United States of the Western World

I. The Trend Toward Western World Unity

Is it a happenstance that such titles as the above are being used on every hand in the secular press as well as in prophetic writings? I think not, for this is to be the final condition of the Western World, according to Scripture.

Sometime ago the front cover of *U.S. News and World Report* carried a picture of M. Paul Reynaud of France, with large white letters emblazoned on a red background reading, "Coming—A United States of Europe." The *Saturday Review* (Nov. 4, 1961, pp. 18-20) published a convincing article by Roscoe Drummond, condensed as the lead article in the *Reader's Digest* (Feb. 1962, pp. 87-90), entitled "The United States of Europe—Hope of the West." At the time of the formation of the Common Market, *Life* (Jan. 9, 1959) carried an editorial, "Birth of Unity for Europe," whose opening words stated:

> On Capitoline Hill in Rome, nearly 2,000 years ago, Caesar's legions went forth to bring the first unified rule to Europe's warring tribes. Since the Roman Empire's fall the unification of Europe has been a dream which neither the sword of Napoleon nor Hitler could realize. But on Rome's Capitoline Hill last week six statesmen, with the peaceful stroke of a pen, took the biggest step yet made toward this dream of centuries.

If a prophetic teacher had tried to summarize the trend in the Western World toward unification in accordance with Scripture, he could not have said it better. If men in secular circles can see these things shaping up, why is the average pulpit so silent and why are the people of God so uninformed?

In similar vein, the lead paragraph in *Time* on that occasion (Jan. 12, 1959, p. 23) read:

> When the history of the 20th century is written, last week is likely to prove one of its watersheds. For in the seven days which spanned 1958 and 1959, Western Europe began to flex its economic muscles for the first time in a decade, and took its biggest step toward unity since the death of Charlemagne 1,145 years ago.

The idea of Western unity was not born yesterday. Lloyd George first used the name "United States of Europe" at the close of World War I, when he foresaw what has since been undeniably proven true; that there is no future for a divided Europe. But it took a while. Churchill was first to grasp the mistake Roosevelt made in playing into the hands of Stalin, as witness his famous telegram and speech (at Fulton, Mo.) on "The Iron Curtain." He saw that Europe and the United States were in grave danger from Russia and urged moving quickly toward closer cooperation if they were to overcome the bear's menace. His warning sounded very much like that of Benjamin Franklin's, when he challenged the struggling, divided colonies with his famous speech in which he advised: "Gentlemen, if we do not hang together, we shall hang separately!"

Since this is taught in Scripture, the Bible student watches these events with great interest. We do not try to make shrewd guesses in the light of the newspapers, but first we get a firm grasp upon what Scripture prophecy says will be the ultimate outcome, and then interpret our newspapers by the Bible. There is nothing in Scripture to determine which cycle of history we are in. We may swing away from the present trend, but the swing will be temporary. The next cycle will swing closer. Only God knows when the last cycle will occur, and men would be wise not to try to become prophets by stating categorically that we are at such and such a point in God's program. This dishonors Scripture, and is in direct contradiction to our Lord's warning not to set any time markers. But the Bible-taught person can certainly recognize that the trend is moving strongly toward fulfillment, even though he properly leaves the time elements with God. However, we are getting ahead of ourselves on our subject.

II. The Scriptural Background to Western Unity

This theme takes us back to the book of Daniel, chapters 2 and 7. In chapter 2, we have a majestic image picturing Gentile world power as man looks upon it, with flags waving, and drums beating, and the intoxication of conquest. But in chapter 7, we see the same thing from God's viewpoint. We see succeeding world powers as savage beasts of the jungle, slashing and attacking one another and fighting to the death. This is the painful, ugly side of war of which General Sherman spoke.

The extent of the period of time which the image of Daniel 2 pictures is easily determined. God revealed it to Daniel, who informed the king, Nebuchadnezzar, that it began with him and his Babylonian Empire. "Thou, O king, art a king of kings: for the God of heaven hath given thee a kingdom. . . . Thou art this head of gold" (2:37-38). This is the beginning of that period of the world's history called by our Lord Jesus Christ "The times of the Gentiles," since Israel had failed to rule properly for God in the theocracy. Daniel was in Babylon because of Jewish disobedience. Jerusalem and the nation were shortly to fall. This, then, is the *terminus a quo.*

The *terminus ad quem* is also plainly revealed in Daniel

2. The image is traced from the head (Babylon) down to the feet with its ten toes, when we read,

> Thou sawest till that a stone was cut out without hands, which smote the image upon his feet that were of iron and clay, and brake them to pieces. Then was the iron, the clay, the brass, the silver, and the gold, broken to pieces together, and became like the chaff of the summer threshing-floors; and the wind carried them away, that no place was found for them: and the stone that smote the image became a great mountain, and filled the whole earth (2:34-35).

This is interpreted as follows by verses 44-45:

> And in the days of these kings shall the God of heaven set up a kingdom, which shall never be destroyed. . . . Forasmuch as thou sawest that the stone was cut out of the mountains without hands, and that it brake in pieces the iron, the brass, the clay, the silver, and the gold; the great God hath made known to the king what shall come to pass hereafter: and the dream is certain, and the interpretation thereof sure.

It is therefore apparent that the times of the Gentiles last from the transfer of God's delegated power to rule from Israel to the Gentiles in the days of Nebuchadnezzar II, and that Gentile world power will continue until it is smashed by the intervention of the supernatural second coming of Jesus Christ, whose kingdom will supersede the kingdoms of this world and "never be destroyed."

This chapter also fills us in on the major transitions of the intervening period between the start and the conclusion of the times of the Gentiles. We should know this order of the succession of kingdoms from history, but it is significant that God proved His uniqueness as God by revealing these facts long before they occurred (Is 44:6-7; 46:9-10; contra 47:12-13).

The next two kingdoms, following Babylon (625-539 B.C.), are the "breast and arms of silver," emphasizing the duality of Media-Persia (named in 8:20) and the "thighs of brass" (2:32), named as Greece (8:21). The usual dates for these kingdoms are 539-331 and 331-323 B.C. respectively.

History tells us that Rome overcame the Grecian empire begun by Alexander the Great, carried on by his generals following his death, and chiefly important in Israel's history as perpetuated in the Seleucid dynasty of Syria and the Ptolemaic dynasty of Egypt. The name "Rome" is not given us in Daniel, but there can be no doubt that Rome is intended, for it was known in literature as the "iron kingdom," taking this imagery from the fact that it was first to forge weapons of this material, and because it was the nation which destroyed the only temple in Jerusalem built after the passing of Media-Persia and Greece from the scene. The A.D. 70 destruction of the city of Jerusalem and its sanctuary are predicted in Daniel 9:26. The Roman Titus did this. Thus, Rome is the fourth world empire in the times of the Gentiles.

However, despite its strength which permitted it to break in pieces and subdue opposing nations (2:40), we are told that "the kingdom shall be divided" (v. 41). It is instructive to observe that three periods of Rome, the fourth world empire, appear to be designated by the Scripture as follows: (1) the legs of iron, (2) the feet of iron and clay, (3) ten toes of iron and potter's clay.

FIRST PERIOD: The Two Legs of Iron (2:40)
The Original Empire (2:33*a*)

Contrary to the usual interpretation, the thrust of the two legs of the image is not primarily concerned with the eventual split of kingdom into Eastern and Western empires. Rome did not divide until hundreds of years after functioning as a unified empire. The two legs primarily emphasized the sturdiness and swift mobility of the united empire, though recognizing inherent differences, as Rudyard Kipling expressed it so well:

East is East and West is West,
And never the twain shall meet.

It was a long while before a tendency to division became apparent when in A.D. 286 Diocletian associated Maximian with himself. But Constantine reunited the empire. However, in building the great "Constantine-ople" (city of Constantine) as a second, eastern Rome, he paved the way for the final division which took place in A.D. 364.

SECOND PERIOD: "Feet . . . of iron and clay" (2:41)
The Intervening Period (2:33*b*)

As mentioned, the eventual two divisioned empire was inherently but secondarily predicted by the two legs. However, that does not explain why each half of the empire fell before its enemies (West, before Odoacer in 475; East, before the Turks in 1453, with the eventual fall of Contantinople); nor does it explain the persistence of Rome in the interim without any definite seats of authority, i.e., clay mixed with iron is essential to the understanding of the fall of the "iron kingdom."

The verse before us (v. 41) says that "the kingdom shall be divided" because it is composed of iron and clay. It was because the iron of Roman imperium (militaristic force as seen today in totalitarian systems) was mixed with the brittle weakness of clay (the popular will, fickle and easily molded, as seen today in Communistic appeals to the common man), that the West and then the East fell (because of lack of internal cohesion). And Rome has continued "divided" into many parts by these two diverse principles, but the important thing is that Rome has continued.

Rome has persisted in the unsatisfactory and weak condition of inward division, but she has persisted! As Urquhart expressed it:

> The whole of Western Europe adopted the language of the Romans, and its inhabitants looked upon themselves as Ro-

mans. The laws and institutions of Rome acquired such a power and durability that even at the present moment they still continue to maintain their influence upon millions of men. Such a development is without parallel in the history of the world.

Rome persisted in the Holy Roman Empire, with all of its weakness, attesting the truth of verse 41; and the Roman (Catholic) Church especially has perpetuated the language, spirit, idolatries, and culture of Rome.

Charlemagne sought to regroup the southern European nations of the old Roman Empire in A.D. 800 in a union which later became known as the Holy Roman Empire. This persisted through medieval times until after the Reformation. A period of nationalistic emphasis, with antagonism heightened by colonial expansion jealousies, characterized the further history of Europe from that time into the modern period. Bitter national envy and hatred carried on into the twentieth century and had a real share in precipitating World Wars I and II. This was especially true of Germany and France (War of 1870, World Wars I and II).

Thus, the "feet" period of the fourth kingdom is the period between the disruption of old Rome and the revival of Rome in its final form.

THIRD PERIOD: "Toes (ten) . . . of iron mixed with potter's clay" (2:42-43) =
Revived Final Form of Fourth Empire

Despite the "divided" condition of the West, Scripture makes it plain that "the deadly wound" of the dismembered empire is going to be "healed" to the consternation of all peoples (Rev 13:3-4). It matters little what the new empire will be called. It may, as we have suggested, be called "The United States of Europe" or "The United States of the Western World"; but the empire is to be reconstituted, for the image smitten by the stone (Christ) is envisioned as being totally intact when it is smitten on the ten toes, its final form. In my judgment it will comprise the whole Western world, all that was Rome and all that has come out of Rome. This would include the western hemisphere, which almost totally came out of Western Europe, the sphere of the *old* Roman world. This ten-divisioned form, represented by ten toes and ten "horns" (Rev 13:1; 17:12-17), is ten kings or kingdoms who cooperate with the Roman "beast" (leader) for an agreed purpose and period of time ("one hour"). At no time in Rome's history has she been divided into ten parts. This final form has not yet arrived but is undoubtedly on the way. It is the revivified Western Entente which makes a treaty with Israel permitting the restoration of temple worship for a period of seven years (Dan 9:27). This inevitably involves a reconstituted Israel with a leader in Jerusalem called "the false prophet," who will be an ally of the Western ruler whose capital is Rome (cp. Rev 13, 17).

Much of this has taken place in the lifetime of many living today. The decline of colonial powers, the sustaining of which led to constant wars among the Western nations, has well-nigh reached its conclusion. One by one the Western nations have lost their colonies and have had all they can do to survive. Weakened by two world wars and pressed into the beginnings of unity by the threat of Russia, things which seemed far off a few years ago are taking place at an accelerated rate.

One of the few results of World War I in prophetic fulfillment was the freeing of Palestine from the Turkish yoke, permitting the return of Israel to Palestine. Despite tremendous odds, the nation was formed in 1948 and has withstood all attempts to dislodge her. Thus, we have two parallel events: (1) the revival of Israel on her own soil as a sovereign nation able to make treaties and (2) the trend toward western unity, which will eventuate in a treaty with Israel concerning the restoration of temple worship.

II. Recent Progress Toward Fulfillment of the Prophecy of Western Unity

The need for unity has become increasingly apparent to the Western world; and with World War II, the United States and Latin America became very much related to all that goes on in Europe. Toward the close of World War II came Benelux, a working agreement between *Bel*gium, the *Net*herlands, and *Lux*embourg. This was followed swiftly by Western European Union in 1948 and NATO in 1949. At this point the United States became a prime mover in the drive toward western unity. No less a person than the great General Eisenhower was the first chief of staff of the North Atlantic Treaty Organization.

Following this came the European Coal and Steel Community (April 18, 1951), while in August 1954 the European Defense Community all but succeeded, but was aborted because of the multiple political divisions of the French Assembly in a weak, pre-deGaulle France. Finally steps were taken to form the six member European Economic Community (popularly known as the Common Market). This was signed on historic Capitoline Hill, Rome's ancient government seat, in the week overlapping the last days of 1958 and the first days of 1959.

Despite deGaulle's monumental hatred of Britain (and the United States) and his intransigence in twice vetoing Britain's attempt to join the Common Market, his death left the way open to further negotiation. For two years prior to the successful completion of consultation, the news media began talking about "The Ten," a very interesting phrase to a biblically oriented person (e.g., Dan 2—ten toes; Dan 7—ten horns)! On January 22, 1972 it finally happened—the six countries signed the enlargement treaty with Britain, Norway, Denmark, and Ireland, bringing the six to ten. To every-one's surprise, Norway has temporarily failed to ratify, but the other three countries did. (This is not to suggest the exact final ten are here identified, but we are on the way.)

This economic giant will have 260 million people and ac-count for 25 percent of world trade as contrasted with only 15 percent for the United States or Russia. It will produce more steel, for instance, than either the United States or Rus-sia. Roscoe Drummond, previously cited, argues that this economic force is far more potent in dealing with Commu-nism than increasing armaments. Russia's previous attempt to bankrupt individual Western nations by use of unfair dis-count-house methods, playing nation against nation in harm-ful competition, have been checkmated. Now Russia is hurt-ing! At the end of the first ten years, the Common Market reports showed that they were 200 to 400 percent ahead of estimates, depending upon the country. The upward trend continues.

The United States is being drawn closer and closer because of monetary and trade problems which require cooperative action. Beginning with the Kennedy Treaty, constant negoti-ations are going on concerning tariffs from the United States to Europe and from Europe to the United States. Already in 1972, as I write, two congressional committees have wrestled with Common Market representatives in Brussels and Com-mon Market representatives have visited Washington. This will increase. For her own good, the United States must sooner or later formally join this economic entity of the West and the sooner the better, if the stability of the dollar is to be forwarded. Cooperation of all the Western World for the common good is the only way. The fiscal future of all nations in the Western World depends upon such a union of efforts. The various sovereign states must come to the place where they see that the only solution to their problems is to delegate their powers to a parliament of Europe which would correspond in many ways to our American federal union.

Former timid steps toward political union of Western Europe are being superseded by blunt warnings from Malfatti (most recent Common Market president) and others to the effect that these nations must move much faster toward political union if they are to hold the dramatic economic gains the Common Market has attained.

Indeed, methods of voting are already under serious discussion, according to their official magazine, *European Community*. Everything is pointing toward a directly elected European parliament by citizens of all the community nations, voting as individuals of Europe rather than as citizens of their respective countries. When this is decided, the final step of political union will have been consummated and the Western World will fulfill the prophecy of the "deadly wound healed."

The latter is as inevitable as the incoming tide. The western hemisphere will be part of this revived fourth "empire." Not a fundamentalist, prophetic teacher, but a keen secular observer of international events (Chet Huntley) spoke the following words in a broadcast on May 2, 1956—words which carry an even more ringing sound to clear-thinking people today, quite apart from prophetic teaching:

> By treaty, by past, by tradition, by promise, by sentiment, by civilization, heritage, language, custom, and purpose, we are today bound to Europe. A loose coalition of states will not do. The formation of an Atlantic Community is the logical conclusion. This reporter can recall most vividly the debate when the European Defense Community was almost a reality. I have only to recall the speeches of Monnet (of France), Henri Spaak (of Belgium), and De Gasperi (of Italy), through which ran the steady premise that a federated Europe could alone become a reality when it is joined by Britain and the United States in an Atlantic Community.

To the student of prophecy the shape of things to come is becoming increasingly plain. Therefore, a United States of Europe, yea, of the Western World, must come. Typical of the complete change of climate is a little news item of a few years back which went unobserved by most people. It told of West Germany being invited by France to train her troops on French soil! Knowing the galling pain and hate of their three wars (Franco-Prussian of 1870, and World Wars I and II), this is nothing short of a miracle! As late as 1955 any such possibility would have been scoffed at. But such things are now reality, and the world is moving swiftly toward the events prophesied by Daniel and other prophets.

Just how far these things will proceed before the Lord returns for His church we cannot know. The cycle could swing the other way. But, if it should, it will return again. At any event, the Western World as revivified Rome (it matters not under what name) will make a treaty with Israel for one seven-year period. The final form of the revived empire will be a ten-divisioned form pictured by the ten toes (Dan 2) and ten horns (Dan 7; Rev 13, 17). Some think the ten-divisioned form will not come till about the middle of the seventieth week. But, in any event, in the middle of the week the Jewish leader will traitorously double-cross his people and break the treaty (Dan 9:27) by desecrating the sanctuary through setting up in the temple an image of the political leader of the western empire (the one with headquarters in Rome, Mt 24:15; Rev 13). He will persecute with devilish cruelty all who refuse to worship the image (Rev 13; Mt 24: 16-22, esp. v. 21). This period is called the great tribulation, the time of Jacob's trouble.

This latter half of the week will be the occasion for the hellish, Satan-inspired form of empire, which will specialize in persecution of believers and blasphemy of heaven and its Christ. These ten kings (kingdoms) shall give their power to the beast "for one hour," i.e., one agreed period (Rev 17: 12-14).

This final form of the empire will continue till Christ returns to earth as the Smiting Stone.

So, pilgrims, lift up your heads. Your redemption draweth nigh!

11

The Power Struggle of the End Time

I. Prelude and Explanation

For as long as I can remember, I have known and rejoiced in the truths related to the future purpose of God with Israel and the nations, the unique place of the church in the economy of God, and the great fact of our Lord's second advent. My father and mother came into a knowledge of these things at the turn of the century, and the entrance of this line of Scripture truth revolutionized their Christian lives, leading to fervent, lifelong Bible study with a library that would do credit to an average pastor. The truth of the imminent coming of Christ led them to an intense desire for a holy life, earnest witness to the unsaved, and dedicated devotion to the cause of missions in calling out a people for His name from among the nations.

As a result, some of the great teachers in biblical and prophetic study were household names, especially since quite a number were guests in our home. I was weaned on the *Scofield Reference Bible* (1909 edition) and Larkin's charts, with liberal doses of Gaebelein, Gray, Torrey, Blackstone, and others. I was taken to Bible conferences at a young age. D. M. Stearns and W. H. Griffith Thomas were neighbors. Later I attended a college and seminary committed to this position, being in the first class at Dallas Seminary and privileged to sit under such men as Lewis Sperry Chafer, H. A. Ironside, A. C. Gaebelein, George Guille, B. B. Sutcliffe and

A. B. Winchester. I have been associated with Philadelphia College of Bible since 1928, and for twenty years of that time served as a pastor who believed in bringing the best American and English Bible teachers to my church. For eight years I directed the Boardwalk Bible Conference in Atlantic City, where most of the outstanding Bible teachers of that era were invited to serve.

I have recited these associations so as to affirm my position with the premillennial, dispensational, pretribulational movement. Therefore, when in this chapter I express a viewpoint that runs counter to the almost universally held position of prophetic teachers, I want to make it clear that I am a member of the *loyal* opposition! I am not trying to undercut the basic unity of the position we all hold dear. Rather, I am offering an alternate solution to one of the areas in which I have felt our hermeneutics as a movement has been faulty. I have found many people confused by a seeming contradiction. It is as though two lines of prophetic exposition go down two different one-way streets which run in opposite directions, and there is no collision because they are not on the same street. It is my conviction that, interpretationally, they are on the same street and should be dealt with together instead of separately.

II. Two Debatable Positions: One Antichrist and One World Ruler

I refer to the almost universally held thesis of prophetic teaching that there is to be a world ruler, Satan's man, who will dominate the whole inhabited earth. There is a collateral view that usually goes along with it, namely, that there is a single individual—whether one identifies him with the universal ruler in Rome or his Jewish ally in Jerusalem—who is to be called *the* Antichrist, despite the objection that our Lord said, "There shall arise false Christs" and "Many false prophets shall rise" (Mt 24:24, 11).

The word "antichrist" is used only five times and all by John in his epistles. A careful examination will establish the fact that the word is never used solely of some one individual who is yet coming in the future and of him alone. Look at the evidence: In 1 John 2:22 and 2 John 7 it is used generally of *any* person who denies the truth that the Lord Jesus came in an actual body (i.e., the heresy of the Gnostics who said that He merely appeared to have, but did not have, an actual body). The 2 John 7 passage says "many deceivers are entered into the world." So this is no future false messiah but false messiahs present in John's day whom he labels "deceivers." In 1 John 2:18 it is used both in the singular and in the plural. This verse and 1 John 4:3 say they have heard of a coming false Messiah, but goes on to say: "this is that spirit of antichrist" which is "even now already . . . in the world." "Whereby we know that it is the last time" is added by 1 John 2:18. If anyone wishes to insist that there is only one Antichrist who can be so labeled, he must also accept the erroneous position that that one (*the*) Antichrist was already in the world as of the first century (in John's day). This leaves no room for *only one* and he a future Antichrist.

To summarize: Both Jesus and John said there were many deceivers, not one; many false prophets, many false Christs. This was true in John's day and will be true all the way through the church age and into the end-time seventieth week, commonly called the tribulation. There never was and there never will be only one who can properly be called "the" Antichrist. Satan's men can always be called antichrists. "Which beast of Revelation 13 is the Antichrist?" has long been a real bone of contention among prophetic teachers. The answer is simple: *Both* are antichrists, and *many* others. Jesus and John said so.

Those who urge the theory of one certain individual Antichrist plainly expect him to be manifest after our Lord Jesus comes in the air to take His church to heaven. Thus, although it may well be true that one superman raised up by Satan may supremely be dominated by Satan and supremely deceive men, the term "antichrist" cannot be limited to that one individual, for our Lord declared there were to be plural "false Christs . . . many false prophets."

In my judgment, a substantial amount of time has been wasted on the platform and in books on prophetic themes arguing which of the beasts of Revelation 13 is *the* Antichrist. Indeed, godly brethren have at times gotten so warm in their debate on this question of which is the Antichrist that fellowship has been cooled, if not broken.

I should like to submit for your consideration the viewpoint that in the end time of the tribulation there is to be not just one great ruler (and/or sphere of authority), but *four* great spheres of political authority backed up by military might. I will submit evidence to support the view that only in the movement and attack of the armies of these four power spheres do we find room for numerous Scriptures to be explained and fulfilled. The usually received idea of a central, universal ruler over the whole inhabited earth will not properly allow for those great tensions and movements of armies of which both Old and New Testament speak. And may I request your gracious forbearance and wise suspension of judgment until I have presented that part of the evidence for which I have space? I shall greatly appreciate your cooperation in reading me through and then searching "the Scriptures daily" to see if these things I present are so (Ac 17:11).

Perhaps it would be well, first of all, to present the two lines of biblical data that seem to collide and require some kind of adequate solution.

III. The Case for the One World Ruler Thesis

In Revelation 13:1-10 we read of the sinister "beast . . . out of the sea" who is commonly identified as the ruler of the revived fourth world empire, which was Rome. The revivification is based upon the statement that the "deadly wound was healed" (v. 3). History records the "death" of the Roman Empire of the West in A.D. 476, and the fall of the last remaining bastion of the Eastern Roman Empire (Constantinople) in A.D. 1453. To every intent and purpose Rome was dead and buried.

But this passage says that the deadly wound will be healed, that the empire that was Rome will be revived. The correctness of this interpretation is affirmed by Daniel 2 and Daniel 7. There in the imagery of the colossus (ch. 2) and of the four beasts (ch. 7), it is made apparent that there is not to be a fifth human empire superseding the fourth. The stone which is cut out of the mountains without hands supernaturally smites the image in its final form ("ten toes"), pulverizes it, and grows into a great mountain filling the whole earth (2:34-35). Daniel 2 also includes the divine interpretation that this is the kingdom of our Lord Jesus Christ which the God of heaven will set up on earth (vv. 44-45). Thus, if the deadly wound is healed and there is not to be a fifth empire of human origin, the revivification of the fourth empire must be the correct interpretation.

The Revelation 13 passage then goes on to say that the Roman beast will "make war with the saints and . . . overcome them: and power was given him over all kindreds, and tongues, and nations," and that all who "dwell upon the earth shall worship him" unless their names are written in the Lamb's book of life (vv. 7-8). This seems at face value to indicate complete sovereignty over the whole earth.

IV. THE SEEMING CONTRADICTION TO THE ONE WORLD RULER THESIS

However, when we turn to the Old Testament we find many prophecies telling of armies marching against Palestine. In addition, our Lord Jesus Christ speaks of Jerusalem being surrounded with armies, of a crescendo of nations warring against nations until the Lord Jesus intervenes by means of

His second coming in power and glory (Mt 24; Lk 21). Let us look at two or three key passages emphasizing this fact.

Turn to the prophecy of Zechariah, chapter 12. We read in verses 2 and 3:

> Behold, I will make Jerusalem a cup of trembling unto all the people round about, when they shall be in the siege both against Judah and against Jerusalem. And in that day will I make Jerusalem a burdensome stone for all people: all that burden themselves with it shall be cut in pieces, though all the people of the earth be gathered together against it.

Again, in verse 9 of the same chapter we read:

> And it shall come to pass in that day, that I will seek to destroy all the nations that come against Jerusalem.

In chapters 38 and 39 of Ezekiel we are told of a host which will come against Palestine and Jerusalem. It will be so large that when God smites the invaders upon the mountains of Israel, it will require seven months to bury the dead. Many expositors are convinced that this is the occasion, mentioned in Zechariah 14:2, when Jerusalem will be actually taken and spoiled in battle, although the successful invader is evidently in the process of withdrawal homeward, according to Ezekiel 39, when five-sixths of his large army is destroyed by God. There is almost universal agreement among prophetic scholars that this army comes from Russia and her satellites, whose ruler is known as "the king of the north" in the pattern of end-time events.

However, the north is not the only area from which assaults against Palestine come. In the prophecy of Daniel, chapter 11, it is said that the king of the south shall first push against the man in Jerusalem, which "push" is quickly followed by the invasion of the king of the north, who comes against the ruler in Jerusalem "like a whirlwind" (v. 40).

Further, we are informed that "tidings out of the east . . .

shall trouble" the Jerusalem ruler, so that he hurries back from the south to "plant the tabernacles of his palace between the seas (Mediterranean and Dead Seas) in the glorious holy mountain (plainly Jerusalem)."

To what do those "tidings out of the east" refer? The Bible does not leave us in doubt. In Revelation 9:16 we are told of an army of two hundred million men. Associated with the announcement is the statement that the four angels binding the River Euphrates are "loosed." A parallel passage in Revelation 16:12 throws a great deal of light on the matter: "And the sixth angel poured out his vial upon the great river Euphrates; and the water thereof was dried up, that the way of the kings of the east might be prepared."

Regardless of what "the drying up" of the Euphrates means, it is clearly connected with the invasion of an army of two hundred millions of men led by the kings of the east (sunrising). This abundantly explains why "tidings out of the east" trouble the man in Jerusalem of Daniel 11.

This should be sufficient evidence to make the issue clear: namely, if there is to be a world ruler "over all kindreds and tongues and nations," how is it possible that armies are able to come at him from the south, the north, and the east? What kind of authority is unable to control his territory any better than that? Here is a ruler supposed to be in complete authority over the earth, and yet the king of the north successfully invades the land and takes the capital city of his ally in the east (the false prophet, ruler over the Jews in Jerusalem). And even more damaging to the theory is the question: How could an army of two hundred million men be raised, come all the way west against him, and presumably successfully invade that part of his territory west of the Euphrates?

I find it difficult to understand by what stretch of the imagination a man could be called a world ruler who has so little power that armies from the south, from the north, and from the east can come against him in startlingly large numbers and, judging by the language of Ezekiel 38-39, Zechariah 14, and Revelation 16, be successful in invading the land and, at least temporarily, in taking the capital city (Jerusalem) of the eastern ally of the "world ruler." The idea is completely untenable to me.

Further, since it is plainly prophesied by our Lord and others that Jerusalem will be surrounded with armies, and since we are told in the Revelation that the armies of the beast and the false prophet will be drawn up at Armageddon when our Lord descends to the earth, how can these things be if there be a universal world ruler? Does he come against himself? Does he surround himself? If not, against whom are his armies drawn up at Armageddon? Against heaven? If against heaven, why not in Jerusalem? Why go up to Armageddon? Or does anyone seriously believe, as I have heard, that a handful of repentant Jews who refuse the mark of the beast could actually mount a sort of Maccabean revolt and, barricaded in Jerusalem, successfully defy the beast and the false prophet? This taxes my credulity!

V. The Suggested Solution to the One World Ruler Thesis

There seems to be a plain contradiction if the Bible teaches a powerful world ruler, but also teaches invading armies from three directions, with Jerusalem surrounded and armies drawn up at Armageddon.

I have a very simple suggestion to offer that solves the whole problem for me, and I trust will commend itself to you. I feel the thing that has confused expositors is the word "world," especially when it is a translation of the Greek word *oikoumene*, which is translated "world" but means literally "the inhabited earth." There is no doubt that to an English-speaking person this means the complete globe. But the first law of hermeneutics of a language, or even translation of a language into another, is that a language means only what it meant to the people who used it in the first instance.

What did the word *oikoumene* mean to the people of the first century A.D. when our New Testament was written?

Fortunately, we have a classic example. In the very familiar story about the events leading to the birth of Jesus, as recorded in Luke 2, we have this statement: "And it came to pass in those days, that there went out a decree from Caesar Augustus that all the world [*oikoumene*] should be [enrolled for taxing]" (Lk 2:1).

Were the Chinese or Japanese enrolled by Augustus? Were the Incas of South America enrolled, or the Iroquois of New York, or even the ancestors of the Russians? Or the Ethiopians? Who were enrolled?

Plainly we have the solution in the use the Romans made of the word *oikoumene*. The *Roman* world was the *only* world to them. All others were barbarians. No one else counted. Scofield has an excellent note here. He says: "This passage is noteworthy as defining the usual N. T. use of *oikoumene* as the sphere of Roman rule at its greatest extent." The *New Scofield Reference Bible* (p. 1078) is even more precise: "The 'world' (Gk. *oikoumenē*, signifying the *inhabited earth*) throughout the N. T. has reference politically to the Roman Empire or the Roman world."

Thus, this first-century passage in a first-century book (Rev 13) must be understood in that light. It is "all kindred, and tongues, and nations" in the Roman "world" that are involved, that part of the world over which the revived fourth empire of the west will have sovereignty. If this view be accepted, then it is perfectly intelligible that kings of the south and the north and the east can and will come against the Roman ruler and his ally. Those nations are *outside* the Roman world, as revived. Thus, there is no contradiction whatever.

VI. Marching Armies in the End Time

The argument above shows that, contrary to the usual conception, in the end time of the tribulation there will be *four* great spheres of political authority backed by military might, not just one. The revived fourth empire is the empire of the West, the "United States of the Western World," composed of all that was once Rome and that which came out of Rome, i.e., the western hemisphere.

Indeed, it would appear that the very pretensions of the defiant "beast" heading the revived fourth empire (Rev 13: 5), will arouse resentment and antagonism in the rulers of other parts of the world: south, north, and east.

At any event, Jerusalem, as the eastern capital of the fourth (western) empire, will be presided over by the ally and lieutenant of the ruler in Rome. This man is the second beast or false prophet of Revelation 13, who makes an image of the Roman ruler, desecrating the restored temple and making further sacrifice impossible (Dan 9:27), as in the days when Antiochus Epiphanes defiled the altar in Jerusalem by sacrificing a sow upon it. This act of the false prophet in Revelation 13 is the "abomination of desolation" spoken of by the Lord Jesus (Mt 24:15), because of which horrible persecution will be the portion of those who do not go along with him.

This arrogant attitude will evidently anger those outside the Roman Empire, and Jerusalem, in the providence of God, will become a mighty magnet drawing the armies of the nations to it that the Lord may destroy them (Zec 12:2-3, 7-9). It is not insignificant that only comparatively recently have Asia and Africa become strong in political and war potential.

Using Daniel 11:40 as our starting point, we shall seek to trace and chart the movement of armies in the end time, leading up to the final destruction of the beast and the false prophet at Armageddon, when our Lord Jesus returns the second time.

The four political areas of the world to be distinguished are listed below and the movements of their armies are charted on the accompanying map:

1. WEST—The Jewish "willful king" in Jerusalem (Dan 11:45, labeled 1*b* on the chart, is allied to the Head of Revived Fourth (Western or Roman) Empire (Dan 2:40-43; 7:7-8) whose headquarters are in Rome (labeled 1*a* on the chart).

2. SOUTH—The king of the south (Africa) who "pushes at" no. 1*b* (Dan 11:40*a*), located in Jerusalem. No. 2 seems to be allied with no. 3 (Dan 11:43*b*; Eze 38:5-6), and his attack is evidently designed to draw no. 1*b* out of position (with his back to the north). No. 2 initially succeeds in capturing Egypt with the special help of Ethiopia and Libya (Dan 11:42-43; Eze 38:5).

3. NORTH—The king of the north (the Assyrian, Gog-Magog, i.e., Russia, etc.; Is 10:24-27; 14:25; Mic 5:5-6; Eze 38-39) in the meantime swoops down, while no. 1*b* has turned south to protect his flank against no. 2 (no. 1*b* is evidently soon able to neutralize the armies of no. 2, for we hear no more of no. 2.) This accomplished, no. 1*b* hastens back to Palestine because of unfavorable tidings out of the north and east (Dan 11:44), but before he can get back, the king of the north (no. 3) has already taken Jerusalem (Zec 14:2; Dan 11:40*b*-43*a*; compare Zec 12:2; 13:8-9) and started his return journey home. However, no. 3 is smitten by God upon the mountains of Israel (Zec 14:3; Eze 38:21—39:4; cp. Sennacherib's destruction, Is 37:36-37) before no. 1*b* can counterattack him. But no. 3's invasion has laid open the eastern flank of no. 1*b* to attack (evidently the meaning of the Euphrates being "dried up," Rev 16:12).

4. EAST—The kings of the east ("sunrising," Dan 11:44; Rev 16:12) now proceed westward with an army of two hundred million men (Rev 9:16), sweeping through the eastern part of the fourth empire with great destruction (Rev 9:17-18). Meanwhile no. 1*b* hastens northward and deploys his army (now strengthened with legions from his

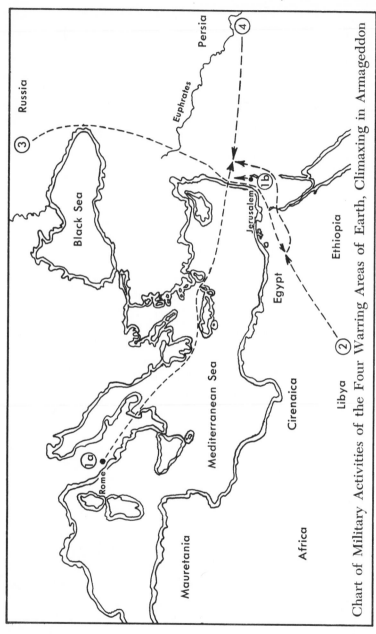

Chart of Military Activities of the Four Warring Areas of Earth, Climaxing in Armageddon

ally in Rome, no. 1*a*) in the valley of Megiddo, readying for no. 4's assault.

Evidently, they (nos. 1*a*, 1*b*, and 4) *never actually join* battle at Megiddo, as it would seem that "the sign of the Son of man" then appears in the heavens (Mt 24:29-30), diverting their attention from each other and leading to further blasphemy on their part (Ps 2:1-3). At this point the Lord Jesus Christ returns (Ps 2:4-9), definitely smiting no. 1*a* and no. 1*b* (as told in Rev 19:11-21 and as alluded to in Dan 11:36*d*, 45*b*, with 12:1); and evidently the Lord also smites no. 4, for "Armageddon" (Rev 16:16) is mentioned in the same context with the kings of the east (Rev 16:12).

By this explanation, we understand (1) how Jerusalem will come to be attacked, (2) the part that the movement of the armies of the south, north, and east play, and (3) why the beast and false prophet have their western empire army drawn up at Armageddon at the time the Lord Jesus descends to set up His glorious earthly kingdom.

VII. Two Explanatory Notes as Postscripts

Two explanatory notes are needed to complete this study.

First, in both Daniel 11 and Ezekiel 38, Libya and Ethiopia are mentioned in such a way as to make it evident that these names are used to identify the king of the south of the end time. It should be immediately pointed out that Ethiopia was *never* conquered by Rome and thus was never in the fourth world empire. Further, only a casual glance at a map of the Roman world of the first century is necessary to make it clear that all Rome ever possessed of the great continent of Africa was the northern tip, which read from east to west as follows: Aegyptus, Cirenaica, Africa (from which later the whole continent was named, as the name of the continent of Asia was taken from the southwest province of what is now Turkey), and Mauretania. I would particularly call your attention to the fact that none of these northern fringe provinces was called Libya. Although Herodotus had no idea of the shape of the continent of Africa, his map of Africa puts Libya south of the coast, thus indicating the interior. The *National Geographic* map of the Roman Empire makes Libya the *whole* of the interior under the Roman lip of North Africa, except Ethiopia to the east. Evidently, therefore, the biblical terms Ethiopia and Libya are to convey the idea of the whole continent excepting the Roman lip on the north coast. Confirming this, Daniel 11:42-43 indicates Egypt is attacked and its treasures taken. Thus Egypt is that part of the Roman Empire the king of the south invades.

Second: The expositors have had a problem in the identification of the antecedents to the "he's" of Daniel 11:40*b* and the verses following. Both Gaebelein and Ironside, from whom I received the basic idea of the movement of armies, think that once the king of the north (no. 3 on the chart) comes on the scene in verse 40*b*, all the "he's" thereafter refer to him, and that thus he sets his tents victoriously upon the glorious holy mountain (v. 45*a*) and is destroyed by the Lord (v. 45 *b*).

I find this thesis objectionable for a number of reasons. First and foremost, this interpretation does not finish the dramatic story of the "willful king," so strikingly begun in 11:36-39. Further, it does not make apparent why the willful king, after blunting the attack of no. 2 (the king of the south), would hurry back home; nor does it show why he would take his army up to Armageddon. Evidently, the king of the south is so closely allied with the king of the north that any victory of the king of the south is counted as also a victory of the king of the north (v. 43). Why then should the "he" of verse 44 be the king of the north? Why should he be disturbed about his own invasion of Palestine and conquest of Jerusalem? This would not be news to him or his ally, nor be anything to cause fear. Thus, the problem is to distinguish the "he's" of verses 40-45.

My suggested solution is to make the "he's" of verses 40*b*-43 refer to the king of the north both in his own activity and that of his ally, the king of the south. I then bring the story back to the willful king in verse 44, which explains that while he is fighting the king of the south, the king of the north has taken Jerusalem (vv. 40*b*-43). Hence, the willful king, hearing these ill tidings out of the north and hearing of the approaching march of the kings of the east toward Palestine (v. 44), furiously completes the defeat of the king of the south and swiftly moves back north to deal with the king of the north and the kings of the east. On returning to Jerusalem, he finds the king of the north has been destroyed by the Lord upon the mountains of Israel. He reestablishes his palace in Jerusalem (v. 45*a*), then goes to Armageddon with his Roman ally to make a stand against the kings of the east. But there he comes to his end (v. 46*b*), being smitten by the Lord Jesus Christ at Armageddon on His way down to the Mount of Olives. All this fits exactly with the context of Daniel 12:1 as being the end of the tribulation period.

12

Gog and Magog, Who and When?

ONE THING IS CERTAIN; no teacher should speak dogmatically on a prophecy like that of Gog and Magog in Ezekiel 38—39. So many different views have been offered that it is difficult to sift, discard, and retain. I shall earnestly advocate the conclusions to which I have come, but I shall do it in the spirit of an investigator, willing to accept any more light that may be thrown upon this great prophecy. Perhaps my attitude has been heightened by the dogmatism with which I have often heard this passage expounded. I suggest these solutions for consideration and study.

But, having said that, there are some things about which the majority of premillennialists are agreed. The most prominent of these is the identification of Gog and Magog with other prophecies about the invasion of Palestine by a future king of the north. Many have identified Gog as the head of what has been called the northeastern confederacy, headed by Russia. It is the details, particularly as to the *time* of the action, regarding which there is disagreement. There are five areas covered in this chapter: the area, the allies, the action, the outcome, and the time of the action.

THE AREA ALLUDED TO

"Son of man, set thy face against Gog, the land of Magog, the chief prince of Meshech and Tubal, and prophesy against him" (Eze 38:2).

The philological and geographical identification arguments

against the generally received premillennial view are not impressive. The evidence seems to point toward a *person* designated as "Gog," who is "prince of Rosh" (the literal of the phrase "the chief prince"), and presides over a *land* called "Magog," which has two chief cities called "Meshech" and "Tubal." Again, there are some who argue on grounds of philology against the following identification, but the weight of the evidence appears to point to it. The name "Rosh" would be a typically variant spelling of Russia. Anyone who has worked with names is not disturbed by the seemingly different orthography. Thus, if Rosh is Russia, Magog would be the *land* of Russia. The suggestion has been made that Meshech and Tubal constitute the old names for the former western and eastern capital cities of old Russia, Moscow and Tobolsk. It is interesting that although in modern times the capital was moved to what was known successively as St. Petersburg, Petrograd, and finally Leningrad, the pendulum swung back to Moscow as the capital of Russia.

The Allies of Russia, the King of the North

In Ezekiel 38:5-6 we are introduced to the allies of the king of the north. Again, we have a problem because of the changing of names during the long time involved since this passage was written. But the nearest ally of Russia could be "Gomer" of verse 6. There is confidence that these are the Cimmerians who have for millennia occupied the area of Central Europe, which may include Germany and other satellites of Russia in that area today. When we say Germany, we mean *East* Germany because, although Rome did some conquering east of the Rhine, the official Roman attitude was that the fallback line was the Rhine. Rome always thought of her empire in Western Europe as extending to the Rhine on the east, and in Central Europe, to the Danube on the north. Chapters 2 and 7 of Daniel, with Revelation 13, make it plain that the deadly wound of the defeated fourth "world" empire (476 and 1453 A.D.), fulfilled in the historical Rome, is going to be healed.

Thus there will be a hegemony of the West which, in my judgment, will include all that was Rome in the past *and* that which came out of Rome (i.e., Rome extended), the western hemisphere. As widely heralded, NATO and the Common Market have signalized the West's realization that she could not afford the luxury of the national jealousies of the past few hundred years any longer. Bled white by World Wars I and II, overshadowed by the growing power of Russia, the West has found herself in the position of the scattered and quarreling American colonies, when Benjamin Franklin advised: "Gentlemen, we must hang together, or assuredly we shall all hang separately."

So, while men are amazed at the revival of Rome (Rev 13:3), the western powers have thrown themselves into each other's arms, both out of a sense of mutual need and in the sway of a sense of destiny, sharing as they do the same ideology. Hence, the territory in Europe of the king of the north will not include territory giving its allegiance to the Western Confederacy with its capital in Rome, so this is why we say, Germany and other Central Europe countries east of the Rhine and north of the Danube.

In addition to Gomer and his bands (or hordes), the next allies to be considered are Ethiopia and Libya (also literally called Cush and Put), mentioned in Ezekiel 38:5. These are also in the important account (Dan 11:40) of the movements of armies in the end time. In line with the interpretation given above of the western revival of the old Roman Empire, it should be pointed out that Rome held only the lip of North Africa. She never occupied the interior. The countries on the Mediterranean from the west to east on the northern lip of Africa were in Roman times called Mauretania (opposite Spain and France); Africa (from which the whole continent later took its name, opposite France and Italy); Cyrenaica, opposite Greece; and Egypt, opposite Asia

Minor. Forays were made against the Ethiopians but they were not conquered. One trouble spot of identification on the old maps is the tendency of many cartographers to put Libya on the coast. If this were true, the mention of Libya here in Ezekiel 38 and Daniel 11 would be confusing, since Ethiopia and Libya are said to be allies of the king of the north and, in Daniel 11:42-43, it is stated that the king of the north will "stretch forth his hand . . . upon . . . the land of Egypt" and "have power over the treasures" by means of the activities of his southern confederates, "the Lybians and the Ethiopians."

It is my conviction that the king of the south mentioned in Daniel 11:40 is an ally of the king of the north, who makes his assault on the vulnerable portions of the territory of Egypt, ruled jointly by the beast (Roman leader in the city of Rome and the head of the Western Confederacy) and his ally in Jerusalem (the Jewish leader called the false prophet in Rev 13). .

The usual interpretation is that the future king of the south is Egypt, evidently because the ruler of Egypt was the king of the south in the intertestament period. That was when the Ptolemaic dynasty of Egypt constantly meddled in the affairs of Israel, while the Egyptian ruler attacked (or was attacked by) the king of the north (the Seleucid dynasty of Syria). These were remnants from Alexander the Great's empire divided among his generals at his death. But, if Egypt is the king of the south in the day yet future to us, then Syria and Iraq would have to be the future king of the north. No major prophetic teachers seem satisfied with this view. The final blow to the theory is that it is Egypt that is *attacked by* the king of the south, as explained in Daniel 11 and here in Ezekiel 38.

The solution is aided by a map issued by the *National Geographic,* in which it is plain that Libya is not on the coast. Cyrenaica is on the coast and was the Roman province there. Libya is the desert *south of* the coast. Herodotus lacked knowledge of the interior of Africa, as did the Romans. His map of Africa looks as awkward today as early maps by Europeans of the western hemisphere. However, he clearly made Libya to be the *interior* of Africa south of the coast. Indeed, he put no other interior identification than Ethiopia with Libya. It seems to me that this fifth century B.C. historian indicates that the interior of Africa, as known then, could be summarized by the two terms *Libya* and *Ethiopia*. Then, in the language then available to describe the territory of the future king of the south, Ezekiel is led by the Spirit to use the two terms which would permit the idea of the whole continent of Africa today, except for that part which later pertained to the king of the west, the Romans, namely, the thin northern lip of Africa on the coast.

This leaves only "Persia" in 38:5. It is certainly known that this area was just beyond the boundary of the old Roman Empire. The Oxford Bible Atlas states that Rome's area was "roughly bounded by the Atlantic, Britain, the Rhine, the Danube, and the Euphrates, and by the Arabian and the Sahara deserts." Whether Persia is a single ally of the king of the north, or stands for the hordes of the kings of the east, who will come with an army of 200 million men (Rev 9 and 16), is not clear for a decisive conclusion. It is indeed possible and even plausible, if we follow the analogy of Ethiopia and Libya being used to stand for the whole continent of Africa. And we do know they are allies of the king of the north. It is not clear whether the kings of the sunrise (East) will come on their own, perhaps even as enemies of Russia, or whether they will come as the third prong of the attack of the armies of south, north, and east against Palestine in collaboration. We are told that the king in Jerusalem, while he has been drawn south (into Egypt) to meet the assault of the invading king of the south, will be troubled by "tidings out of the east and out of the north," as though both groups are marching at the same time against Palestine (Dan 11:44). Thus there is nothing to hinder prearranged assaults by all three as allies, or by the first two (south and north) as allies and the east independently.

It is plain, therefore, that these names in Ezekiel 38:5-6 carry far greater meaning than has been commonly attributed to them. In any event, the king of the north makes his assault after having cultivated and obtained allies to the south and the east, in addition to the nations immediately contiguous to him.

Years ago, when Bible students stated that the Bible indicated that the king of the north would be Russia and Germany with Russia as the head nation, people were obviously unconvinced. Even as late as World War II this seemed incredible. Russia had just been stopped at the Mannerheim Line of Finland, who held out an unbelievably long time against the great colossus of Russia. At that time no one would have dreamed that Russia in a few short years would become the great military power that she is. With the defeat and occupation of Germany by Russia for the first time it was apparent that prophecy was in process of fulfillment, getting ready for the time God's clock would strike.

The same may be said of the east and the south. Except for Japan no one in the Far East had any military power. Then in quick succession, China (where the scholar was lauded and the soldier despised), Korea, the Philippines, the nations of former Indo-China, Indonesia, Malaysia, and finally Pakistan and India have developed awesome military power. And at long last Africa is awaking to militarism and unity. All of these movements toward unity and military power are simply getting the kettle simmering for the boiling process yet to take place in God's time when He is going to "make Jerusalem a cup of trembling . . . and a burdensome stone for all people: all that burden themselves with it shall be cut in pieces, though all the people of the earth be gathered together against it. And it shall come to pass in that day, that I will seek to destroy all the nations that come against Jerusalem" (Zec 12:2-3, 9).

THE ACTION

We have somewhat anticipated this portion by the remarks made in the previous section. There, however, we were identifying the "who are involved" rather than the sequence of events. My conclusions as to the order of events are largely based on the sequence of Daniel 11:40-45, when read with Ezekiel 38—39 and Zechariah 14.

The king of the south pushes at the southern territory (Egypt) particularly committed to the care of the Jewish leader in Jerusalem by his ally and overlord, the head of the western world with headquarters in Rome. It would appear from Daniel 11:42-43 that the king of the south will be successful in actually invading Egypt and taking some of its treasure in behalf of his ally, the king of the north.

By this prearranged assault, the king of the south draws the Jewish king away from Palestine and his capital, Jerusalem, giving the king of the north opportunity to make an assault against Jerusalem. I understand Zechariah 14:2 to indicate that this assault by the king of the north will be successful; that Jerusalem will be taken, the population mauled, and many taken captive. Certainly, the elaborate description given in Ezekiel 38 of the attack of Gog, the king of the north, makes it clear that it is a gigantic, horrendous assault. Every indication is that, except for the intervention of God, nothing but success would crown the campaign, brilliantly conceived by the feint from the south to get the defender out of Jerusalem and off guard.

Of course, in recent years the papers are full of Russia's attempt to dominate the Middle East. But one thing that has not often been pointed out is the fact that this is not a new idea to Russia. Russia has not been unified and strong enough to do much before, but even Peter the Great, who was czar of Russia from 1672 to 1725, urged this policy on them: "We must progress as much as possible in the direction of

Constantinople and India. He who can get possession of these places is the real ruler of the world."

He went on to explain that he who controlled the cross-roads of the world, represented by the Middle East, would split the world and be able to say what he wished to both East and West, because he would be straddling the world.

Thus, Ezekiel 38:9 describes Russia's coming against Palestine like a storm (cf. v. 18). The masses of his army are described in terms of warfare (weapons and equipment) of the day in which Ezekiel was writing. It is not helpful to prophecy, nor is it good exposition, to push the literal in such cases. Had God used, centuries ahead of time, a description of weapons yet to be developed (e.g., tanks, airplanes), this would have been confusing to Christians through the centuries. We understand that God is revealing that a large, well-equipped army will assault and will be initially successful. Daniel 11:40 describes the invasion similarly, "like a whirlwind."

The Jewish king evidently blunts the assault of the king of the south, for nothing is further said of him; and hearing disturbing news (Dan 11:44) out of the east and the north, he hastens homeward. Of course, the news alluded to was the fact that the king of the north had invaded his land and taken his capital city; and, as though that were not enough, the kings of the sunrise are marching toward his country with their vast army of 200 million men. So, he hastens back, only to find a ruined Jerusalem, mauled by the invasion of the king of the north (so much so that he has to set up "the tents of his palace between the sea and the glorious holy mountain," Dan 11:45, ASV). But to his joy he finds the king of the north's army has been supernaturally destroyed. Yet, there is no time for relaxing. The kings of the east are on their way with their huge army! Therefore, now joined by his Roman ally and his troops, he hastens north to Megiddo to draw up battle defenses against the kings of the East.

We are not told that a battle takes place between them.

Evidently at this strategic time the sign of the Son of man appears, causing them to turn their attention from each other to Christ, whom they blasphemously defy. Suffice it to say, they do this to their own destruction, as recorded in Revelation 19. Christ slays them with the brightness of His coming, on His way down to the Mount of Olives, where His feet will touch as prophesied. Nothing is specifically said about the fate of the armies of the kings of the East, but the last mention of them places them at Armageddon (Rev 16:12, 16). Presumptively, therefore, their armies are destroyed at the same time as the western armies of the beast and false prophet, in accordance with God's stated purpose in Zechariah 12:9 to destroy the armies of all the nations of the world.

THE OUTCOME OF GOG'S INVASION

Ezekiel's language rises to rhetorical heights. God's face is said to be against Gog (38:2; 39:1). "I will turn thee back, and put hooks into thy jaws" (38:4). He has spoken in jealousy for His land in the fire of wrath against the invader (v. 19a). Thus there is to be "a great shaking" (v. 19b); an earthquake (v. 20); internal dissension (v. 21); pestilence, blood, overflowing rain, and great hailstones (v. 22).

The result is that five-sixths of his army is destroyed on the mountains of Israel (39:2). Presumptively, the king of the north does not want to get caught on this narrow strip of land between the desert and the sea, when he hears the Jewish leader is returning from Egypt and his Roman ally is moving toward him. Probably worst of all is the news that the eastern kings' gigantic army is now moving into the eastern portion of the western empire, since the invasion of the king of the north has made invalid the eastern defenses (drying up of the Euphrates). So the king of the north tries to return home, when supernaturally he is destroyed "on the mountains of Israel," like an earlier king of the north, Sennacherib of Assyria (Is 37).

So great will be the loss of life that it will require seven months to bury the dead (Eze 39:12), and special men will be employed even after that to bury bones that are continually found (39:11, 14). Further, it will take seven years before all the material of war is finally disposed of (39:9).

Six Views as to the Time of the Invasion

Probably this is where the greatest lack of unity has been apparent. It would seem wise to eliminate two of the least likely viewpoints before considering those that are more likely. These two views are at opposite ends of the spectrum and require little attention.

First, there are some who see no distant invasion, but have identified this invasion as one by a king of the north (probably Nebuchadnezzar II of Babylon) shortly after Ezekiel's prophecy. This will not fit, for Ezekiel 38:8 and 38:16 plainly say that the invasion envisioned is "after many days . . . in the latter days." Further, it will be in a time when there are "unwalled villages" (v. 11), which certainly could not fit in with Palestine of that day. Finally and most important, Nebuchadnezzar had already invaded Palestine before 600 B.C. and the dates for Ezekiel's prophesying are 593–560 (Whitcomb).

Second, there are those who persist in confusing this Ezekiel 38–39 invasion with a later mention of Gog and Magog in Revelation 20. A careful reading will show that the only similarity is the name. The Revelation 20 event is after the one thousand-year reign and represents a final attempt of Satan, after his release from the pit, to stir up trouble against Christ. Evidently, quite a few born during the one thousand-year period (who have yielded feigned obedience to Christ but have not been converted) will seize the opportunity to join Satan's revolt. Clearly, also, the northern lands provide most of the group who rebel. However, they presumably do not arrive at Jerusalem. They just start toward it, only to be destroyed by fire from heaven. Everything in the Ezekiel prophecy implies a tribulational setting.

The next two less likely views are the third and fourth. The third view suggests that the time is at the *beginning* of the millennium. This is based on verses 8 and 11 of Ezekiel 38, especially the thought of "dwelling safely." The fourth view is similar. It holds that the invasion is at the beginning of the tribulation period and likewise depends upon the phrase "dwell safely," on the theory that the tribulation period starts peacefully (cf. Rev 6:1-2).

Both of these views are invalid. There is a great deal of difference between "being in no known danger of assault" and "dwelling safely." No doubt, immediately after Israel signs the seven-year treaty with the West, there will have been much political power exerted to insulate the Arabs, so that a temple in Jerusalem can be built under the protection of the western ruler in Rome. It is possible that this could be the time for an assault from the north. However, so climactic is the assault, so extensive its overthrow by God, so drastic its damage to Jerusalem, which would by this time include a temple, that it does not seem to fit the picture of the movements of various other armies in addition to the king of the north. It seems to belong to the latter part of the tribulation period.

As to view 3, in the early millennium, it is contradictory and inconsistent with all that is told us about the absolute sovereignty of Christ, ruling with a rod of iron, to conceive of such an invasion being allowed to take place at any time in the millennium, and certainly not that early in it. For at the Lord's return to earth after the destruction of the armies, the civilian populations are tried. Unbelieving Jews and Gentiles will be purged from the kingdom. Thus, where would vast numbers of rebels come from early in the millennium? Especially is it unthinkable that large areas of the world would hold such attitudes toward Christ, or be able to mount so large a campaign.

This leaves us with two views most likely to include the

correct one. In the fifth view the destruction of the northern army is equated with the destruction of the armies at Armageddon. And finally, the sixth view makes the destruction a prelude, shortly before Armageddon.

The chief objection to the Armageddon identification is that neither in Ezekiel nor Daniel nor Revelation is a destruction of a northern army mentioned in connection with Armageddon. For instance, it cannot be proved that the armies of the kings of the east are destroyed at Armageddon; but it can be suggested on the basis that the last mention of the eastern armies is in a context with Armageddon (Rev 16:12, 16).

But nowhere is there a mention of Armageddon in a context of the army of the king of the north. A great destruction is not limited to Armageddon. God has done that before, as mentioned with Sennacherib, the earlier king of the north. There is also nothing that can be cited against a destruction of the northern army prior to Armageddon.

Following the sequence earlier suggested in this message seems to put everything in place and in harmony with Scripture. Thus in Daniel 11:40:

1. There is first an assault by a king of the south.
2. There is then an assault by a king of the north. It would appear that precisely at this point God would intervene with destruction in the terms of Ezekiel 38—39.
3. The rumor of the kings of the east (Dan 11:44) becomes actual (Rev 9:13-18; 16:12, 16).
4. God destroys them (the armies of the east) and the armies of the beast and false prophet at Armageddon where they have met for battle with each other. (Otherwise, why is the western army drawn up at Armageddon? Against whom?) But God will be against both of them!

This, then, is a suggested solution. In the meantime, look up, not around! So, take courage and move on toward tomorrow! The best for the church is yet ahead!

13

The Sinister Men

PROPHECY is important and extensive, not only in the books usually thought of as prophetic books, but in many other Bible books as well.

In a book like Daniel, where there is so much prophecy, it is important to be alert to two things. First, to distinguish those prophecies which have already been fulfilled from those prophecies yet to be fulfilled. Second, to observe the intimate detail in which those already fulfilled prophecies came to fulfillment. By watching the method of their fulfillment, we can learn what to look for in current and future fulfillment.

Both aspects of prophecy are therefore important and should be kept in balance. Fulfilled prophecy should not be neglected in favor of unfulfilled, nor vice versa. And certainly prophecies yet to be fulfilled must not be confused with, or subordinated to, prophecies already fulfilled.

Those who accuse us premillennialists of overzealous interest in prophecy *yet* to be fulfilled, spend disproportionate time and space in seeking to prove that these men are actually historical characters in prophecy *already* fulfilled.

There has always been substantial interest among Bible students in attempting to establish the identity of the men who, in the future end time of the world's history, will seek to "wear out the saints of the most High" (obviously God's "Israel"), like the man described in Daniel 7:25.

Certainly God has seen fit to provide abundant detail in many parts of His prophetic Word concerning these men, awesome in their hate and, within the permission of His will, remarkably effective in their persecution and destruction of large numbers of believing Israelites who will reject their specious claims and courageously look for their true Messiah's return to deliver them from these monsters of iniquity. This is not only true of the Old Testament, but is a constant emphasis of the New Testament as well (e.g. Mt 24:9, 15-24, 29-31; Ro 11:23-26; Rev 6:9-10; 7:2-4; 13:7, 9-10; 14:9-12; 18: 4-6, 20; 19:2, 15, 20; 20:10).

Although there has been a considerable body of literature written about the leader of the future revived fourth (Western-Roman) empire, brought before us in Daniel 2 and 7, there has been far less written about the future men of chapters 8 and 11, and particularly about the man of chapter 8. Most of that written about the man of chapter 8 has labored the fact that he is to be distinguished from the future man of chapter 7, designated "the little horn," although the phrase occurs in both chapters. Very little has been written about the sinister man in chapter 8 per se.

Further, although there has been almost complete unanimity among permillennial writers in equating the future man of Daniel 2 with the future "little horn" of Daniel 7, there has been considerable difference of conclusion as to who is the future man of chapter 8 and who the future man of chapter 11. Few writers have given attention to any possible correlation between the end-time men of chapters 8 and 11, such as they have repeatedly affirmed in equating the man of chapter 2 with the man of chapter 7.

Despite all the careful writing to distinguish "the little horn" of Daniel 8 from "the little horn" of Daniel 7 (e.g., note on 8:9, *New Scofield Bible,* p. 910), it is unfortunately true that the average Bible readers (and even earnest students of prophecy) are generally confused and tend to equate them, unless cautioned not to do so. Since this is true, it is easy to see why few writers have spent time comparing the future men of chapters 8 and 11. They have been preoccupied with the men of chapters 7 and 8. It is the purpose of this study to inquire into this neglected theme and throw light, if possible, on the two sinister men of the future brought to our attention in chapters 8 and 11.

How Many Antichrists: One, Two, or Many?

An almost casual acquaintance with the book of Revelation reveals that there are two important enemies of Christ and of "God's Israel" prophesied under the designation of "beasts" in Revelation 13. Although there are a number of interesting distinctions between the two, it is equally clear that they share a great deal in common. Certainly, they are so closely allied that they work together as though one. I am sure that this fact has led to the almost humorous result (if it were not basically distressing) that some very excellent expositors have been so insistent on their view of which of the two is the Antichrist that they have almost come to swords points over the identification. Indeed, I have known men who had their fellowship cooled by too-warm debates over the matter. I remember two devout Bible teachers who, on every occasion I happened to be with them, managed to get the conversation around to some added point which each felt—since their previous meeting—made clearer the fact that the one they identified as the Antichrist was the one, if properly interpreted.

Naturally this has been distressing to all serious prophetic students, and confusing to a young man trying to make correct identifications, as was my case at the time. Fortunately for me, a good many years ago I came to the conclusion that this debate was not only profitless, but basically in error. My reason will be found in chapter 11 on "The Power Struggle in the End Time." In essence, my point is that our Lord never referred to *one* Antichrist. He flatly stated the opposite, as witness:

> "Many shall come in my name, saying, I am Christ" (Mt 24:5).
>
> "Many false prophets shall rise" (Mt 24:11).
>
> "Then if any man shall say unto you, Lo, here is Christ, or there; believe it not. For there shall arise false Christs (plural), and false prophets (plural), and shall shew great signs and wonders; insomuch that, if it were possible, they (plural) shall deceive the very elect" (Mt 24: 23-24).

Thus, there is not to be just one Antichrist. Our Lord said there would be "many." The answer, then, to the perennial question, "Which of the two beasts of Revelation 13 is the Antichrist?", is unequivocally: "both!"

IRONSIDE'S SUGGESTION

One of the special bonuses which came to the first class in Dallas Theological Seminary (1924-27) was the privilege of having H. A. Ironside available as one of the visiting Bible teachers for two months, rather than the usual one, of the school year. (This was possible because he had not yet accepted the pastorate of the Moody Church, which, from then on, precluded his giving more than one series of lectures per year.) This availability extended far beyond his thrilling classes to personal conversations. Being both personable and generous with his time, he was often sought out by students for his solution to Bible problems. While working on a course thesis for "The New Testament Mysteries," I asked his advice about the important passage on this subject in 2 Thessalonians 2, "the mystery of iniquity," which was already at work in Paul's day but would come to its climax in the end time.

Ironside came up with a very illuminating idea which I have fervently wished he had included in one of his excellent books, because it helped me and has helped others with whom I have shared it, in and out of classes. He suggested that, as we read the Old Testament and a substantial part of The New, there appears to be *only one* man who is the great enemy of God and Israel. It is only when we get to Revelation 13 that we find that there are two particularly sinister enemies, much as we read about the resurrection all through the Bible, as though it were one event at one time (e.g., Jn 5:28-29), only to come to Revelation 20 and find that there are two resurrections, not synchronous but separated by 1,000 years.

Just as we take the light of Revelation 20 back into our study of previous Scripture, so we may take the light of Revelation 13 back into previous Scripture. Without that light, no one could definitely assert that there was more than one great enemy of Israel in the end time. The similarities of the two men are so great that previous Scripture combines them as though they were one.

So Ironside suggested that in 2 Thessalonians 2, we may throw the light of Revelation 13 back on it and see, very probably, both men, as follows:

"The first beast" may well be described by the words of 2 Thessalonians 2:3-4 as the "man of sin . . . who opposeth and exalteth himself above all that is called God, or that is worshipped; so that he, as God sitteth in the temple of God, shewing himself that he is God." Then, verses 8-10 may well be a description of "the second beast" of Revelation 13 in the words: "Then shall that Wicked (one) be revealed" (i.e., after the departure of the Holy Spirit and the church with Him—the presently restraining power of verses 5-7) ". . . even him, whose coming is after the working of Satan with all power and signs and lying wonders (e.g., the miraculous image of Rev 13:1-15), and with all deceivableness of unrighteousness in them that perish."

This is an intriguing suggestion, and confirms what our Lord said concerning multiple "Christs"/"false prophets," though the overriding emphasis of Old and New Testaments seems to prepare us for only one striking person with supernatural (but not omnipotent) powers who will, like his master Satan, deceive and persecute the people of God. It is interesting that we must arrive nearly at the end of the Bible (Rev. 13) before we are clearly told that there are two men actually involved, closely allied, whereas up to that point, we would never be able to say dogmatically that there is more than one man before us in 2 Thessalonians 2, and other passages.

Some might wish to counter with the fact that other men will, in the end time, come against Palestine, such as the king of the south, the king of the north and, presumptively, advancing kings from the east, implied in "tidings out of the east will trouble" the man who is reigning in Jerusalem in the end time (Dan 11:44). However, it should be made very clear that these men do not come to attack "God's Israel." In fact, our Lord plainly implies that in proportion as God's remnant can flee from Jerusalem and Palestine to other portions of the world, their relative safety will be increased (Mt 24:15ff.). These people may persecute a fleeing remnant but it is a side issue. Thus, they do not come against Palestine for this purpose at all. Rather, it is my conviction that the loudmouthed boasting of Satan's man infuriates these rulers of other portions of the world, and they come to defeat him and stop his boasting. (In the chapter on "The Power Struggle in the End Time," I take the position that it is a great mistake to hold the usual idea of one man/one world ruler; that, rather, there are *four areas* of power matched by military might, with kings of east, north, south, and the west, the latter being the revived fourth empire of Daniel 2 and 7.) Suffice it to say that ultimately the reason is stated in Zechariah 12:2-3, 9, that God draws these armies against the man in Jerusalem that he might "destroy all the nations that come against Jerusalem." The western empire leaders are, of course, also destroyed by God at Armageddon (Rev 19:17-21). It is they who assault God's Israel (Rev 13:7, 15; 12:12-17).

In the light of what has been said thus far, it becomes all the more important to identify accurately the sinister men of the future in the book of Daniel, with help from all the Bible. Since it is already generally accepted that the end-time man of Daniel 2 and 7 is the man in Rome, ruling over the ten-divisioned revival of the fourth empire (Rev 13:3; 17:10), I shall give my attention to the men of chapters 8 and 11; which brings us to the question, How shall we go about it? It is my purpose, first, to examine the historically fulfilled portions; second, to look closely at the future man of Daniel 11; third, at the future man of Daniel 8. And finally, ask: Are they two different men? If so, whom? Or to ask, Are they more properly to be equated? And, if so, who is the man so equated?

HISTORICAL BACKGROUND TO THE HISTORICAL TYPE OF THE END-TIME MAN OR MEN IN DANIEL 8 AND 11

Before we are in any position to seek to identify the future man or men of Daniel 8 and 11, we must get the flavor of the passages involved, see the context, and carefully trace how the near-view fulfillments of these prophecies have taken place. Only by this approach can we discover where the transition is to be found between the fulfilled and the yet unfulfilled portions, complicated as it is by the necessity of mentally inserting the whole church age, which was not revealed—although in the plan of God—until after Israel had rejected her Messiah in a valid offer of Himself as King (e.g., Mt 13:11, 17, 34-35; Eph 3:1-5, esp. v. 5; Col 1:25-26). To this period of 2,000 years, not foreseen by Old Testament prophets (1 Pe 1:10-12), one must add nearly 200 further years to get the whole period of time which must be mentally inserted interpretationally between the passage concerning the historical Antiochus Epiphanes and his antitype who is yet to come in the future. We have our Lord's own precedent for this interpretational method. When He went to His home-town synagogue in Nazareth, and began reading from the Isaiah scroll (61:1-2), Luke 4:16-21 tells the story of how He stopped His quotation in the midst of a sentence, before the words ". . . to proclaim . . . the day of vengeance of our God," because these words did not apply to His then present ministry on earth, and would not be fulfilled until the events of the tribulation period immediately preceding His second coming to the earth.

Daniel 8 spends much more detail on the relation of the second (Persian) empire and the third (Grecian) kingdoms than does chapter 11. In contrast, chapter 11 gives an abundance of detail concerning what happened between Alexander the Great and Antiochus Epiphanes in the third (Grecian) kingdom, not given in chapter 8. Both chapters show deep concern over what will happen to the Jewish people through the wicked cruelty of Antiochus. Both chapters say things about the historical Antiochus, already historically fulfilled, which become graphic illustrations of a yet future and more awesome enemy of Israel in the great tribulation. Thus, in both chapters the near and far-view overlap, and then skip to the yet to be identified end-time monster. It is of great importance to see that some details could not possibly have been fulfilled by the historical Epiphanes. For instance, the historical Antiochus died at Tabor in Persia, while the future man will meet his end *in Palestine,* the place of "the glorious holy mountain" (Mount Zion) "between the seas" (the Mediterranean and the Dead Seas, 11:45).

Now to address ourselves to the portion historically fulfilled. In the vision at the beginning of chapter 8, Daniel sees a ram pushing westward, northward, and southward. This is precisely stated by verse 20 to be Media/Persia (with two horns, v. 3), Media later becoming eclipsed by Persia (the higher horn) in the joint kingdom.

Similarly, in Daniel 11 the Persian kingdom is brought before us in verse 2, beginning with the current monarch, Cyrus II the Great (559-530 B.C.). Cyrus was followed by his son, Cambyses II (530-522 B.C.). After Cambyses came Gaumata, a rebel impostor who is sometimes counted but often skipped in the count of Persian kings because he had no right to the throne. His revolt was put down by Darius I Hystaspes (522-486 B.C.). Then came Xerxes I the Great (486-465 B.C.). Many expositors count him as "the fourth" of verse 2c, although some—by not counting Gaumata—feel Artaxerxes I (465-425 B.C.) is the man intended, a man who surpassed his predecessors.

There is no problem in either chapter in identifying Alexander the Great, the "mighty king" of 11:3, founder of the third (Grecian) empire of the four empires preannounced in Daniel 2 and 7. He is seen in 8:5 as "the notable horn" of the he-goat (Grecian) kingdom (8:21), who smashes into and overcomes the ram (Persian) empire (8:6-7).

Scripture is gratifyingly precise in its identifying details! For instance, as Babylon had as its national symbol the winged lion (7:4), so the ram and he-goat symbols are easily read by the student of history, even if 8:20-21 had not actually named the kingdoms involved. Persian kings wore a ram's head of gold instead of a crown, and the guardian spirit of Persia was pictured as a ram with two horns. Persian coins bore the ram impress. Similarly, the goat symbol was often used of Macedonia, the portion of Greece where Alexander's father, Philip, was king and where Alexander was brought up. Caremus, an early king of Macedonia, called his city Aege (later Edessa), which meant "the goat city." These are not coincidences but evidences of the significant way God makes clear the true import of visions when He uses that method of communication.

Alexander's death is dramatically foretold: "the great horn" is "broken" (8:8, 21-22; 11:4). Alexander died at the age of 32 (323 B.C.). His four generals ("not of his posterity," 11:4b; "four notable ones," 8:8, 22) murdered his sons and split the kingdom four ways. Daniel 8 gives no details whatever of that which immediately followed. Indeed, it skips from Alexander to Antiochus Epiphanes (8:9ff., 23). Observe that 8:9 does not say "one of them," i.e., one of the four generals, but "out of one of them," i.e., a later man out of one of the four kingdoms carved out by the generals.

But Daniel 11 provides some extensive data on the intervening period between Alexander and Epiphanes, beginning at verse 5. Of the four kingdoms formed by Alexander's generals, only two come into the purview of prophecy, and that only because they affect Israel. Bible-stated directions relate to Palestine, so when we read in 11:5, "the king of the south," it refers to the first king of the Ptolemaic dynasty of Egypt, Ptolemy I Soter (323-285 B.C.). Likewise, "the king of the north" (11:6) refers to a second part of Alexander's split kingdom, north of Palestine. This was the Seleucid dynasty of Syria and Armenia.

There follows one of the most detailed series of predictions of future events in the Bible. The intimacies of fulfillment are a striking proof of the divine origin of the Scriptures and are so declared to be by God (Is 46:9-10; 47:12-13; 48:3, 5).

As we look through this section, it is crucial to observe that regardless of whether the attack comes from the north (Syria) against Egypt, or from the south (Egypt) against Syria, Israel and Palestine bear the brunt of the coming and going of the respective invader's army. Israel suffers regardless of who wins.

The first ruler of the Seleucid line in Syria was Seleucus I Nicator (312-281 B.C.), who was simply a subordinate at first of Ptolemy I of Egypt ("one of Ptolemy's princes," 11:5), but in time he gained his independence and surpassed Ptolemy I.

An attempt at peace, by intermarriage of the two kingly lines, was not successful (11:6). Antiochus II Theos (261-246 B.C.) divorced his wife, Laodice, and disinherited their son, Callinicus. By previous agreement with Ptolemy II Philadelphus (285-246 B.C.), Ptolemy then gave the Egyptian princess, his daughter Berenice, in marriage to Antiochus II. But Laodice engineered the murder of Berenice, her child, and her entire retinue. Then, Ptolemy, Berenice's father and protector, died.

But "a branch out of her (Berenice's) roots" (11:7), her brother Ptolemy III Euergetes I (246-222 B.C.), invaded Syria, avenged his sister, and returned to Egypt with valuable booty (11:8-9). An attempt by Antiochus II at reprisal failed (11:9). He was badly defeated and a storm destroyed his fleet.

The career of one of the more important Syrian kings, Antiochus III the Great (223-187 B.C.), is described next in 11:10-19. He was successful at first (11:10) but was stunned by his defeat at Raphia by Ptolemy IV Philopator (223-203 B.C.) in an attempt to invade Egypt. However, Antiochus was more successful in his next expedition because the boy king, Ptolemy V Epiphanes (203-181 B.C.), was checkmated through the opposition of a group of rebel Jewish residents of Egypt ("robbers of thy people," 11:14). Ptolemy's best soldiers ("chosen people," 11:15) were defeated near Sidon by Antiochus III (11:16).

Later, Antiochus III's strategy to obtain Egypt backfired. He entered into a treaty of peace by giving Ptolemy V his daughter in marriage. The girl was Cleopatra, evidently very beautiful (11:17). But his daughter sided with her Egyptian husband against her father. Whereupon Antiochus gathered an immense army and fleet and attacked Asia Minor and Greece (11:18), but Ptolemy and Cleopatra invited the protection of the Romans. Lucius Scipio defeated Antiochus III, thereby causing "the reproach . . . to cease" (11:18), i.e., the reproach against the Romans for their previous failure to protect Egypt and Greece. Antiochus III died ignominiously while on his way home from Greece, when he aroused the fury of worshipers by attempting to plunder their temple to get tribute to give to Rome (11:19). His successor, Seleucus IV Philapator (187-175 B.C.) sent Heliodorus into the "kingdom" (Judah) to plunder that temple ("the glory of the kingdom"), but on his return Heliodorus poisoned his master, who died "neither in anger, nor in battle" (11:20).

ANTIOCHUS IV EPIPHANES: THE AWESOME ARCHETYPE OF THE END-TIME MAN (OR MEN)
(Dan 8:9-14, 23; Dan 11:21-35)

Much as the previous kings hurt Israel, whether from Egypt or Syria, none can be compared with Antiochus IV Epiphanes (175-164 B.C.). In his deceitful actions, character, and fiendish cruelty, climaxed by his desecration of the temple altar, he aptly illustrates and foreshadows the future monster of iniquity revealed in the closing predictions of these chapters (8:23-25; 11:36-45). But he does not fulfill them! I say this because the Lord Jesus Christ in Matthew 24:15, long after Antiochus Epiphanes, plainly says that 11:31 (cp. 8:11-13) has a yet future fulfillment, in addition to anything that the historical Antiochus did in partial fulfillment.

Truly this man was "a vile person" (11:21). He was a past master at flattery and treachery (8:25; 11:21-23). He despoiled Palestine in a far more systematic and devastating way than any of his predecessors (8:9-13, 24; 11:24). Though shrewd and clever, selecting for himself the title Epiphanes (i.e., "Illustrious"), he was called Epimanes (i.e., "Madman") by his detractors.

His first expedition against Greece was highly successful (11:25-26). A grim bit of ironic humor is seen in the prediction of 11:27 (cp. 8:23), where Epiphanes is pictured as sitting with the Egyptian king at what was ostensibly a "peace" table, while both men, under the cover of honeyed words, vie to outdo each other in tricks of semantics; at the same time, each knows that the other is lying! But the problem is, what is the lie and what is the truth?

Later, a second expedition against Egypt was not successful. The Greeks and the Romans intervened (11:29-30). This expedition underlines the insincerity of the "peace" talks of 11:27. History records that the Roman general drew a circle around Epiphanes with his sword on the ground and, as it were, put him "under house arrest," forbidding him any further access to Egypt.

A false rumor reached Jerusalem that Epiphanes had been slain in Egypt. The populace were delirious with joy. However, their premature response to the false report infuriated Antiochus and he viciously punished the Jews on his way back to Syria. Indeed, "his heart" was set "against the holy covenant" of God with Israel (11:28; 8:10-11). Unfortunately for Israel, prior to this, he had been successful in securing quite a following of apostatizing Jews in his Hellenization program. He seized the occasion to pollute the sanctuary by sacrificing a sow on the altar, making further sacrifice impossible for a period of 2,300 days, not quite seven years (11:31; 8:11-14).

Many godly Jews resisted and were put to death with brutal cruelty. Many were sold into slavery. The hearts of Jews were sorely tested. Tatford suggests that 8:11-12a should be considered a parenthesis and that a better wording of verse 12a would be: "And a time of trial was appointed unto the continual burnt offering by reason of transgression." Some Jews remained true and their courageous resistance led to the Maccabean revolt which liberated Israel from Syria's yoke (11:33-35).

The events of these passages (11:30-35; 8:9-14, 23) are literally but partially fulfilled. They are typical. The two aspects overlap the historical fulfillment of Epiphanes' day with the horrendous yet to be fulfilled events of the great tribulation, as Christ predicted (Mt 24:15-22). The *type* is Antiochus Epiphanes. The *antitype* is the willful king of 11:36-45 (also called "the king of fierce countenance" in 8:23-25). There will be a greater defilement of the temple in the end time (Rev 13:14-15). The Jews will likewise be divided then into two groups, the apostate and the faithful.

THE WILLFUL KING OF DANIEL 11: THE SINISTER MAN
OF THE END TIME (vv. 36-45)

It has been seen thus far that in chapters 8 and 11 the Holy Spirit has led us through a survey of important men and events during the second (Persian) and third (Grecian) empires. The men most delineated have been Alexander the Great, Antiochus III the Great, and Antiochus IV Epiphanes. The last named has been given particular prominence because he cruelly assaulted Israel and desecrated the temple, causing sacrifice to cease. In this latter, he became a glaring type of a more wicked and powerful person who will painfully hurt the Israel of God, i.e., true Jewish believers looking for deliverance at Messiah's return to earth (Mt 24:15-31). The climax of this future man's fury will also result from the desecration of the temple, causing sacrifice to cease (Rev 13:14-15).

Who is the man of whom 11:36-45 speak? What are the various views?

Amillennial expositors have denied any break between verses 35 and 36 and have seen the historical Antiochus as the fulfillment of the remainder of the chapter. This is, of course, impossible because the man in view is foretold to be present "at the time of the end" (v. 40). Other reasons for the necessity of seeing a considerable body of time between the historical Antiochus and the men of the tribulation period, yet future, have been given earlier in this chapter. It should therefore be borne in mind that a gap of approximately 2,200 years has already intervened.

Among those who see a future man as the only valid position, there has been a natural tendency to assume that this man will be another and final "king of the north," of whom Antiochus was an apt type. This analogy seems bolstered by the fact that in chapters 2 and 7, the end-time man is plainly one who as "the little horn" comes out of the ten-horned beast (cp. ten toes of the image), i.e., out of the final form of the fourth western (Roman) empire as revived. That interpretation is further affirmed by the fact that the supernatural stone (Christ) smites the image of chapter 2, not on the head, but on the feet replete with ten toes.

So those who hold the "king of the north" view ask, why should not this end-time man of chapter 11 be a horrendous expanded replica of Antiochus Epiphanes, and come out of the north (third, Grecian empire) to harass Israel in the end time as Antiochus did in what is now history?

There are good reasons why this is not the case, however tempting the analogy. In the first place, the most obvious reason is that that *fourth* empire *succeeded* the third empire, and will be around in its revived form at the time of the end. This is what is meant by the healing of "the deadly wound" of the sixth form of old Rome, which seemed to have died forever in A.D. 476 in the West, and 1453 in the East (Rev 13:3; cp. "the other is yet to come," 17:10). This reconstitution of the fourth kingdom is utterly unexpected and without precedent, and will cause great amazement (Rev 13:3-4). In the chapter, "The United States of the Western World," however, I seek to demonstrate that there are abundant and striking evidences of the growth of unity in the Western World, which will eventuate in the "healing" of the fourth empire, which historians have long ago written off.

Further, there is no passage of Scripture that even faintly suggests that the third (Grecian) empire is to be revived. On the contrary, the viewpoint of prophecy is that the four empires which God revealed to Nebuchadnezzar through Daniel were to succeed each other, not by destroying the previous empire, but by absorbing it: using its skills, attainments, and expertise, and profiting by its political and military ability.

To support this viewpoint on the four kingdoms, one should remember that the whole image is envisioned as being intact and standing when the stone smites the final form of the fourth empire. Further, to change the figure to the wild beasts of the jungle of chapter 7, the fourth beast is not described as a lion or bear or leopard, but as a strange sort of *composite* creature. The cue is given us in Revelation 13:2, where we see the fourth kingdom pictorially described in its revived form: "And the beast which I saw was like unto a leopard, and his feet were as the feet of a bear, and his mouth as the mouth of a lion." In other words, the fourth beast combines and continues the qualities that characterized the three previous kingdoms, which one by one conquered and absorbed one another until the fourth beast culminates as a combination of the three with itself. Hence, there is no first, nor second, nor third kingdom as an entity, either in the past after Rome took over, nor in the future. The fourth kingdom *is all four* of them, constituting *one* final beast in its final form. Thus there is no room in this fact for the theory of a third kingdom as revived and running alongside the revived fourth kingdom. The three ceased to exist, having been absorbed in and superseded by the fourth, which alone is said to be revived.

Another view has been advanced by some expositors, namely, that the man of 11:36ff. is the king of the north," (v. 40), in the sense that Syria was geographically part of the old Roman Empire, so in this geographical area a future man will arise and in the end time come and fight against the eastern ally (in Jerusalem) of the leader of the fourth empire (in Rome). This view does not commend itself. In the chapter already alluded to, "The Power Struggle of the End Time," I have raised a very real problem occasioned by the all too usual interpretation that the fourth revived empire is a "one ruler over all the earth" affair. I ask in that chapter how this can be, because successively the king of the south, then the king of the north, and finally the kings of the east (the latter with 200 million men) come against the eastern hub of the empire (Palestine). How can a man be said to be a world ruler who has no more control over his subjects than that?

But when one compounds that problem by suggesting that

the king of the north is from Syria, which was within even the *old* Roman Empire, and that this man—so close geograhically—could mount an invasion against his superiors and attack either Palestine or/and Egypt (as differing expositors declare), makes a preposterous hypothesis. What would the man in Rome and his eastern ally in Jerusalem be doing if they would not be aware of the hate and treachery of a man so close geographically, and so crush his rebellion before it got off the ground? Such incompetence is absurd in any kingdom worthy of the name. And, further, since most expositors identify the king of the north with Russia/Germany and her satellites (Eze 38-39), one would have to say that the northern invasion, as far as reaching Jerusalem is concerned, is successful (Zec 14:2-3). The whole proposition lacks clarity and coherence.

Further, it should be pointed out that, except for Egypt, no attacks were historically made against Palestine from any other direction than from the north. No one attacked across the desert from the east. With only two natural harbors in Palestine (Haifa and Joppa), no worthwhile assault could be made from the west by sea. So whether it was Syria, Assyria, Babylon, Persia, Greece, or Rome, the direction of attack was uniformly described as being "from the north." To limit "the north" to any one of the nations involved from time to time in attacks upon Israel, and to put future prophetic events in the straightjacket of a past and gone identification (such as Syria), is very poor hermeneutics, to say the least.

Then, since Syria became a part of the Roman Empire and could never again be legitimately designated as "the king of the north," by the same token it is my conviction that a colossal mistake has been made in the almost universal identification of Egypt as the "king of the south" of the end time, simply because this was the case during the days of the wars between the two kingdoms of the third empire, headed by two of Alexander's generals, the Seleucid dynasty of Syria in the north and the Ptolemaic dynasty of Egypt in the south.

Thus, just as Syria became part of the *fourth* empire, *so did Egypt.* Neither could any longer be considered *third* empire. In the chapter referred to previously, I have included a map of the first century A.D., showing that the following nations on the northern lip of Africa were part of Rome, namely, from east to west: Aegyptus, Cirenaica, Africa, Mauretania. Except for the Nile valley (Egypt), Rome never conquered any other part of Africa beyond the northern lip. Ethiopia and all of Africa, except the northern lip, were never in the Roman Empire.

Therefore, as the king of the north of verse 40 cannot be Syria, but some other power much further north (i.e., the Russian confederacy), so the king of the south cannot be Egypt. In fact, both Ezekiel 38 and Daniel 11 list Ethiopia and Libya as being allies of the king of the north in his assault on Palestine. They are said to be "at his steps" (11:43) and they are successful in their invasion of Egypt; acting in his behalf they have "power over the treasures . . . and over all the precious things of Egypt." So Egypt is not the king of the south doing the invading, but Egypt is invaded by "the king of the south" acting as ally of the "king of the north."

The map that Herodotus drew of Africa, crude as it was, plainly shows Libya to be what we call "the desert" south of the lip of North Africa. It was the great unknown interior. Of course, Egypt and Ethiopia were known and listed. Carefully constructed maps of first century A.D. Roman territory put Libya south of Cirenaica, south of the coast; not on the coast as occasional inaccurate maps show. Thus, I take it, in modern language these ancient descriptions are supposed to be understood as the continent of Africa, except for that part which was Roman and again will be in the fourth revived western empire. The strong trend to come of age on the part of the nations of Africa (e.g., the Organization of African States) is not window dressing, but preparation for what Scripture calls "the king of the south," who, in the end time, will "push at" the soft belly (Egypt) of the eastern end of the fourth empire, requiring the nearest associate of the man in Rome to rush to the rescue of his southern province, Egypt. This nearest associate is the man in Jerusalem, who moves quickly south to blunt the invasion, but not before Egypt has been entered and booty taken. This is precisely the occasion of the pre-planned assault of "the king of the north," who swoops down like a whirlwind against Palestine and Jerusalem when the Jerusalem leader has turned his back to overcome the attack on Egypt from the south (v. 40).

Thus far we have, I hope successfully, ruled out the identification of the willful king as: (1) the historical Antiochus Epiphanes; (2) some subordinate rebel king of Syria who, though in the fourth revived empire, treacherously attacks Jerusalem; and (3) the Russian confederacy, usually collated with Gog and Magog. Plainly it could not be the nations from the far east, since they come against Palestine and the willful king (vv. 44-45).

If these are eliminated, there are only two left who could possibly fulfill the requirements to be the willful king, namely, the head of the fourth empire with headquarters in Rome, or his Jewish ally in Jerusalem.

For a number of reasons I rule out the Roman leader. First and foremost, the whole scene of activity is Palestine. This is seen both by the fact that the man being attacked has his headquarters in Jerusalem (v. 45), and by the further fact that all directions in Scripture follow the familiar pattern of Old Testament geographical idiom: kings are mentioned as being "north" or "south" of Palestine. To argue that because the man in Rome possesses Palestine as part of his dominion, hence is seen present in his eastern subordinate, is both gratuitous and unlikely. The far more natural interpretation is to say that, if Palestine is being attacked, the man in Jerusalem is the one being attacked, and thus is the one being described. This being the case, the man in Jerusalem must be the willful king.

However, there are other and stronger reasons. The

description of this man in verses 36-39 fits a Jew much better than a Gentile. It is true that, as some expositors suggest, the words could be applied to a Gentile, but they apply much more naturally to a Jew. Observe the following:

"Neither shall he regard the God of his fathers" (v. 37) fits the Jewish context best. It could be said of a pagan (certainly unlikely of a professing Christian, as some have suggested) that he will reject the "gods of his fathers," as the word could be translated; but the Old Testament is replete with references to the covenant God, who makes promises to the *Jewish* fathers, Abraham, Isaac, and Jacob. For instance, God appears in the burning bush as "the God of Abraham . . . Isaac . . . and Jacob" and Moses says he will tell the people of Israel that "the God of your fathers (Abraham, Isaac, and Jacob) hath sent me unto you" (Ex 3:6, 13; cp. Deu 1:11; 4:1; Jos 18:3; 2 Ch 13:12; 28:9; Ezra 8:28, etc.). Why imagine a pagan when a Jew would meet the situation better? Does not this fit the man who reigns in Jerusalem? Is he not reigning when sacrifices are being made in a temple? Why would a pagan do this? Why do the Scriptures emphasize that he is a traitor to his people in causing sacrifice to cease when he breaks the covenant (Dan 9:27)?

Again, the next phrase, "nor the desire of women" (v. 37) makes more sense of a Jewish apostate who ignores the true Messiah, i.e., in the light of the historic "desire of (all Jewish) women" to have the honor of being the mother of Messiah.

The signs and wonders he will cause the image of Revelation 13:13, 15 to produce are indicated in Daniel 11:36 and 39. The wording of verse 38 would strongly point to his making this image of the Roman beast ("a foreign god") and his demand that all shall worship it.

The willful king anticipates Messiah's rewards to those who have been faithful to Him (Is 40:10; 62:11) in his rewarding of those apostates faithful to him, dividing the land among his followers (v. 39b, "for gain" equate reward).

Finally, the lofty pretension of this Jewish apostate leader (vv. 36, 37c), in which he shares with the Roman leader but exceeds him, are such that Paul applies, yea almost quotes these words, concerning the "man of sin" in 2 Thessalonians 2:3-4.

These considerations seem to point more dramatically to the Jewish apostate in Jerusalem than to any other man. Fittingly, "he shall come to his end, and none shall help him" (v. 45), not even his powerful associate in Rome. They are judged together by the returning Christ (Rev 19:20).

The King of Fierce Countenance of Daniel 8: The Sinister Man of the End Time

We have already examined the historical fulfillments of chapter 8 in respect to Alexander the Great's defeat of Persia, his death, the partition of his kingdom into four parts, and the most notable of the Seleucid kings of Syria who harassed Israel, Antiochus IV Epiphanes (8:9-14, 23).

We found that these details dovetailed with the historic fulfillment of chapter eleven's prophecies concerning the same persons (although many more persons were added in the chapter 11 data). There was nothing but unanimity.

We find an overlap in chapter 8, as we did in chapter 11, in a near and far view of Antiochus Epiphanes. But, as in chapter 11, there are details concerning a future antitype which were obviously not fulfilled by Antiochus. This overlap is particularly true of the description of Antiochus' fiendish character, his venomous hatred of the Jews, and his desecration of the temple, described in verses 9-14 and 23. Verse 23 is a strong transition overlap verse between the historical Antiochus and his future antitype. It moves to the future while acting as a bridge with the past.

The deceitful strategy of the end-time antitype is declared in verse 25. Verse 24b emphasizes his malignity in his hatred of, and attempt to seduce and destroy, the faithful in Israel. Verse 25b reiterates his self-vaunting pride, and v. 25d the bravado with which he will foolishly seek to stand up against the Lord Jesus Christ. Plainly, he will be allied with some other powerful person (v. 24a). His utter defeat is foretold in verse 25e.

It is evident that there are certain similarities to things we have said about the man in 11:36-45, but similarity does not prove identity. It is necessary, therefore, to weigh all possible identifications before arriving at a final conclusion. This we shall do.

NEAR VIEW REVIEW

First of all, it should be apparent that this "little horn" of 8:9 (which title some also refer to vv. 23-25) must not be confused with "the notable horn" of 8:5, 8, 21-22. That was the historical Alexander the Great who lived and died quite a while before the rise of the "little horn" of chapter 8.

Second, this person is not to be confused with "the little horn" of chapter 7 (vv. 8, 11, 20-21), because that man comes up amid ten horns (7:7-8, 24-27), which represent not the third, but the final, ten-divisioned end-time form of the fourth kingdom (cp., the ten toes of chapter 2). Whereas, the man in Daniel 8:9 is primarily a near-view "little horn" already historically fulfilled in Antiochus Epiphanes and coming out of the third kingdom. Whether the term "little horn" has any far-view application in Daniel 8 is debatable.

Third, since the ten horns do represent the final form of the fourth (western) kingdom, it is doubtful if there is any near-view application at all to the "little horn" of chapter 7. It appears there is only a *far* view, for he comes up after the ten horns are present (the ten-divisioned revived empire).

Hence, in the near view, "the little horn" of chapter 8 is Antiochus Epiphanes of the Seleucid dynasty of Syria, coming as he does "out of one of the four notable ones" (Alexander's four generals, who inherited and partitioned his kingdom). This cruel, crushing, crafty, enigmatic person was awesome and convincing in his deceit, filled with hatred toward the Jews. His antitype will have the same qualities, only heightened.

FAR VIEW: THREE VIEWS EVALUATED

First, it is my conviction that this future antitype is not the western fourth revived (Roman) leader, residing in Rome, and brought to us in chapters 2 and 7. The very fact that the man in Rome has already been delineated twice makes unlikely the need of a third rehearsal, particularly in a chapter immediately following chapter 7. The strong contrast between the fourth and third kingdoms, inherent in chapters 7 and 8 respectively, would argue against it. (See note, *New Scofield Reference Bible*, p. 910, on Dan 8:9). As we shall see later, some of the terminology would seem to argue for another solution.

Second, the most natural interpretation would be to have the antitype of the future come out of the *third* kingdom, "the king of the north" of the end time as Antiochus was in the near view of Daniel 11. This view would lead us to identify the man as the future end-time king of the north, "the Chief Prince of Rosh (Russia)," as per Ezekiel 38:13 (*New Scofield*, margin 1). This future invader of Palestine will be destroyed supernaturally by the Lord on the mountains of Israel (Eze 38:18—39:4), in the same way as the army of Sennacherib of Assyria, another earlier historical "king of the north," was supernaturally destroyed (Is 37:36-37). This future king is also called "the Assyrian" (in Is 10:24-25 and 14:24-25), and "Gog and Magog," with headquarters in Meshech (Moscow—west) and Tubal (Tobolsk—east) in the Ezekiel passages (38:1-2; 39:1). As mentioned, Daniel called this future man, "king of the north" (11:40). (See chapter 12, "Gog and Magog, Who and When?")

Far from being the western empire leader, this man will be the bitter rival of the Roman beast and his ally in Jerusalem, the apostate false prophet (Rev 13:11-18). Indeed, it is against the eastern part of the fourth (western) kingdom land, in its final ten toes/ten horns form that the king of the north mounts his assault (Dan 11:40-43).

This is a very natural interpretation and many expositors follow it. I formerly gave this identification priority. But as previously explained there are a number of good reasons, in my judgment, for rejecting this view.

The third view, and the one I have become increasingly convinced is the correct one, is to identify this future man of chapter 8 with the same man we accepted for this role in chapter 11.

As we saw there, most premillennialists make a shift from the historical "king of the north" (Antiochus Epiphanes) in 11:21-35 to a future willful king at verses 36-39, no matter whom they identify as the willful king. I have always been committed to the position that the antitype of Antiochus is the Jewish apostate leader in Jerusalem (the false prophet of Rev 13:11-18) who is allied with the beast of Revelation 13:1-10. I do this because this willful king is attacked by both the king of the south and the king of the north (Dan 11:40). It would seem ridiculous to make the willful king a future "king of the north," for why would he attack himself?

In chapter 11, we have an abrupt shift from the historical Antiochus (11:21-35) to the willful king at verse 36. I have been increasingly impressed that we have exactly the same thing, the same sudden switch, in chapter 8. If this be the case, chapter 8 may very well parallel chapter 11, in much the same way that we have seen chapter 7 parallel chapter 2. The latter two chapters have been identified by premillennialists, with complete unanimity, as being two perspectives of the same thing, the four world kingdoms which begin with Nebuchadnezzar II and conclude with events leading to the second coming of Christ, featuring the beast of Revelation 13:1-10, the awesome leader of the fourth revived western (Roman) empire.

In similar manner, in chapters 8 and 11, all expositors agree that the climactic figure in the *near* view is Antiochus Epiphanes. Why may we not have a parallel in the end-time figure? Why may not this sinister man of the end time be the same man, none other than the second beast of Revelation 13:11-18, that horrendous antitype of Antiochus, whose subtlety and ferocity against the Jews made him an apt illustration of this future monster who will double-cross his own people in the midst of the seventieth week of Daniel 9, by desecrating the sanctuary, and precipitating the great tribulation.

Only views two and three are real options, and I strongly lean toward this third view as having much more going for it and fewer problems.

14

The City from Outer Space

I. INTRODUCTION: THE METHOD OF JEWISH WRITINGS

THE NEW JERUSALEM! How wonderful are the thoughts which the very mention of this name evokes! How glorious a description is given to us in this last portion of the last book of our Bible, the book of Revelation, the unveiling of Jesus Christ in all His glory, with accompanying scenes that stagger the imagination.

It has been almost uniformly assumed that because we in the Western World have a habit of writing things sequentially and chronologically, this must be the Bible's way of writing. This is both true and untrue. Many times the story proceeds chronologically. But many times, the story goes back of the immediately previous chapter or paragraph to an earlier (often much earlier) time. Two examples will suffice as illustration. When one finishes Genesis 5 he is clear up to Noah. When one opens Genesis 6, we are taken back to Adam's children and their posterity. In Genesis 10, we are taken well along the genealogical route to names, persons, and some events (e.g., Gen 10:8-11) which are later than the story of Genesis 11:1ff. It can easily be shown that this is the Hebrew method of writing which we find often in the Bible and certainly in the book of Revelation. Every scholar emphasizes the heavy Jewish element in the book of Revelation. Indeed, in the 404 verses of Revelation, 278 contain references to the Jewish Scriptures. It is therefore in keeping with the method of Jewish thought and writing to expect, after a sequence of events, a backtrack to something earlier in time or sequence.

The book of Revelation has an interesting format in relation to the seven seals, seven trumpets, and seven bowls (vials). It goes like this:

1 2 3 4 5 6—intercalation (or parenthesis)—then 7

To be specific: Chapter 6 announces seals 1 through 6; at this point there is the intercalation or parenthesis of chapter 7, part of which goes back to a time before a single seal is opened or judgment poured forth (vv. 1-3). Then after the intercalation of Revelation 7, the seventh seal is brought before us in 8:1ff, where we find that the seventh seal is composed of seven trumpets!

Here again we have 1, 2, 3, 4, 5, 6 trumpets in Revelation 8-9, then the insertion of an intercalation from 10:1—11:14 before we get to the seventh trumpet at 11:15-18. This method of writing might be helpfully illustrated by a simple diagram, thus:

```
                SEALS              │
 1   2   3   4   5   6  │ 7  (which is composed of
─────────────────────────────────────────────────────
                       │    1  2  3  4  5  6  7   TRUMPETS)
```

Cp. 7 bowls (vials)

When we later get to the seven bowls or vials of wrath of chapters 15-16, there is a slight change in format. The fall of "Babylon" (Rome) has been briefly forecasted in 14:8 and emphasized in 16:19 under the sixth bowl. Although there is a parenthesis between bowls six and seven (16:13-16), we have substantial added detail placed *afterward* in the parenthesis of 17:1—19:10. So the idea of added detail is still there, whether it is inserted between the sixth and seventh of a sequence, or placed after the seventh.

II. ASSISTANCE FURNISHED US BY UNDERSTANDING
THIS METHOD OF WRITING

The usual interpretation of the book of Revelation by pre-millennial scholars ignores certain important signals given us in the intercalation of 10:1—11:14 between trumpets six and seven. They improperly assume that the rest of the book, following the seventh trumpet and beginning at 11:19, flows chronologically and sequentially beyond what has been traced from 6:1 through 11:18. In my judgment, this is an unfortunate and major mistake in hermeneutics which ex-positors should have been warned against by a remembrance of the fact, already illustrated, that Hebrew-oriented writers often finish a series of events and then dip back to a time previously covered, for the inclusion of further important detail. I understand this to be the situation arising when we get to the end of the seventh trumpet in 11:15-18.

To get the problem before us, I quote Revelation 11:15-18:

15 And the seventh angel sounded; and there were great voices in heaven, saying, The kingdoms of this world are become the kingdoms of our Lord, and of his Christ; and he shall reign for ever and ever.

16 And the four and twenty elders, which sat before God on their seats, fell on their faces, and worshipped God,

17 Saying, We give thee thanks, O Lord God Almighty, which art, and wast, and art to come; because thou hast taken to thee thy great power, and hast reigned.

18 And the nations were angry, and thy wrath is come, and the time of the dead, that they should be judged, and that thou shouldest give reward unto thy servants the proph-ets, and to the saints, and them that fear thy name, small and great; and shouldest destroy them which destroy the earth.

This is obviously a kaleidoscopic, non-chronological sum-mary of a large number of great events which are packed into these four verses comprising the delineation of the seventh trumpet. It will be obvious to the reader that at least seven factors, which I now arrange chronologically, are encompassed in this seventh trumpet as follows:

(1) "thy wrath is come" (v. 18a) announces the wrath of God against the nations, a familiar description of the judgments poured out by God upon the world during the tribulation period.

(2) and (3) "And the nations were angry" (v. 18a) describes the resentment and resistance of the nations against God in His plan to place His Son in sovereignty over the earth (cp. Ps 2, especially vv. 1-3), to which challenge Jehovah responds with derision and judgment at the second coming of Christ (Ps 2:4-9), summarized in Revelation 11:18e as the time that He will "destroy them which destroy the earth" (cp. Rev 19:11-21).

(4) "the time . . . . that thou shouldest give reward unto thy servants the prophets, and to the saints, and to them that fear thy name, small and great" (v. 18d): This is plainly the time that, following His intervention at His second coming, Christ judges *living* Jews and Gentiles, rewarding the righteous ("sheep") with welcome into His earthly kingdom (vv. 15, 17), and severing the wicked ("goats") from the righteous by exclusion from His kingdom (Eze 20:34-38; Mt 24:43—25:46).

(5) "the time of the dead, that they should be judged" (v. 18b), a statement that includes both the last battalion of the first resurrection (of *righteous* dead) before the thousand-year kingdom begins (for they must "reign with Christ") and the second resurrection (of *wicked* dead) after the thousand-year kingdom. These two groups are carefully distinguished in Revelation 20:4-6.

(6) the kingdom reign of Christ (vv. 15, 17), which is later stated to be for 1,000 years (20:4-5). Verse 15b is rendered by the *New English Bible,* "The sovereignty of the world has passed (notice past tense) to our Lord and

his Christ." The *New American Bible* says, "The kingdom of the world now belongs to our Lord and to His Anointed One." The *New American Standard Bible* uses ". . . has become the kingdom. . . ." Although all three versions indicate their understanding of the similar phrase of verse 17 to mean "thou hast begun to reign," the *New American Standard Bible*, in all candor, gives the literal in the margin as "thou didst reign." This agrees with the *King James Version* which says: "thou hast taken to thee thy great power, and hast reigned." I hasten to include the seventh declaration of verses 15-18, in order to make a point relative to these comments under (6):

(7) "and he shall reign for ever and ever" (v. 15c). It is apparent from this declaration that, included in this sweeping kaleidoscope summary of 11:15-18, we are to see not only the mediatorial, thousand-year kingdom of Christ on earth but also the eternal kingdom into which the millennial kingdom flows. Thus, by the time we have finished the seventh trumpet, we have been introduced, in this summary, not only to great events of the tribulation period and the return of Christ to earth (with its striking consequences), but we are to understand that Christ has not only begun His reign but "has reigned" for one thousand years; and will keep on reigning, with Father and Spirit, for eternity.

This is a very important fact that must necessarily guide the interpretation of the rest of the book. Here we find ourselves only approximately halfway through the Revelation, but we have run out of time at 11:18! Not only is the tribulation over but, to every good intent and purpose, the thousand-year reign also ("thou hast reigned"). We find ourselves beyond the end of time and into the eternal kingdom.

The usual interpretation by premillennialists of the book of Revelation ignores these facts and tries to put the seven vials or bowls of wrath (Rev 15-16) chronologically in the tribulation but following the trumpets in point of time. This seems manifestly impossible in the light of what has been demonstrated above from the wording of 11:15-18. We are beyond the millennium into eternity when we finish 11:18. There is no "time" after 11:18.

It is precisely at this point that the method I have been urging comes to our rescue and harmonizes our hermeneutics. Our proposition has been that a thing is not necessarily later than something preceding it in this book, but that often a sequence of events is run through, and then backtracks in harmony with the Hebrew method of writing: picking up the story at some previous point of time and bringing other relevant material into the review, while pressing toward the end already arrived at in the earlier account of the sequence. It might be described as a review with added details!

It is interesting that God so often plants keys to proper understanding at easily seen places. In the intercalation of 10:1—11:14 between the sixth and seventh trumpets, two very significant keys are plainly held up for us to look at and to use! In 10:6 and 7 we are told that when the seventh angel sounds the seventh trumpet: "the mystery of God shall be finished . . . there shall be time no longer." In other words, as far as the time-ages are concerned, we have run out of time and are over into eternity. In harmony with this John is told, in 10:11, "Thou must prophesy again concerning (lit.) many peoples, and nations, and tongues, and kings." This is exactly what we have from 11:19 through chapter 20—a review and reiteration of what is going to happen on earth to nations and kings during the last half of the tribulation period, ending with the return of Christ and His kingdom reign. But all this is rehearsed with particular emphasis on Israel, the people who alone had the ark of the covenant (11:19); the people who gave birth to the man child who would "rule all nations with a rod of iron" (12:1-5). The monsters who will fiendishly assault Israel are paraded before us in

Revelation 13 (cp. 12:6, 10-12, 13-17). And the bowls (vials) of wrath parallel the seven trumpets.

It should also be remembered that the scroll Jesus Christ took from the Father's hand in 5:1 was "written within *and* on the backside." That is why we must start over again at 11:19. The front side of the scroll takes us up to 11:18, where time ceases and the eternal kingdom ensues. The backside of the scroll picks up the story again, but this time in regard to how *Israel* is affected; and takes us through to the same place we had arrived at in 11:15-18, i.e., the end of time and the beginning of eternity. Thus, we are brought to the passage now to be discussed, namely 21:9—22:5.

III. THE PRINCIPLE OF SUSPENDED DETAIL APPLIED TO REVELATION 21:9—22:5

Although there are a few items I shall come back to later in this section, I would like to get ahead to the particular question of how to interpret 21:9—22:5. In the light of what we have just been demonstrating, namely, the pattern of the book of Revelation which goes through a sequence of events but then feels free to come back and start over again with some added details, we should get some further light on the passage before us by applying the principles learned from earlier format.

First, let us trace the order of events which precede our passage. Let me list them:

(1) The coming of the King of kings in power and great glory! (19:11-16).

(2) Armageddon ("hill of slaughter") (19:17-19, 21). On our Lord's way down to the Mount of Olives, He swoops past the armies of the Western hegemony led by the beast and the false prophet (and very likely the armies of the kings of the east—Rev 16:12-16) and destroys them, calling the birds of heaven to a great banquet of soldiers' flesh (vv. 17-18, 21).

(3) The beast and the false prophet (delineated in chapter 13) are caught red-handed in treacherous rebellion against Christ and cast alive into the lake of fire (19: 20).

(4) Satan is bound and cast into the abyss ("a bottomless pit") for the duration of the 1,000-year reign of Christ (20:1-3).

(5) The completion of the *first* resurrection—the remaining battalions (20:4-6). Certainly we have here in verse 4 the battalion of the tribulation martyrs (cp. 6:9-11; 13:7). And, although many Bible teachers have assumed that Old Testament saints, Gentiles and Jews, will already have been raised with the church before the tribulation (1 Th 4:13-18; 1 Co 15:51-52), it is my conviction that the Old Testament saints are raised here, at the end of the seventieth week as the kingdom is being brought in by Christ. The only two Old Testament passages that predict the resurrection of the Old Testament saints speak of it in a context which shows the tribulation has already taken place (see Dan 12:1-3; Is 26:19-21). In the words of our Lord, it is definitely "after the tribulation of those days" (Mt 24:29).

(6) The judgments preparatory to the kingdom age take place (20:4). These are not specified here, but must include the Old Testament saints who are raised and the tribulation saints who are raised, as well as the *living* Jews and *living* Gentiles who are divided between "sheep" who enter the kingdom and "goats" who are slain and excluded from the kingdom (Eze 20:34-38; Mt 25:41). Just as plainly, the *wicked* dead are not raised at this point of time but await the *second* resurrection after the 1,000 years (20:5-6).

(7) The reign of the redeemed of all ages with Christ during the 1,000 years, 20:4-6. Actually nothing is told us here about the kingdom age; just the fact that Christ reigns and Satan is bound. Dozens of extended passages

in the Old Testament and some in the New have already fully portrayed what it will be like to have Christ reigning over the earth. (This is further demonstration of the method of Scripture which tends to give a sequence of things in short, crisp order, leaving the detail to other portions of Scripture, so the reader will not get sidetracked from the order of events.)

(8) Satan is loosed for "a little season" after the 1,000 years are completed (20:3, 7-9). He goes forth to deceive and finds many, evidently from among those born during the period, who have posed as believers but who prove their hearts are unregenerate by gladly welcoming a chance to rebel against Christ. They are destroyed by fire from heaven.

(9) Satan is cast (hurled) into the lake of fire (20:10). There is no such thing as annihilation. The beast and false prophet are still there after 1,000 years.

(10) The heavens and earth which now exist will be purged by fire (20:11; cp. 2 Pe 3:10-12).

(11) and (12) The great white throne judgment, following the *second* resurrection (20:11-14). The second resurrection is composed of the wicked of all ages. They are raised after the 1,000 years (20:5).

Plainly, at this point, we are over into eternity!

There is no disposition to debate this fact among Bible-believing people, regardless of their views of prophecy prior to this point. The story of God's dealings with man would be utterly incomplete without knowing just what God proposes to do after His purposes on earth have run their course. What will happen to those who reject His light and His mercy? What will happen to those who are redeemed by His grace which was set free to act in righteousness through the sacrifice of our Lord Jesus Christ upon the cross?

The Bible has foretold this again and again. One of the closely reasoned portions which sharply contrasts the destiny

of the righteous and the wicked is Romans 2:2-11. It is both
to be expected and fitting that God would conclude this
order of events, beginning at the return of Christ to earth,
with the eternal destiny of the wicked in the lake of fire (Rev
20:14-15; 21:8) and the eternal destiny of the righteous, in
fellowship with God (21:3) in the New Jerusalem (21:1-7).

As has often been pointed out, chapter divisions were not
part of the original text. They were added to make possible
the compilation of a concordance. At this point of Revelation we see one of the unfortunate breaks which tends to confuse the proper understanding of this portion.

The chapter ending of Revelation 20 has been misplaced.
The eternal destiny of the righteous in the New Jerusalem
should never have been torn from its integral relation to 20:
11-15 by this mistaken interruption at 21:1. The unit section
is 20:11 through 21:8. The new chapter should have begun
with 21:9 and continued (through another unfortunate break
at 22:1) to 22:5, after which the epilogue of 22:6-21 con-
cludes the book.

This very confused divorcing of what should be joined and
joining of what should be distinguished has made it almost
inevitable that the average reader would never dream of
making a unit break after 21:8. He continues reading on at
verse 9. Is it not about a beautiful city that he has just been
reading about in the previous verses?

However, this improper divisoning has contributed toward
a more serious effect, even among able expositors. The similarities in things that are said about the city of 21:1-7 and the
city of 21:9—22:5 have lulled expositors into confusing similarity with identity. Although some expositors have interpreted the passage as a pictorial and spiritual description of
the bride of Christ, the spiritual qualities of the church, a
woman rather than a *city,* I see a *literal city* here, accompanied by spiritual qualities. Cities do have character (e.g.,
11:8; 17:1, 5, 18). The only question is whether there is anything different between what is said about the city in 21:1-7

and what is said in 21:9—22:5. I believe there is and I believe the distinctions lead to an important decision of interpretation.

IV. THE NEW JERUSALEM IN ETERNITY

However properly and helpfully one may interpret the language used to picture the virtues of the church as "the holy city, new Jerusalem. . . . the bride, the Lamb's wife" (21:2, 9-10), if language means anything, there must be a city, a dwelling place. Jesus said, "I go to prepare a place (not a condition) for you" (Jn 14:2). He said He was coming back to take us to that place (Jn 14:3). Abraham looked forward to a heavenly city which "God . . . hath prepared" (Heb 11:16). . . . "a city which hath foundations, whose builder and maker is God" (Heb 11:10). The New Jerusalem is a city and it has foundations (Rev 21:2, 10, 12-21). It is prepared by God, for it comes down, not from heaven, but out of heaven in the sense that God is the designer and fashioner of it (vv. 2, 10). To equate these promises, quoted from John and Hebrews, with just an experience that is "heavenly" or even with the dwelling place of God, "the heaven of heavens. . . . the third heaven" (Neh 9:6; 2 Co 12:2) is to miss the point that the eternal dwelling of the redeemed is a *place* prepared by God, distinct from the third heaven. It comes down from God (the Preparer), not out of the third heaven and is thus utterly distinct from it.

In similar analogy, hell (hades/sheol) is not the place God is going to use for the eternal destiny of the lost, nor is eternal judgment just an experience. It is an experience in a place, the lake of fire. Hades/sheol is emptied and its occupants are hurled into the lake of fire (Rev 20:14-15). To try to spiritualize the lake of fire as being only an experience is to do despite to Scripture. Hell (hades/sheol) is temporary; the lake of fire is eternal. It is a *place*. So is the New Jerusalem.

As an aside, there seems to be what amounts to a con-

spiracy to symbolize and deliteralize the lake of fire. It is
true that if it is not literal, then the symbolic language could
be argued as being worse (whatever that is). But that is
not the problem. Of course, it will be horrible beyond imagination. That is not the point. The Word of God says it is a
place. It seems strange to me that such passages as the parables of Matthew 13, where everything symbolic is explained
by our Lord (e.g., "the field is the world; the reapers are the
angels," etc.), never once does He suggest that "fire" is a
symbol by saying "the fire is . . ."! Why not, if it is a symbol?
Further, to let our limited knowledge argue against the plain
statements of God is to move on very dangerous ground. Years
ago Professor Schwarze, of New York University, challenged
the idea that fire would dissipate. He insisted that the white
dwarf stars were already "lakes of fire," already in existence.
God could make another one or use any one of these already
here. Now that we know much more about the breakdown of
atoms, our old ideas that fire would dissipate as heat and
smoke are untenable. The intense pressure on the broken
down molecules permits no escape. If man can make asbestos
to endure fire, can't God make the human body to have the
same quality? And if "the lake of fire" is just a symbolic experience, why should God raise the bodies of the wicked at
all? If it is only spiritual suffering, why have bodies?

And, finally, to the argument that Satan is a spirit and
hence could not suffer literally in a lake of fire, for spirits
do not have substance, I respond: Who says spirits do not
have substance? Of course, not physical substance, but substance—spiritual substance. Otherwise, what is the point of
our Lord's words when He draws back the curtain of the unseen world in Luke 16 and shows men in rest ("Abraham afar
off, and Lazarus in his bosom") and in pain ("dip the
tip of his finger in water, and cool my tongue; for I am
tormented in this flame")? If one argues that corporeality
is necessary to feeling, then until resurrection bodies are given
them, heaven is populated by a limitless number of ghosts of

men (and angels) who neither see, nor hear, nor find themselves able to communicate. Indeed, after we get resurrection bodies, God is still Spirit and we would not be able to see Him, if a spirit has not substance.

Perhaps the easiest illustration is the story of Elisha and his servant at Dothan (2 Ki 6:13-17). The Syrian king sent charioteers to capture Elisha, and when his servant saw them surrounding Dothan, he cried out for fear. So Elisha prayed: "Lord, . . . open his eyes, that he may see." And he did see horses and chariots of fire protecting them from the Syrians. Yes, spiritual substance can be seen; not with physical sight, but with spiritual sight. We shall see God!

So away with arguments against the possibility of literality based on our ignorance of the "other" world, the "spirit" world, the "unseen" world!

Thus, the hermeneutics that would spiritualize both the lake of fire and the New Jerusalem rest upon faulty premises. Certainly there are great spiritual issues, experiences, suffering, and joy encompassed in the language. But *both* eternal abiding places are unquestionably *places*, with accompanying thoughts of reality and literality, both for the saved and for the unsaved.

Having said that, I do not pretend that we can, with our finite minds and lack of knowledge, understand some of the grand descriptions given us in these great words of 20:11 through 22:5. That is not the point. I simply submit that we should not reject the probability of a literal city, with literal walls, literal gates, literal foundations, and literal measurements, because of our limited capacity to understand.

I haven't the slightest idea what a great city, designed as a 1,500-mile cube would look like or how it would be suitable. I just know those are the measurements and the shape announced. And I believe it.

My soul thrills to these majestic descriptions, and particularly to the emphasis of God personalizing it all, and treating us as gloriously expanded and wonderfully appreciative indi-

viduals (21:3-4, 22; 22:3-4)! The purity, beauty, and glori-
ousness of that place beggars language. How wonderful to
be there! And to abide there forever!

V. THE NEW JERUSALEM IN TIME

There can be no debate about the New Jerusalem in eternity. But I would like to submit a thought proposed by Ironside, Scott, and others, that the city will not only be the *eternal* abode of the righteous, but that beginning at 21:9 (where
a new chapter should begin, anyway), we have a description
of that city accompanied by a number of statements that
would suggest that this city is related to earth *during time—*
that is, during the millennium.

First, observe verse 24, where we read: "And the nations . . .
shall walk in the light of it" (the clause "of them which are
saved" is omitted in the better texts, although the result is
inconsequential to the point I am making).

I find nowhere in Scripture any suggestion that peoples
will continue as nations, as national units. Those who composed various nations, whether saved or unsaved, are there,
in the eternal abodes. But nations "in heaven"? This idea is
utterly foreign to the Scriptures related to eternity. Certainly one would never argue for the unsaved being grouped
as nations in the lake of fire.

What then are these nations of verse 24 and where are
they? That is not too difficult to establish. Our Lord is King
of kings. Prophecy is full of statements concerning nations.
For instance,

> And many nations shall come, and say, Come, and let us go
> up to the mountain of the LORD, and to the house of the God
> of Jacob [i.e., the millennial temple, Eze 40—48]; and he
> will teach us of his ways, and we will walk in his paths: for
> the law shall go forth of Zion, and the word of the LORD
> from Jerusalem (Mic 4:2).

In the Bible, the earthly Jerusalem is never confused with the

heavenly Jerusalem. It remains for confused modern inter-
preters to do that! So, these nations are upon the earth and
God's temple is in Jerusalem on earth. Hence, if nations are
said to "walk in the light of" the New Jerusalem, it could not
be in eternity but only in time; the nations are not in heaven
but upon the earth. Hence, if this prophecy is to be fulfilled,
the New Jerusalem must appear and be related in some way
to this earth before earth's destruction (2 Pe 3:7). Indeed, it
is not only said that the saints will reign *on* the earth, but
over the earth.

Second, how can this be explained? The language of verse
24 suggests it, "the nations . . . walk in the light of it," and this
city is seen "descending out of heaven from God" (v. 10).
Thus, since it does not replace earth, but comes down toward
earth, it would appear that it comes close enough to the earth
for these words to be fulfilled: "the nations . . . shall walk in
the light of it." Ironside has helpfully suggested that it will
hang over the earth like a gigantic chandelier. Men will see
"heaven" ruling and we shall have here, as Moses once wist-
fully said, "the days of heaven upon the earth" (Deu 11:21).
They will walk in the light of Jerusalem the Golden! This
gigantic 1,500-mile cube, with its glorious beauty, will remind men of earth that "the most High ruleth in the kingdom of men" (Dan 4:25). Men will be very aware of the
closeness of heaven and earth and the right of heaven to rule.
Certainly Jesus Christ will literally and physically come back
to the earth to reestablish the throne of David. And we shall
come with Him. But any conception that He must sit on a
literal throne in the earthly Jerusalem 24 hours a day for
1,000 years is born of well-intentioned ignorance. Elizabeth
is queen of England when she is in Buckingham Palace, Paris,
or South Africa, as well as on rare state occasions when she
may actually sit on that throne. Our Lord is King of kings
and Lord of lords. He will delegate substantial power. Some
of us believe that resurrected David will have the honor of
reigning over Israel as Christ's viceroy. What could be more

fitting than to have One, who is Himself ruled by heaven, rule over the earth from the New Jerusalem, in plain view of all the nations?

Third, the above consideration leads us to the last half of the verse: "and the kings of the earth shall bring their glory into it" (v. 24b, NASB). Also: "And in the daytime (for there shall be no night there) its gates will never be closed; and they shall bring the glory and the honor of the nations into it" (vv. 25-26, NASB). How could this be possibly related to eternity? In time, the gates of the overhanging New Jerusalem, always open for ingress and egress, are entered by the great ones of earth, who not only worship and give fealty to the Lord Jesus in the earthly Jerusalem, but from time to time, in the New Jerusalem. Transportation is no real problem to God! There is point and purpose to these passages if we envision the New Jerusalem being related to the millennial earth with its kings and lords answerable to the Lord Christ. Any attempt to relate these concepts to the New Jerusalem after the 1,000 years, after the great white throne judgment, after nations as units have been forever dissolved and individuals are related to God as individuals in either the New Jerusalem or the lake of fire, becomes futile and invalid. These details could be related to time only if something like this suggestion of the gigantic chandelier is the explanation *during,* and *not after,* the 1.000 years.

Fourth, but the most significant reason for suggesting a relationship of the New Jerusalem to this earth during time, specifically the thousand years, is brought to us in verses 1 and 2 of the twenty-second chapter. There we read of the river, the tree of life yielding twelve kinds of fruit (each appropriate to its month), and then the bombshell to any idea that this passage is talking of eternity: "and the leaves of the tree were for the healing (or health) of the nations."

Notice these things inappropriate to eternity, but entirely appropriate to time: (1) nations—already discussed; (2) twelve months—since when did heaven run by clocks and calendars! How utterly fantastic!; (3) and, most amazing of all, these nations need health or healing! By no stretch of the imagination or allowance for language flexibility could it ever be argued that people in eternity are going to be healed or kept healthy by monthly use of certain leaves from a certain kind of tree!

If one reads carefully about the reign of the Son of God during the thousand years, there is not the slightest suggestion that anyone dies during that period except under the judgment stroke of the rod of iron. Isaiah 65:20, in the literal rendering of the last clause, states: "a sinner dying at a hundred years will be but a child." In other words, in proportion to the extended life that will be characteristic of the millennium, 100 years is childhood. If Methusaleh lived 969 years in the vile and violent society just before the flood, with disease and murder rife, why should not those born during that period (or who come into the period alive from the tribulation period) live through it, with disease removed, the curse of Genesis 3 on nature removed, without wars, with no food problem, etc.? But even then, this extension of life becomes more meaningful if we heed these words of Revelation 22, that there will be a supernatural lengthening of life by use of the leaves of the tree of life. McClain has suggested that the original tree of life in Eden was not something which would forever give life if one ate once; but rather if one kept on eating. It would therefore be in full keeping with this conception (of something that perennially sustained life) that the leaves of the tree in the New Jerusalem would provide for that continuous extension of life predicted of those who go into or who are born during the millennium. A mystery is thus solved, namely, how could they live through the whole period (if they are not among those who are rebellious and slain with the rod of iron)? We have our answer and we have a reason why these things about the New Jerusalem, so different from the needs of the eternal state, are brought before us in the special, second description of it, after the sequence of events leading to the eternal destiny of the wicked and the righteous had been concluded at 21:8.

The relation of the New Jerusalem to time, millennial time, now makes sense and a far better solution to the section is available, rather than the idea of carelessly tacking it on as a postlude to the New Jerusalem in the eternal scene. It is hoped that this solution approves itself to the readers who may well have been puzzled by some of these statements.

VI. A NOVEL COROLLARY SOLUTION

It is commonly understood by premillennialists that the redeemed of all ages will share in the millennium *on earth*. This poses a problem which is not often mentioned but which nonetheless has disturbed many earnest Bible students and puzzled expositors. Evidently because devout students of the Word recognize that they must reverently avoid going beyond what God has revealed, they have tended to "skip" this problem. After all, there are some mysteries we must be willing to leave with God, and they feel this well may be one of them. But is it?

I refer, of course, to the question in the millennium, how will those who enter that period in resurrected bodies relate to those who enter with *non*resurrected bodies, that is, those living Jews and Gentiles who come in saved from the tribulation period?

The general supposition is that we will live side by side, as it were, in the same earth areas and environment; but this would make for some strange situations. I have never heard any attempt to discuss the matter explicitly with suggested solutions, so I shall attempt a solution, coherent with the line of thought we have just exposited in section VI above.

My wife and I live at 330 Harrison Avenue in a Philadelphia suburb. We have neighbors on each side of us, and neighbors on the other side of the street corresponding to the three houses on our side. Suppose God, in line with the usual view, placed my wife and me at 330 Harrison Avenue during the millennium, but with neighbors other than the present ones. Look at this hypothetical chart:

Jews from before Christ (resurrected) 327	Gentiles born during the millennium (nonresurrected) 329	Jews martyred in the tribulation (resurrected) 331
HARRISON AVENUE		
328 Living Jews from the tribulation (nonresurrected bodies)	330 The Masons from the church age (resurrected bodies)	332 Living Gentiles from the tribulation (nonresurrected bodies)

1. My wife and I reside at 330, two church age believers in resurrected bodies.

2. In 328, to our left, is a Jewish family who received Christ as Lord during the tribulation period, were rescued by our Lord at His second coming, and entered the millennium in *non*resurrected bodies.

3. In 332, to our right, is a Gentile family who came out of the tribulation also. The father, wife, and two children were saved early in the tribulation period.

4. In 331, directly across the street from them, are a Jew and his wife who believed on the Lord Jesus during the tribulation but were martyred for their faith by Satan's monster of iniquity for refusing to bow down to the image of the beast, set up in the holy place (Mt 24:15; Rev 13:14-15). They also have resurrected bodies.

5. In 329, next to them and directly across the street from us, there is a Gentile father and mother, each of whom were *born* of saved Gentile parents during the early part of the millennium. *Their* parents entered the millennium, like those in 328 and 332, when Christ came back to set up His kingdom. These *second* generation parents have a

little boy three years old and a baby on the way. (Each of those in 329 will have to be saved like people in any preceding age; for sadly, each would be capable of sinning brazenly and openly, resulting in their being smitten by Christ's "rod of iron," or even be guilty of posing as loyal citizens until opportunity is given to show their true inner feelings when Satan is released at the end of the 1000 years, perishing with him in his abortive rebellion.)

6. In 327, to their right, is a Jewish family who lived before the time of Christ and died looking for a *heavenly city* which God *had prepared for them* (Heb 11:16). They are in resurrected bodies.

To summarize, the people residing in 327, 330, and 331 have glorified bodies. They do not cohabit with their wives and do not produce children. They do not have old natures. They cannot sin. They have never-dying, never-aging bodies. There is no suggestion in Scripture that they will eat food or be sustained by it.

On the other hand, families living in 328, 329, and 332 do NOT have resurrected bodies. They will eat, sleep, play, cohabit with their wives, have children, and probably work in the earth, which, though curse-freed, will have crops that need to be tilled (Amos 9:13-15).

How would this neighborhood get along together? Will we all " go to church" together? Or, will we all go up to Jerusalem together (Zec 14:16-17; Mic 4:1-2)? If so, how? Will "their" kids play in "our" backyards? Will the nice people in 332 invite all five neighbor families to a barbecue on their spacious lawn? Will I offer to drive the young pregnant wife and her little boy (in 329) to the supermarket in my Zippo Eight, while her husband is tilling the earth outside of town? Will these neighbors play horseshoes together? What will my wife and I, and the people in 327 and 331 do at night while those in 328, 329, and 332 are sleeping, since we have permanent, resurrected bodies that need no sleep?

What sort of community would it be with people who cannot sin living side by side with those who can? To add to the complications, just what would be the relationship between those in 328 and 332, who are saved but can sin, and that young couple in 329, who could not only sin but might reject Christ's claims and remain unsaved? Why would God put mixed-up groups like this in tens of thousands of neighborhoods all over the world?

However, if we accept the solution suggested under section V and believe that the New Jerusalem will be related to *time* as well as later to *eternity*, then things begin to unwind in our thinking. Certainly Christ and all resurrected saints will return to earth in resurrected bodies to join in His day of triumph and exaltation. But that Christ, or we in resurrected bodies, will remain on earth all through the thousand years has been assumed and not stated. As previously suggested as far as Christ is concerned, implicit in the titles "King of *kings*" and "Lord of *lords*" is the thought that He will heavily delegate authority, and perhaps David will be His earthly regent over Israel.

Suppose that, during the millennium, Christ and those believers of previous ages who have resurrection bodies, live in the New Jerusalem and the people with *non*resurrected bodies live on earth. Kings of the earth would "bring their glory and honor" into the New Jerusalem and earth's inhabitants' longevity would be assured by the provison of the "leaves of the tree of life for the healing [health] of the nations." Each *kind* of people, resurrected and nonresurrected, would be in suitable habitats. There would be full cooperation between the New Jerusalem and province Earth and full submission to King Jesus. But we would have a really viable solution to the puzzling problem of all kinds of people from all kinds of ages living all mixed up together in earth's neighborhoods.

May *this* be the solution? Think it over!

And now, just before we conclude, consider one more solution.

VII. Postscript

Premillennialists have been very dogmatic in saying that only the wicked dead will be judged at the great white throne. One can easily see why. The translation of the church, both dead and living, has accounted for their judgment at the judgment seat of Christ. If my previous suggestion is adopted, the Old Testament dead and the dead of the tribulation period are judged at the return of the Lord to the earth at the close of the tribulation. Similarly the living at the time of Christ's return to earth are divided into "sheep" and "goats" in the judgment of the (living) Jews and Gentiles (as individuals, not nations). Thus it has been assumed that, with the great white throne judgment of all the wicked, our Lord's words that everyone of us will give an account to God will have been fulfilled. But wait!

Those who in natural bodies live into the millennium, counted "worthy of life" at the judgments concluding the tribulation, will have children. These children will have children, on and on for 1,000 years. That constitutes a mighty host of people when it is remembered that war, disease, malnutrition, murder, and other usual decimators of society are not present, because the Lord is reigning over earth's golden age. When will those *born during* the 1,000 years be judged, since Jesus said every man must be judged? If this does not take place at the great white throne judgment, when will it? If those saved during the thousand years are judged at the great white throne, this may well be the solution to those significant words of Revelation 20:15: "And whosoever was not found written in the book of life was cast into the lake of fire." But this obviously cannot include those whose names will be there in the Book of Life! Those saved during the millennium, who live through the period, who reject the final appeal of Satan precisely because they are saved people, these would rightfully appear to be judged out of the books, just like all other people of the human race, at the only judgment left, the judgment of the great white throne!

God never leaves loopholes. He always does things decently and in order. "Shall not the Judge of all the earth do right?" (Gen 18:25). INDEED HE WILL!

Scripture Index

OLD TESTAMENT

GENESIS

1:26-30	39, 107, 119
2:7, 15-17	39, 140
3	91, 117, 245
3:14-19	39
5, 6	229
9:12-16	23
10:8-11	229
11	34, 35
11:1	229
11:31-32	29, 31, 32
12	34, 35
12:1-4, 7	28, 29, 30, 31, 32, 33, 39, 40, 89, 115
12:10-20	37
13	34, 38
13:5-9	31, 33
13:14-17	40
15	34, 35, 39
15:1-7, 18	31, 39, 40, 89
17:1-21	38, 40
18:12	38
18:17-29	16, 34, 40, 251
19	15
22	34, 35
22:15-18	29, 30, 31, 34, 38, 40
24:43	56
26:2-5, 24	40
28:12-15	40
29:20-21	57
32:29	153
35:9-12	40
46:3-4	40
48:14-16, 19-20	40

EXODUS

2:8	56
3:6, 13	223
3:14-15	154
19	108
19:3, 5, 8	35, 36
20:13, 14	92
32	69

LEVITICUS

11:44	155
17:11	132, 139
26:3-10	78

DEUTERONOMY

1:11	222
4:1	222
11:21	243
18:15-19	115
24:3	92
30:1-10	153

JOSHUA

4:6-9	76
5:13	15
18:3	223
24:2	29

JUDGES

13:17	153

1 SAMUEL

7-8	128
8:6-7, 19-22	108

2 SAMUEL

7	88

I KINGS

3:1	67
11:1-8, 9	67
11:29-40	68
12:28	68

2 KINGS

6:13-17	241
8:19	73
16:2	59
18:2	59

1 CHRONICLES

15:20	56

2 CHRONICLES

13:12	223
28:9	223

EZRA

8:28	223

NEHEMIAH

9:6	239
9:10	154

PSALMS

2:1-3	189, 232
2:4-9	91, 149, 189, 232
8	107
8:6	120
19:1-6	107
22:22	154
46	56
48:10	154
68:25	56
72:8	40
76:10	17
103:19	15, 19
111:19	154

PROVERBS

30:19	56
31:1-9	67

ECCLESIASTES

2:3	67
4:13	67
7:25-28	67
12:9-13	68

SONG OF SOLOMON

1:3	56
6:8	56

ISAIAH

1-12	48
2:2-4, 11	149
2:3	88
5:1-2	80
6	153
6:1	48
6:1-5	15
6:9-10	96
7:1-9	49, 54, 60, 61
7:1—9:7	48
7:10-16	43, 44, 47, 48, 49, 50, 51, 52, 53, 54, 55, 56, 57, 59, 60, 61, 63, 64
7:17-25	50, 55, 60
8	62
8:1-22	50, 51, 52, 53, 54, 55, 60, 61, 63, 73
9:1-7	51, 53, 63, 154
10:24-27	187, 226
14:24-25	63, 187, 226
24:22	135
26:19-21	236
30:31	63
36	51, 73
37	51, 73, 200
37:7, 30-38	51, 74, 187, 226
40:3-5	118
40:10	223
42:8	155
44:6-7	167
46:9-10	167, 213
47:12-13	213
48:3, 5	69
50:1	69
60:5	95
61	93
61:1-2	79, 210
62	93
62:11	223
65:20	93, 122, 245

JEREMIAH

10:6	155
31:34	154

EZEKIEL

1:1-28	14, 16, 17, 19-21, 22, 23-27
20:34-38	232, 236
21:26, 27	17, 93, 120
37	119
38-39	63, 182, 184, 187, 189, 192, 193, 194, 195, 196, 197, 198, 199, 200, 202, 203, 220, 221, 226
40-48	242

DANIEL

2	166, 175, 181, 205, 206, 209, 210, 217, 225, 226-27

2:32-33   168-69
2:34-35   167, 181
2:36-38   103, 108, 166
2:40-45   88, 167-69, 181, 187
4:17, 25, 26   16, 90, 103
4:32, 35   16, 90, 103, 107, 243
5:21, 23   103
7   166, 175, 181, 205, 206, 209, 217, 219, 226-27
7:4, 7-8, 9-11   107, 187, 212, 225
7:13-14, 18, 24-27   103, 204, 212, 225
8   205, 206, 210, 211, 217, 224, 226, 227
8:5-8   168, 211, 212, 225
8:9-20   168, 205, 211, 212, 215, 216, 224-26
8:21-26   63, 168, 212, 215, 216, 224-26
9:26, 27   168, 171, 175, 186, 223
10:12, 13   18
11   183, 189, 205, 206, 210, 211, 217, 226
11:2-4   211-12
11:5-19   63, 214
11:20-35   215-16
11:36-39   189
11:40-45   40, 182, 186, 187, 189, 190, 191, 209, 211, 215, 217, 219, 221, 222, 224, 226, 227
12:1   18, 189, 191
12:1-3   236

HOSEA

1:1-11   66, 69-75, 77, 79
2:1-23   70, 75-77, 79, 80, 81
3:1-5   69, 70, 77, 82, 84, 85
4:12-13, 15-17   70
11:1   47

JOEL

1:8   57-8

AMOS

9:13-15   77, 91, 247

MICAH

4:1-7   16, 78, 88, 108, 242, 248
5:1-6   53, 187

ZECHARIAH

12:2-3   182, 186, 187, 209
12:7-10   88, 108, 128, 182, 186, 209
13:8-9   187
14   184
14:1-4   63, 81, 88, 148, 182, 187, 220
14:5-17   81, 88, 91, 148, 248

MALACHI

4:6   116

NEW TESTAMENT

MATTHEW

1-10   87, 100, 102
1:1—11:1   89
1   59
1:18-25   44, 45, 47, 53, 57, 61-64, 156
2   89
2:6   53
2:19-21, 23   47
3:1-5   87, 100, 105, 108
3:12   141
3:17   89
4   89
4-10   100
4:8   120
4:12, 17   108
5-7   90
5:20-35   90-92
6:33   102-4
7:13   118
8:1—11:1   92
9:34   93
10:5-15   76, 108
11:2—12:45   89, 93
11:7-13   88
11:20-30   95, 144
12   93, 97, 99, 101, 108
12:22-37   94, 103, 109, 125, 144
12:38-50   95, 128
12:46—28:20   89
13   87, 99, 103, 105, 240
13:10-17   96, 98, 100, 210
13:34-38   96, 99, 100, 210
13:40-50   100
15:8   48
16:18   99
17:11   116
18:3   105
19:3-12   92
19:23-28   103, 105, 116
21:31, 43   103
23:37-39   108, 128
24   182
24:1-15   175, 178, 186, 205, 207, 209, 215, 216, 217, 236, 247
24:16-36   108, 144, 178, 189, 205, 207, 216, 217, 236
24:43—25:46   232
25:1-13   57
25:31-46   88, 93, 123, 136, 236
26:27   103
26:29   144
27:18   94
28:18   121, 160

MARK

1:1-8, 14-15   108
4   103, 105
4:26-29   104
6:11   144
9:43, 45   141
13:32   144
14:25   144
15:10   144

LUKE

1   44, 59
1:1-4   163
1:27   62

1:30-33   88, 108
1:38   45
2   44, 59
2:1   185
3:1-18   108
3:17   141
4:16-21   108, 210
10:12   144
11:2   155
13   103, 105
15:18   104
16   240
16:27-31   127-28
17:23, 30, 31   144
18:24-25   105
19:11-14   128
19:35-40   88
21   182
21:34   144
22:20   104
24   131, 139

JOHN

1:18   157, 159
1:46   45
3:3-8   90, 105, 108
4:29   15
5:22   15
5:27   159
5:28, 29   134, 208
5:45-47   126
6:39, 40, 44, 54   144
7:5   95
8:41   45
8:56   144
11:24   144
12:31   120
12:39-41   15
12:48   144
14   130
14:2-3   239
14:30   109, 120
19:10-22   88
20:9   63
20:22   140
21:24, 25   104, 163

ACTS

1-11   128
1:3, 6, 7, 8   88, 114, 116, 127
2:17, 20   144
2   126
3:17-20   110, 111, 112, 125-26
7:51-60   127-28
15:14, 15   128
17:11   180
17:24-28   107
17:30-31   134, 144
26:7   76

ROMANS

1:20   22
2:2-11   145
2:16   144
4:13-16   37
5:12   132
6:12-14   109
8   130
8:15-32   91, 117
8:17   160
9-11   28
10:9   130
11:1-6, 11-12, 22-27   108, 128, 205
11:33   20
13:1-7   17, 108

13:12	144, 147
14:17	108

1 CORINTHIANS

1:7, 8	144, 149
1:22	93, 126
1:30	157
2:8	126
3:13	144, 147
4:3	144, 145
5:5	144, 146, 149
6:2-3	123
13	130, 139
14:8	137
15	130
15:1-11	130
15:12-19	132
15:20-28	109, 128-29, 133
15:29-34	136-37
15:35-50	133, 137-39, 145
15:51-58	135-37, 141-42, 236

2 CORINTHIANS

1:14	144, 146, 149
4:14	109, 120
5:11	134
5:19	126
12:2	103, 239

GALATIANS

2:17-18	70
3:16	89

EPHESIANS

1:10, 11	42, 123
3:1-5	97, 210
4:20	146
4:30	144

PHILIPPIANS

1:6, 10	144, 146-47, 149
2:9-11	107
2:16	144-47, 149

COLOSSIANS

1:16-17	107, 157
1:25-26	97, 210
2:3	157
2:9	46

1 THESSALONIANS

4	150
4:13-18	135, 141, 236
5	149-50
5:2, 4	144, 147

2 THESSALONIANS

1:8	123
1:8-9	146
1:10	144
2	207, 209
2:2-10	144, 146, 149-51, 208, 224

1 TIMOTHY

1:15	156
3:16	46
6:15	162

2 TIMOTHY

1:12, 18	144, 146
3:1	144
3:16-17	92
4:8	144, 146

HEBREWS

1:2	144
2:3	93
2:5	120
2:5-8	107
2:12	154
6:5	93
6:13	38
9:22	156
9:27	132
10:4, 5	156
10:7	89
10:8-10	156
11	130
11:3-6	46
11:10, 16	239, 248

JAMES

2:26	132
4:4	69
5:3	144

1 PETER

1:5	144
1:10-12	96, 97, 98, 210
2:11-17	108
3:22	107

2 PETER

1:11	109
2:9	144
3:3, 7	14, 146, 243
3:10-12	144-47, 149, 237

1 JOHN

2:18, 22	179
4:3	179
4:17	144

2 JOHN

1:7	179

JUDE

1:6	144

REVELATION

1-7	230
1:1	155-56
1:4-5	156
1:7	128
1:8, 11	157-58
1:12	183
1:13, 18	159
2:18	159
2:26-27	108
3:1-10	180
3:12, 14	160
3:21	16, 88, 108
4:3	23
4:8	160
5:1	235
5:1-7	160
5:5, 6, 9	160-61
5:9-10	121, 161
5:9-14	124
6:1-2	202
6:1—11:18	231
6:6	161
6:9-11	205, 236
6:16	161
6:17	145
7:1-2	230
7:2-4	205

8:1	230
9	196, 230
9:13-18	203
9:16, 17, 18	183, 187
10:1—11:14	230, 231, 234
10:6, 7, 11	234
11:8	238
11:15-18	108, 121, 124, 230-35
11:19	231, 235
12:5	91, 145, 161
12:6, 10-12, 13-17	235
12:12-17	209
13	171, 175, 179, 185-86, 193, 206, 207, 209
13:1-2	171, 219
13:1-10	227
13:3-4	170, 210, 218
13:5	186
13:7-8	181, 236
13:7, 9, 10	205
13:7, 15	216, 217, 247
13:11-15	208
13:13, 15	223
13:13-18	226-28, 247
14:3-4, 20	16
14:8	230
14:9-12	205
14:10	141-42
15	123, 230
15:3	161
16	123, 184, 230, 234
16:12-16 ,17-18, 21	187, 189, 200, 203, 235
16:14	145, 230
17	171, 175
17:1, 5, 18	238
17:1—19:10	230
17:10	210, 218
17:12-17	171, 176
17:14	162
17:15	95
18:4-6, 20	205
19	162, 200
19:2, 18, 20	205
19:11-16, 17-19, 21	163, 235
19:11-21	189, 232
19:11—20:6	108
19:16	162
19:17-21	209
19:19	147
19:20	226, 236
20	27, 201
20:1, 2, 7, 10	107
20:1-3, 4-6	134, 135, 236
20:1-5	88, 136
20:3, 5, 7-9, 10, 11-14	237
20:4-6	134-36, 232, 236
20:10	122, 205
20:11-15	91, 134-36, 238
20:11—22:5	241
20:13	208
20:14-15	141-42, 238-39
20:15	250
21:1-7	238
21:1-8, 9	238, 242
21:8	246
21:9, 24	242
21:9—22:5	235, 238
21:10, 24	243
21:22, 23	162
21:24, 25, 26	244
22	245
22:1-2	244
22:3-4	242
22:5, 6-22	238, 242
22:16, 20	162